GINO K.PIOVESANA S.J.

RECENT JAPANESE
PHILOSOPHICAL THOUGHT
1862–1996
A SURVEY

INCLUDING A NEW SURVEY BY NAOSHI YAMAWAKI
THE PHILOSOPHICAL THOUGHT OF JAPAN
FROM 1963 TO 1996

JAPAN
LIBRARY

RECENT JAPANESE PHILOSOPHICAL THOUGHT

First published 1963 [Original Survey 1862–1962] by Enderle Bookstore, Tokyo

This third revised edition first published 1997 by
JAPAN LIBRARY

Japan Library is an imprint of Curzon Press Ltd
St John's Studios, Church Road, Richmond, Surrey TW9 2QA

British Library Cataloguing in Publication Data
A CIP catalogue entry for this book
is available from the British Library

ISBN 1–873410–65–4

Printed & bound in Great Britain by Bookcraft, Midsomer Norton, Avon

PREFACE TO THE THIRD EDITION

In the autumn of 1994 Mr Hans Enderle, Managing Director of Enderle Book Co. Ltd., Tokyo, wrote: 'About 30 years ago we published a book by Prof. Gino Piovesana then professor of the Jesuit University here (Sophia University) entitled *Recent Japanese Philosophical Thought*. It was later also published in the US by St John's University Press and also translated into Japanese.

'It has been out of print for years, but, believe it or not, we still keep getting orders for it. For years, I have been thinking it would be nice if the book were available again. As far as I can tell, there still isn't anything comparable in English. I have been in touch with the author who now lives in Italy. He is getting along in years obviously, but has arranged for one of his former students, now a professor [Naoshi Yamawaki] to bring the book up to date somewhat.

'There just isn't a large enough English market in Japan alone for us to feel confident in publishing the book again and we have been looking for a publisher in either England or the US. The author has suggested your company.'

Gino Piovesana was delighted with the news when it was subsequently agreed that this third revised edition should be published by Japan Library. Sadly, however, Fr Piovesana died in February 1996.

We are most grateful to Mr Hans Enderle for his assistance and support in connection with this new edition, and to Prof. Yamawaki for what he calls a 'brief outline' of the many changes that have taken place in the 30 years since the book first appeared, bringing the volume fully up to date. Our thanks are also due to Jeremiah L.Alberg, S.J. for the excellent translation of Prof. Yamawaki's contribution. It was not possible to include Prof. Yamawaki's survey in the original Index, hence the separate sub-Index.

PAUL NORBURY
Publisher
February 1997

PREFACE

There would seem to be no special need to justify the publication of this survey, given the fact that no single comprehensive study covering the last hundred years of Japanese philosophical thought has appeared in a Western language. The book by Tsuchida Kyōson is too old, and out of print besides, while the more recent work edited by Kōsaka Masaaki is a history of thought in general up to 1912. If we exclude a few sketchy articles, no adequate introduction to recent Japanese philosophy exists.

A justification is required instead to explain the nature of this book, which is called a "Survey", and does not pretend to be a history of philosophical ideas in Japan. The unassuming subtitle is not due to special modesty, but to the fact that for the moment nothing more could be done. Even in Japanese there is no standard work continuing the pioneering historical investigation of Asō Yoshiteru which treated the development of philosophy in Japan during the first decade of the Meiji period (1868-1880). Unfortunately, although many books on Japanese thought have been printed after Asō, he has had no real successor, partially because pre-war writers were too intent on explaining the "spirit" of Japan, and in the post-war years, the stress is on a social, if not Marxist, history of ideas.

Therefore, at the moment, the best which can be done is to give an introductory survey of Japanese thinkers, rather than a history of systems and philosophical ideas, for which the basic studies are still wanting. Writing as the author does in post-war Japan, it not superfluous to add that the thinkers discussed will be evaluated not on the basis of their "progressive" or "reactionary" political ideas and attitudes, but—as far as it is possible—on the basis of the consistency and value of their speculative thought.

A word of explanation and apology for more basic defects of this survey is in place. First of all, since my native language is not English, my writing lacks that smoothness and clarity which the subject requires. Secondly and even more important, are the inadequacies in handling the vast Japanese material which this survey entails. Japanese sources, as every scholar in Japanese studies is painfully aware of, are not the easiest documents in the world to understand and evaluate. Specific difficulties are to be found in rendering Japanese terms and ideas in a Western language. Furthermore, the selection of sources and points of emphasis will not meet with unanimous approval. In explanation, I can only say that recent Japanese philosophical thought covers practically all the trends of the world, from its philosophical beginnings to the latest philosopher, with a vastness and quantity of publication that nobody can pretend to have complete familiarity with.

Non-Japanese readers will also be surprised because too little is said about Buddhist and Confucianist thought. Recent Japanese philosophical thought, means in Japan, predominantly, if not exclusively, the Western type of philosophical thinking, as is explained in the book itself.

These and many other reasons which it would be tedious to enumerate should, perhaps, have induced me not to rush in where more qualified scholars have feared to tread. But the need for some such study, which I felt when I came to Japan in 1949 and later through my years of study under

Professor Mutai Risaku at Keiō Universitty, seems to be acute. It is felt by professional philosophers and by students of things Japanese. These and other readers can judge for themselves whether the present book is of assistance and can join.me in the hope that it will soon be complemented if not supplanted by better studies.

More than the usual perfunctory thanks must be added here to all who have helped me through this work: Prof. Mutai Risaku for many insights into Japanese philosophical trends; Miss Sandra Sims for her assiduous work on my English; Miss Kawasaki Michiko for secretarial work concerning the Japanese sources. In addition, special acknowledgement is due to several Fathers on the staff of Sophia University, who in different capacities have been of great assistance: J. Blewett, A. Jones, J. McKechney, F. Mathy, P. Milward, J. Pittau, J. Siemes, and A. Stawowy.

Obviously, the interpretations and shortcomings are the responsibility of the author alone.

Gino K. Piovesana, S.J.

Sophia University
Tokyo, May 1962

EXPLANATORY NOTE

Japanese names of persons are given, according to the Chinese-Japanese custom, with the family name first. Pen names and alternative readings of an author's given name have been placed in parentheses.

Long vowels are indicated by a macron over the vowels, ā, ō, ū, with the exception of familiar city names like Tokyo and Kyoto.

In the footnotes and in the Selected Bibliography when no reference is given to the publisher's place it is always understood that it is Tokyo.

CONTENTS

Chapter I

EARLY EMPIRICISM, POSITIVISM, AND EVOLUTIONISM
1862—1885

The Beginning of Western Philosophy

During the early part of 1862, the draft for the first lectures on Greek and European philosophy to be given in Japan was prepared at the Center for the Investigation of Barbarian Books (Bansho Shirabe-sho)[a] by Nishi Amane[b] (1829-97). In order to distinguish it from Buddhist and Chinese thought, Nishi used the term *Kitetsugaku*[c] for Western philosophy. *Kitetsugaku* was a new word, the result, maybe, of discussion between Nishi and his friend and colleague at the Center, Tsuda Mamichi[d] (1821-1903), who developed an early interest in philosophy. The new term became known in 1874, when Nishi printed it in his work *Hyakuichi shinron*[e] (A New Theory on the Hundred and One [Doctrine]).

More important than the term (Nishi was the originator of most of the Japanese Western philosophical terminology), a new discipline was introduced into Japan. Today, philosophy in the Western sense of the term is taught as a compulsory subject in most Japanese colleges and universities. Oriental thought is reserved to specialized courses. The ordinary freshman must undergo a general introduction to Western philosophy,

a. 蕃所調所   b. 西周   c. 希哲学   d. 津田真道   e. 百一新論

stress being laid on the specialty of the professor, who is well acquainted with Western thought and has often studied abroad. As a result, a great majority of students have a smattering of Kant's categories, Hegel's dialectic, Marx's theses, and Heidegger's or Sartre's existentialism, but know almost nothing of Buddhist or Confucianist philosophy. A cursory look at philosophical textbooks, which, due to the enormous student population of Japan, increase in number every year, will confirm this point. They are but introductions to Western philosophy.

However, this does not mean that Western philosophy had more socio-cultural influence upon Japanese mentality than their own oriental heritage, which is absorbed through thousands of other ways. Culture is not made up of philosophy only; even less are other socio-political trends, affecting both Western and Oriental people, determined by pure theory. Cultural "lags" occur more frequently than suspected. Because of the religious and doctrinal overtones of Buddhist and Confucianist thought, those who study philosophy usually mean the Western type of thinking. Western thought was imported mostly after the second opening of Japan, beginning with the Meiji Restoration in 1868.

The limitations of this survey allow for only a brief examination of the so-called Kirishitan[a] or Christian century of Japan. It began in 1549, when the first Catholic missionaries came to Japan, and ended in 1614, when hostilities against the foreign religion became official. In 1552, the Jesuit press of Amakusa[b] published a book of Fray Louis de Granada which, to some extent, was based on the philosophy of Aristotle. Later,

a. 切支丹   b. 天草

Pedro Gomez's *Breve Compendium* discussed Aristotle's *De Anima*. This work contained such distinctions as *"Intellectus agens"* and *"Intellectus possibilis."* The two *Summæ* of Thomas Aquinas and St. Augustine's *Confessions* were used in the seminaries conducted by Catholic missionaries. However, the persecution of Christians, and the seclusion policy enforced by the Tokugawa[a] Shōguns practically extinguished any foreign influence on religious and philosophical thought.[1]

Frequently scholars such as Arai Hakuseki[b] (1657-1725) and Hirata Atsutane[c] (1776-1843) are said to have been influenced by Western ideas. Yet this influence did not bring Confucianism or Shintoism any closer to Western forms of philosophy. In a recent edition of the sources of Japanese thought, the following precursors of Western philosophy are listed: Andō Shōeki[d] (about 1700), Minagawa Kien[e] (1734-1807), and Miura Baien[f] (1723-1789). Kaibara Ekken[g] (1630-1714) could also be included because of his work *Taigiroku*[h] (Grave Doubts), which shows a critical and rationalist mode of thinking.

Among these men, the most interesting is Miura Baien. He is also noted for having formulated a theory, similar to that of his contemporary, Adam Smith, on the Origin of Price *(Kagen)*[i], as well as for establishing a form of Gresham's law on the circulation of bad money.

a. 徳川   b. 新井白石   c. 平田篤胤   d. 安藤昌益   e. 皆川
淇園   f. 三浦梅園   g. 貝原益軒   h. 大疑録   i. 価原

1) For Fray Louis de Granada see: J. Lopez Gay S. J., La Primera Biblioteca de los Jesuitas, in *Monumenta Nipponica*, vol. XV n. 3-4, 1959-60, p. 159. For Pedro Gomez see: J Schütte S. J., Drei Unterrichtsbücher für Japanische Jesuitenprediger aus dem XVI. Jahrhundert, in *Archivum Historicum S.J.*, vol. VIII, 1939, pp. 223-56

Miura's philosophical views were incorporated in three books, the most metaphysical being *Gengo*[a] (Deep Talks). He revised this work thirty times, setting forth his *Shūrigaku*[b] or "Discipline of the Natural Order," based upon *jōri*[c] or "the logic of things." Miura's form of logic was a version of dialectic of reality, and was strongly pervaded by a positivist and rationalist spirit which did not respect authority or tradition.[2]

Miura's positivist spirit was no doubt influenced by Dutch writing and cultivated by *Rangaku*[d], Dutch Science, which consisted of anatomy, medicine, astronomy, geography, and military science, i.e., gunnery and coastal defense. Notwithstanding the seclusion policy, the Tokugawa allowed a few Dutch traders to remain in Deshima[e], an isolated section of Nagasaki. Shōgun Yoshimune's[f] edict of 1716 granted some freedom to translate and study books of Dutch Science. Other more ideological books were smuggled into Japan by Dutch merchants, and from China.

The influence of these illegal books is readily apparent. For example, the *Bunken manroku*[g] (Casual Records of Things Heard and Seen) written by Takano Chōei (Nagahide)[h], contains a survey of the history of philosophy which goes from Thales up to Kant, as well as a criticism of Aristotle's lack of an empirical approach to natural sciences. Takano did not have a specific term for philosophy. He used the word *Gakushi*[i],

---

a. 玄語   b. 修理学   c. 条理   d. 蘭学   e. 出島   f. 吉宗
将軍   g. 聞見漫録   h. 高野長英   i. 学師

2) *Nihon tetsugaku shisō zensho I. Tetsugaku-hen* 日本哲学思想全書 1 哲学篇 (Complete Collection of Japanese Philosophy and Thought vol. I: Philosophy), ed. by Hasegawa Nyozekan 長谷川如是閑. Shimizu Ikutarō 清水幾太郎. Sa'gusa Hiroto 三枝博音. Heibonsha, 1957

which means in context "general or the most important learning." Takano, who is considered a precursor of Western philosophy in Japan, is known as well for his bold, progressive ideas concerning the opening of Japan to the West; ideas which he promoted in many books and pamphlets.

As such notions were unwanted at that time, Takano was obliged to go into hiding more than once to escape the police. In 1840 he was captured and sentenced to life imprisonment. He escaped in 1844. However, the police again pursued him, and he took his life by harakiri to avoid the sword of the emissaries sent to get him.[3]

As an historical curiosity, the oldest philosophical books known in Japan were Lewes's *Biographical History of Philosophy*, 1843, and Kant's *Anthropologie*. The latter was brought to Japan by the merchant C. E. Boedinghaus, a German, who, no doubt, passed as a Hollander, and who had occasion to meet Nishi Amane.[4]

Two Pioneers: Tsuda and Nishi

The career of Nishi, as well as that of Tsuda and many leading intellectuals of the Meiji Restoration, is typical in that it indicates the burden laid upon the pioneers of Western knowledge. These men usually came from a clan of samurai or from a physician's family. They received classical Chinese training, and went to Nagasaki[a] or Edo[b] (the former name of Tokyo)

---

a. 長崎　　　b. 江戸

3) Kuwaki Gen'yoku 桑木厳翼. *Meiji no tetsugaku-kai* 明治の哲学界 (Meiji Philosophical World), Chūōkōronsha, 1943, pp. 10-12

4) Asō Yoshiteru 麻生義輝, *Kinsei Nihon tetsugaku-shi* 近世日本哲学史 (History of Recent Japanese Philosophy), Kondō Shoten, 1943, pp. 124-27

for Dutch Science. Then they were sent abroad. When they returned, they were given official duties in the new government, and were rewarded with a peerage at the end of their careers. Nishi was born in Iwami[a] province (Shimane[b] prefecture) in the castle town (Tsuwano[c]) of the Tsuwano clan. His father was a physician. Tsuda Mamichi (Shindō) was born in Okayama[d], and came from a samurai family. The two went to Edo for study; Tsuda in 1847 and Nishi in 1852. After completing their studies, they were attached to the staff of the Bansho Shirabe-sho. There, the two men developed an interest in philosophical problems; so much so that Nishi even prepared a few lectures on the subject. However, philosophy was not highly regarded by the authorities in charge of the Center for Western Studies.

In June, 1862, Nishi, Tsuda and fifteen others were sent to study abroad. The group, under the leadership of the future admiral Enomoto Takeaki[e], was composed of naval cadets, while Nishi and Tsuda were to study mostly law and political science. They departed from Shinagawa[f], a port which is now a part of Tokyo, stopped briefly at Nagasaki and reached Rotterdam a year later. Nishi and Tsuda went to Leyden, where, after polishing their Dutch, they had S. Vissering for economics, law and political science and C. W. Opzoomer for philosophy. Tsuda adapted the lectures of Vissering and published them in 1868 in the *Taisei kokuhō-ron*[g] (A Treatise on Western Public Law). In the same year Nishi rendered Vissering's lectures on International Public Law *(Bankoku kōho)*[h] into Japanese, as he was obliged to teach that subject when

a. 岩見   b. 島根   c. 津和野   d. 岡山   e. 榎本武揚
f. 品川   g. 秦西国法論   h. 万国公法

be returned to Japan. Nishi translated R. Ihering's *Der Kampf ums Recht*, and wrote an introduction to public law, the *Kōhō teroku*[a], which was published in 1882.

Tsuda is remembered for his translation of Vissering's *Statistics*, the *Hyōkiteikō*[b], which was the first of the genre in the Japanese language. As far as philosophy is concerned, Comte's positivism and the empiricism of J. S. Mill were quite in favor in Leyden. According to Tsuda's testimonial, Nishi was inclined toward idealistic philosophy, while he himself was more positivist, if not materialist.

Nishi and Tsuda left Leyden for Paris in October, 1865, where they met another well-known intellectual and political leader of the early Meiji era, Mori Arinori[c]. Leaving from Marseille and journeying through Alexandria and Suez, the group arrived in Japan on the 28th of December.

Among the books which Nishi brought back were many works by Comte and Mill. Cousin, Montesquieu and Hegel's *Phänomenologie des Geistes* were also included. There were many books on naval and military science, the information of which enabled Nishi to compile a military dictionary, as well as more readable material such as Dickens' *A Tale of Two Cities*, and several books of J. Verne, an author widely read in the middle of the Meiji period by science-minded Japanese.

Upon their return, the two men were assigned to the Kaisei-sho[d]. This was an offspring of the former Center for Western Studies (Bansho Shirabe-sho) which developed into the Kaisei School and eventually became Tokyo University. Dutch was no longer the language of Western learning. When

a. 公法手録　　b. 表記提綱　　c. 森有礼　　d. 開成所

traveling abroad, the Japanese realized that English, French and German were of greater value. Nishi even taught French to the last Shōgun, Keiki[a], around 1867. At that time Nishi was in Kyoto, having left Edo in September, 1866, to move to Osaka[b] with the Shōgun. The final days of the Tokugawa Shogunate were approaching. Nishi proposed two plans of reform to the de facto ruler of Japan. The first plan preserved the rights and privileges of the Shōgun: he was to be president of the Upper House, with power to dissolve the lower one. The second plan was more realistic, though less acceptable to the ruler. He was advised to retire peacefully to Hokkaidō[c] and develop that desolate region, giving the sixteen-year-old Emperor and his ministers a free hand in the main part of Japan.

However, events, not plans, were decisive. Nishi, although he sided with the losing faction, that of the Shogunate, did not end his career. In November, 1868, he assumed charge of the Numazu Military School[d] and a year later he was at the Ministry of Military Affairs (Hyōbusho)[e] in Tokyo. He taught at the Ikueisha[f] and produced, during 1870-1873, the majority of his philosophical books. His manuscripts indicated that from September, 1871, for more than a year, he gave lectures to the Emperor Meiji on Western history and philosophy.

Nishi and Tsuda became members of a famous group founded by Mori Arinori called *Meirokusha*[g]. This name was derived from the sixth (*roku*)[h] year of the Meiji era, 1873. Other members of this group were Kanda Kōhei[i], Katō Hiroyuki[j], Nakamura Masanao[k], Nishimura Shigeki[l] and Fukuzawa

---

a. 慶喜   b. 大阪   c. 北海道   d. 沼津兵学校   e. 兵部省
f. 育英舎   g. 明六社   h. 六   i. 神田孝平   j. 加藤弘之
k. 中村正直   l. 西村茂樹

Yukichi[a]. Under the motto "Civilization and Enlightenment" (*Bummei kaika*)[b] this group of "Illuminists" (*keimōshugisha*)[c] take the lead in diffusing Western progressive ideas and customs throughout Japan.

Both Nishi and Tsuda wrote important articles in the magazine *Meiroku Zasshi*[d], the organ of the group. The most debated question at the time was whether or not intellectuals should participate in political life by taking up governmental duties. Nearly all of the *Meirokusha* were in official positions with the exception of Fukuzawa Yukichi. He remained aloof, and preserved his independence. He was, therefore, not really committed to conservative or autocratic trends.

Tsuda became superintendent of the police in Shizuoka[e]. He was later promoted to the position of judge, with the power of framing laws. He then became Secretary of the Foreign Office, traveling to China as envoy with Date Muneki[f]. He became member of the Tokyo Academy and Chairman of the House of Representatives in 1890. The same year he was made a member of the House of Peers and was nominated to the rank of count and baron.

Nishi, on the other hand, worked more in the educational field, planning new programs. He was elected president of the Tokyo Academy in 1879, and was re-elected seven times. Nishi also went to the House of Peers in 1890. Like Tsuda, he was titled count, and posthumously made a baron. Nishi was most fortunate to have Mori Ōgai[g] as his biographer. Mori, by profession a doctor but much more famous as a novelist, was related

a. 福沢諭吉　　b. 文明開化　　c. 啓蒙主義者　　d. 明六雑誌
e. 静岡　　f. 伊達宗城　　g. 森鷗外

to Nishi by marriage and was born in the same locality, Tsuwano.[5]

Little is said about Tsuda's philosophical activity, for his writings on the subject were limited in number. However, he developed an early interest in philosophy; apparently it never died, as indicated by the works of Nishi Amane. Nishi tried more than once and to no avail to refute Tsuda's naturalism and materialism. This naturalism was most apparent in a short essay entitled *Seiri-ron*[a] (On the Nature of Things) written by Tsuda in 1868. Another essay, *Yuibutsuron*[b] (Materialism) appeared in the Journal of the Tokyo Academy in 1862.

In Leyden, Tsuda declared himself a positivist; Nishi, on the other hand, favored Kant. Actually, however, Nishi was impressed not by Kant's critical epistemology, but by his work *On Eternal Peace*. Tsuda's early "energy" (*tenki*)[c], the unlimited and undetermined pervading element of all things, grew increasingly scientific and positivist after contact with the ideas of the French Encyclopedists and the materialist and positivist philosophy flourishing in Europe at the time. Yet, in spite of his activities, Tsuda remained more legal expert than philosopher or thinker. Kuwaki[d] attributed to Tsuda many legal terms such as *Mimpō*[e], meaning Civil Law[6].

a. 性理論   b. 唯物論   c. 天気   d. 桑木厳翼   e. 民法

5) *Nishi Amane den* 西周伝 (The Biography of Nishi Amane) is to be found in the complete works of Mori Ōgai 森鷗外 like *Ōgai zenshū* 鷗外全集 vol. 9, pp. 3-110, Iwanami Shoten, 1937. See also R. F. Hackett, Nishi Amane, A Tokugawa-Meiji Bureaucrat, in *The Journal of Asian Studies*, vol. XVIII: N2, Feb. 1959, pp. 213-25

6) Kuwaki G., *Meiji . . .*, o.c., pp. 91-115; Nagata Hiroshi 永田広志, *Nihon yuibutsuron-shi* 日本唯物論史 (History of Japanese Materialism), Haku-yōsha, 1949, pp. 94-97

Philosophical Works of Nishi Amane

Nishi Amane fully merited the name of father of Japanese Western philosophy. He was credited with the creation of a great part of Japanese philosophical terminology, much of which is still in use today. Nishi did translation, adaptation and, to some extent, original work. His terminology was polished and perfected by Inoue Tetsujirō[a] during the period from 1881 to 1882. Inoue also edited the *Tetsugaku Jii*[b], a *Dictionary of Philosophical Terms*. This work was completely revised in 1912.

The pioneering efforts of Nishi cleared a path not too difficult for others to pursue. Indeed, the most strenuous part was uniting the ideographical Chinese-Japanese characters with the novel Western ideas to form a clear, accurate terminology.

To give but one example, in 1874 Nishi adopted the term *Tetsugaku*[c] for philosophy. This word was an abbreviation of *Kitetsugaku*, which, in turn, was an abbreviation of *Kikyū tetsuchi*[d], Science of Questing Wisdom, or Love of Wisdom, according to Greek etymology. In his early manuscripts Nishi wavered, using terms like *Kyūrigaku*[e] (natural philosophy), *Rigaku*[f] (Science of *ri*[g]: reason; today it indicates natural science), *Seirigaku*[h] (Science of the nature of things; today it means physiology). Later he realized that, to Western thinkers, the word philosophy also denoted "mental philosophy," that is, philosophical psychology and moral philosophy as well. The above terms were abandoned, and Nishi adopted *Tetsugaku*,

a. 井上哲次郎　　b. 哲学字彙　　c. 哲学　　d. 希求哲智　　e. 窮理
学　　f. 理学　　g. 理　　h. 性理学

which became the standard word for philosophy, partly on account of his position in educational affairs.[7]

True, Nishi, like all other Meiji pioneers of Western learning, had some Chinese books for reference. But they were no more illuminating than Western sources. There was little set terminology, if any at all, in China. Typical of the Chinese framework of thought rather than due to Chinese characters was Nishi's explanation of philosophy given in the *Hyakuichi shinron*. Nishi stated that philosophy was the message to clarify and indicate the Way to Heaven *(tendō jindō)[a]*. This elucidation was surely Confucianistic, but not quite Western. However, Nishi's *Hyakugaku renkan[b]* contained a competent analysis of the term philosophy.

It is not easy to determine exactly when Nishi actually wrote his many manuscripts although the printed ones were dated. Yet, the dates differed from the actual time of writing. His collected essays, *Nishi sensei ronshū[c]*, appeared in 1880, but only at present is a compete edition in preparation.[8]

a. 天道人道   b. 百学連環   c. 西先生論集

7)   See Asō Y.. *Kinsei . . .*, o.c., pp. 315-16 for the evolution of the Japanese philosophical terminology. *Kitetsu* 希哲 seems to come from *Kiken* 希賢 (the quest for wisdom or perspicacity) or from *Shikiken* 士希賢 (the searcher after wisdom) terms to be found in the *Taikyokuzusetsu* 太極図説 by Shūrenkei (Chou L'en-ch'i, 1017-73) 周 濂渓. See Kazue Kyōichi-Sagara Tōru 数江教一, 相良享, *Nihon no rinri* 日本の倫理, Ōbunkan, 1959, p. 144. See also p. 255, footnote 10

8)   *Nishi tetsugaku chosaku-shū* 西哲学著作集 (Collected Philosophical Works of Nishi) ed. by Asō Yoshiteru 麻生義輝, Iwanami Shoten, 1933. A good chronological table is added, pp. 335-51, and an explanation of Nishi's works, pp. 355-405 *Nishi Amane zenshū* 西周全集 (The Complete Works of Nishi Amane), Nihon Hyōronsha, 1944, ed. by Ōkubo Toshiaki.

Reikon ichigenron[a] (Monism of the Soul) was among Nishi's oldest works. This contained a type of monistic animism combined with a positivist's scorn for metaphysics, termed *Kūriron*[b], the Abstract, or Empty Theory. Another essay of importance, the *Shōhaku tōki*[c] (a title which defies translation), attempted a classification of different sciences; it was comparatively complete for even sociology was included. Philosophy was represented by the Chinese character *ri*, which has a greater ideological history than our word "reason." Written in 1873 were *Bimyōgaku-setsu*[d], (Aesthetics), and *Shakaitōron-setsu*[e], (Socialist Theory), a work in which Owen, Saint-Simon, and Fourier were criticised according to the ideas of Vissering. Nishi, therefore, was the first to introduce socialist thought into Japan, although Katō Hiroyuki, too, wrote on socialism about the same time. W. Learned also brought in socialism. He came to Japan in 1875 and taught at Dōshisha[f], the Protestant school, later a university, in Kyoto.[9]

The *Seisei hatsuun*[g], (The Relationship between the Physical and the Spiritual), was a work of great political importance. It was composed of two sections, the first of which was a history of philosophy, concluding with Comte, in which Nishi

a. 靈魂一元論　　b. 空理論　　c. 尚白割記　　d. 美妙学説　　e. 社会党論説　　f. 同志社　　g. 生性発蘊

大久保利謙 only the first volume came out in which the *Hyakugaku renkan* 百学連環 and *Hyakuichi shinron* are included. The same Ōkubo is now re-editing the complete works of Nishi: *Nishi Amane zenshū*, Munetaka Shobō, 1960; and the first volume is already out, in which the philosophical works are printed. For a commentary on the *Hyakuichi shinron* see: Kuwaki Gen'yoku 桑木厳翼 *Nishi Amane no Hyakuichi shinron* 西周の百一新論, Nihon Hōsō Shuppan Kyōkai, 1940

9) See Asō Y., in *Nishi tetsugaku chosaku-shū* . . ., o.c., p. 390, and Asō Y., in *Kinsei* . . .. o.c.. pp. 263-65

showed his sympathy for the French positivist. This exposition of Comte was, acording to Asō Yoshiteru[a], the best historian of early Meiji philosophy, a translation of Lewes's *Biographical History of Philosophy*. Kōsaka Masaaki[b] observes that Nishi, because he borrowed from Mill, did not follow Comte's subordination of the socio-cultural sciences to the biological.[10]

The *Hyakuichi shinron* (A New Theory on the Hundred and One [Doctrine]), published in 1874, apparently dates back to the years 1866-67. This work was significant not only because it introduced the new term for philosophy, but also for its programmatic title in which the "One Doctrine" represented a new discipline: philosophy harmonizing all other sciences. Confucianism was discussed, primarily in the first section, but morality was not confused with the actual system of governing the country as the Old School was wont to do. Nishi's progressive thinking came out even more clearly in the second section of his work, where Comte's theory of the three stages, (referred to as places—*basho*[c] in Nishi's terminology), as well as Mill's a priori and a posteriori principles were discussed. Interpreters of Nishi's thought, such as Asō and Kōsaka, point out that his a priori principle was physical, governing the world of nature, while his spiritual or a posteriori principle governed man. Nishi's moral law was therefore contrasted to his law of nature, although the two should have been combined into a harmonized whole. The philosophy of Nishi was systematized according to three elements: *chi-jō-i*[a], that is, wisdom, sentiment and volition.

Another notable work, dating from 1870 to 1873, although it may have been written earlier, was the *Encyclopedia*. In Japanese it was entitled *Hyakugaku renkan*, (The Link of the Hundred Sciences); the English subtitle "Encyclopedia" was given by Nishi himself. The manuscript of this work was discovered in 1932. Nishi drew from it during his lectures at the Ikueisha school from 1870 through 1873. Nevertheless, it was not an encyclopedia in the ordinary sense of the word; it had no alphabetical order. It was rather a systematic classification of branches of Western learning, based on a similar English work. Definitions in English were abundantly given. The introduction, of which two drafts exist, is of special interest because it presented Mill's "new logic," his reduction and induction and other logical terms, as well as his ideas of political truth and freedom. Comte's theory of three stages or places was again discussed.

It is apparent from the scope of his writings that many philosophers were known to Nishi. However, his preference was clearly not for Kant or Hegel, but for the positivists such as Comte and Mill. Nishi's liberal ideas on political problems too were evident. The first section of his *Encyclopedia* covered the "common sciences;" that is, history, geography, literature, philology, and mathematics. The second section dealt with the "particular sciences" commencing with the "intellectual": theology, philosophy, politics and economics, ethics, aesthetics and jurisprudence. Other sections of the second part contained de-

a. 智．情．意

finitions of various natural sciences. The customary historical survey was given.

Concerning philosophy, besides the above mentioned definition, love of wisdom, Nishi remarked that while religion is based on belief, philosophy is based on reason. He briefly described the different branches of philosophy. Logic *(chichigaku)* [a], the Law of Thinking, was originated by Aristotle and renewed by J. S. Mill. Psychology *(shinrigaku)* [b] presented the problem of the union of man's soul with his body. Ontology *(ritaigaku)* [c] was defined as the doctrine of being as *tai* [d], that is, being as substance. Ethics *(rinrigaku)* [e], as explained by Nishi, comprised man's obligations to the Sublime Being, "between ourselves and to ourselves."

For all its magnitude, Nishi's *Encyclopedia* was introductory. It was intended to clarify and explain the branches of Western learning to Japanese pupils. In the discussion of religion, Buddhism and Confucianism were mentioned. Therefore, some doubt arises as to the validity of the statement of Kōsaka declaring that Nishi's work was comparable to the work of the French Encyclopedists. Still, the merits of Nishi must not be underestimated, even if on a much more modest scale.

At the Ikueisha school Nishi taught logic for the most part. The contents of his lectures were included in the *Gogen shinhan* [f] and in the *Chichi-keimō* [g], published in 1874. His logic was based on Mill's *System of Logic, ratiocinative and inductive.* These works of Nishi were no doubt the first manuals on logic

a. 致知学   b. 心理学   c. 理体学   d. 体   e. 倫理学   f. 五
原新範   g. 致知啓蒙

in Japan. The first book contained an adaptation of Comte's division of sciences; in the second, Mill predominated. Only a a hundred copies of the *Chichi-keimō* were originally printed However, in 1881 the students of the Shihan Gakkō[a] (Normal School) printed a second edition. As director of the school Nishi would not thrust his textbook on the Logic professor Kikuchi[b]. Consequently, the students themselves were responsible for the new edition of Nishi's work.[12]

For the *Meirokusha* journal of October, 1875, Nishi wrote the *Jinsei sampō-setsu*[c] (The Theory of Three Treasures of Life), those being health, knowledge and wealth. The spirit of the Meiji times was reflected in this work; old Confucianist ethics were criticized and utilitarian principles were advocated. In another essay, published two years earlier, Nishi maintained that happiness consisted of the harmonic development of spiritual and physical aptitudes.

Nishi was never among the most progressive Westernizers. As director of the Shihan Gakkō he proposed a moral eclecticism, combining Eastern and Western ethics. This proposition was quite in tune with the mounting reaction against the ultra-westernization of Japan, a feeling in vogue ten years before.

Nishi made a translation of Mill's *Utilitarianism (Rigaku)*, suggested to him by the Abbot of the Nishi Honganji[d], Suzuki Keijun[e], with whom he was on good terms. The translation came out in 1877. For the Ministry of Education he translated Joseph Haven's *Mental Philosophy*. This translation, printed

a. 師範学校   b. 菊地   c. 人生三宝説   d. 西本願寺
e. 鈴木慧淳
12) See Asō Y., *Kinsei . . .*, o.c., pp. 292-308 for Nishi's logic; for psychology see pp. 309-15

in 1878, was used for a time as a textbook.

Nishi's interest in psychology (limited to philosophical and rational, for experimental was introduced into Japan later, by Motora Yūjirō)[a], was manifested in a lecture given at the Tokyo Academy in 1886. Among his last philosophical works, Nishi wrote an essay on logic in 1884, titled *Ronri shin-setsu*[b]. Another work was his *Seisei tōki*[c], a treatise on psychology written in *Kambun*[d] (the old Chinese style), which emphasized the role of the will. According to Asō, Nishi spent a great deal of time writing it. It was started around 1873, was newly drafted two years later, and taken up again in Nishi's last years, spent at his villa in Oiso[e]. Death prevented him from completing the treatise.

In conclusion, it can be said that although Nishi did not have the "system" attributed to him by Kōsaka, Comte-Mill empiricism and positivism was evident in many of his works. A kind of eclecticism was natural, considering the task of the pioneers of Western thought in Japan. Those men faced a multitude of different trends in the West; at the same time, they felt it their duty to adapt them to their Eastern heritage. Nishi made no special effort to unite the two ways of thinking. He was satisfied merely to introduce Western thought. Some amusing applications resulted as, for example, in the case of Mill's a priori and a posteriori principles previously mentioned.

The Evolutionism of Kato Hiroyuki

Although the *Meirokusha* has been mentioned and the lead-in role played by this group of "Illuminists" in spreading liberal

a. 元良勇次郎   b. 論理新説   c. 生性剳記   d. 漢文   e. 大磯

and utilitarian ideas in early Meiji times has been discussed, much more should be said.

In 1875 Fukuzawa Yukichi (1834-1901) wrote the *Bummeiron no gairyaku*[a] (The Outline of Civilization) which put forward a theory of history based on Guizot and Buckle. This work declared that mankind has passed through three stages: savagery, barbarism, and civilization. Barbarism was characterized by agricultural and feudal stages; Japan was included here. Civilization was characterized by liberal and scientific phases, into which Japan was destined to enter. Fukuzawa stressed that civilization was made neither from upper nor from lower stratas; he held that it was formed by the intellectuals of the middle class. This viewpoint was typical of the "Illuminist" group, which at this time advocated a democratic government.

Fukuzawa's middle-class liberal outlook was also stated in his other book *Gakumon no susume*[b] (The Encouragement of Learning), written in 1880, which began with the famous words "Heaven creates no man above man, no man under man." Unfortunately, the limitations of this survey prohibit a detailed analysis of Fukuzawa, whose interesting personality truly deserves a comprehensive study in a Western language.[13]

---

a. 文明論の概略   b. 学問のすすめ

13) For the *Meirokusha* 明六社 see: Asō Y., *Kinsei* . . ., o.c., pp. 1-13; 135-85; 267-81. *Japanese Thought* . . . ed. by Kōsaka, o.c., pp. 61-65. Of Fukuzawa Yukichi 福沢諭吉 there is in English: *The Autobiography of Fukuzawa Yukichi*, transl. by Kiyooka Eiichi, Hokuseidō, 1960. The most complete biography in Japanese is: Ishikawa Kammei石河幹明, *Fukuzawa Yukichi den* 福沢諭吉伝, 4 vols., Iwanami Shoten, 1932-33. The most complete edition of his works is: *Fukuzawa Yukichi zenshū* 福沢諭吉全集, Iwanami Shoten, 1958 ff. planned in 21 vols., at present 18 vols. are published. About Fukuzawa see: *Japanese Thought* . . . ed.

For philosophical importance among the *Meirokusha*, Katō Hiroyuki (1836-1916) must be listed next to Nishi and Tsuda. Katō was more of a political thinker, a social Darwinist, than a philosopher. Nevertheless, his social thought had a very systematic materialist and evolutionist basis. This was not too common among the eclectic thinkers of early Meiji times.

Katō was first a teacher at the Kaisei School; later, in 1877, he was the organizer of the new Tokyo University, as well as its president in 1881 and 1900. His numerous educational activities influenced the introduction of German thought into the foremost academic educational center in Japan. Katō was typical in that he showed in his evolving views the "tour de force," which many of the former "Illuminists" made in passing from liberal and utilitarian ideas of the first decade of the Meiji period to more conservative views in the second decade. Another characteristic of Katō was that, in order to support autocratic trends, he did not refer to the Oriental heritage, as did the majority of the thinkers who will be studied in the next chapter. Katō remained a Westerner; he absorbed Western ideas, specifically racial evolutionism and materialism, which were adapted to strengthen anti-democratic tendencis prevalent from 1886. As recent history proves, autocracy and the "raison d'etat" can be fostered by extreme idealism as well as by extreme materialism.

Katō's autobiography states that although he was obliged to study military science, his interests lay in philosophy, ethics,

by Kōsaka, o.c., pp. pp. 68-84: *Fukuzawa Yukichi no hito to shisō* 福沢諭吉の人と思想 (Fukuzawa Y. as Man and Thinker), Iwanami Shoten, 1940, a series of studies by different experts.

and law. Around 1860-62 he wrote a political tract for private
circulation which had the mild Arcadian title of *Tonarigusa*[a]
(literally, Neighboring Vegetation). This tract criticized absolute monarchy and aristocratic despotism, and advocated a
constitutional monarchy. Allegedly, the criticism was directed
at neighboring China. However, all understood that Katō really
meant Japan. From 1868 to 1874 when more freedom was allowed, he published three books, works in which his liberal
ideas were made even more explicit. In his last, *Kokutai shinron*[b] (A New Theory of National Polity), published in 1874, he
dared to affirm that it was time to cast aside the characteristic
Japanese servility toward superiors which made the people
"cattle and horses" and "slaves of the Imperial Will." Consequently, he was forced to resign from his post of Genrō-in[c], a
position in the first Senate, before the Meiji Constitution of
1889. The conservative *Kokugakusha*[d], or National Scholars,
persuaded the authorities to suppress Katō's works.

In 1882, his *Jinken shinsetsu*[e] (A New Theory of Human
Rights) based on Darwin's natural selection refuted the "chi-
meras" upheld before, namely, that man was born with the rights
of liberty, equality and self-government. Katō declared that
rights were born with the state, that heredity and environment
explained the differences between men.

Darwinism, Haeckel's monism, Gumplowicz's racial anthro-
pologism, etc., were developed in what a student of Katō's
thought, Tabata Shinobu[f], termed his greatest work, *Kyōsha no
kenri no kyōsō*[g] (The Struggle for the Rights of the Strongest)

a. 鄰草   b. 国体新論   c. 元老院   d. 国学者   e. 人権新説
f. 田畑忍   g. 強者の権利の競争

published in 1883. It was published also in German under the title *Der Kampf ums Recht des Stärkeren und seine Entwicklung*. Little comment is here necessary. Katō had an obvious preference for dialectical contradictions in nature and in the world of man. This was a well known argument, exploited by all social Darwinists in the last century as well as in the beginning of the present. I do not intend to enter into the reasons why Katō made such a change; they were, naturally, quite philosophico-scientific according to Katō. For the historians indicated in the notes, the reasons of Katō's new view ranged from the class interest of Marxists to the more ideological reasons, such as those considered by Kōsaka and Tsuchida Kyōson[a], another historian of Japanese thought.[14] All these reasons have good points; none are totally satisfactory. At any rate, the fight for civil rights and democracy was losing ground in Japan. A few years later the new Constitution would end a period so promising from a liberal point of view. Katō, more than any other of the early liberal "Illuminists," was in the forefront, supporting the changing trend.

In addition, Katō published *Dōtoku hōritsu no shimpo*[b] (The Progress of Moral Law) in 1894, *Shizen-kai no mujun to shinka*[c] (Contradiction in Nature and Evolutionism) in 1906,

---

a. 土田杏村   b. 道徳法律の進歩   c. 自然界の矛盾と進化

14) *Japanese Thought* . . . ed. by Kōsaka, o.c., pp. 87-94; 152-59. Tsuchida Kyōson, *Contemporary Thought of Japan and China*, London 1927, pp. 40-41; 152; 58. For Katō Hiroyuki's 加藤弘之 political activity see books like R.A. Scalapino, *Democracy and the Party Movement in Prewar Japan*, Berkeley 1953, pp. 55-56; 71-72; Ike Nobutaka, *The Beginnings of Political Democracy in Japan*, Baltimore 1950, pp. 114-17; G. B. Sansom, *The Western World and Japan*, New York 1951, pp. 434-35

and other books and articles on ethics, such as *Nature and Ethics, Responsibility*, both of which were published in 1915. Katō's position was unchanging. His ethics were based on a materialist and egoist conception of man. This conception was criticized by Ōnishi Hajime[a]. Ebina Danjō[b], president of Dōshisha University, too, attempted to show the inconsistency of Katō's materialism with the Emperor cult and veneration for ancestors. To these critics, Katō replied with a bulky book of more than three hundred pages, the *Meisōteki uchūkan*[c] (Superstitious World View) published in 1908. This book bluntly restated his materialistic views and dislike of Christianity.[15]

Philosophy and Foreign Professors at Tokyo University

As previously mentioned, Tokyo University was organized from pre-existing education centers, under the direction of Katō, in 1877. From this time on, philosophy was taught in the University, although real chairs with more specialized professors came only in 1886, with the re-organization of the University into the Tokyo Imperial University[d]. English was used as a teaching language. Japanese professors had English textbooks, from which translations were made. This partly explains the success of English empiricism and utilitarianism, as well as the vogue of Bentham's and Spencer's ideas in academic circles. English editions of Rousseau and Montesquieu were also translated into Japanese.

As ethico-political problems occurred primarily during this

a. 大西祝   b. 海老名弾正   c. 迷相的宇宙観   d. 東京帝国大学
15) Tabata Shinobu 田畑 忍, *Katō Hiroyuki* 加藤弘之, Yoshikawa Kōbunkan. 1959, pp. 156-63, whom I have followed for my brief sketch. Bibliography at pp. 208-11. See also Asō Y., *Kinsei . . .*, o.c., pp. 256-62

period, the president of Brown University, Francis Wayland's work *Elements of Moral Science* was read in Japan, even before the Meiji Restoration of 1868. His *Elements of Political Economy* was even more widely circulated. Similarly, Mill's *Representative Government* was more often read than his *System of Logic*. Other widely assimilated books on ethical problems were *Self Help and Character*, both written by Samuel Smiles. His translator was Nakamura Masanao (Keiu, 1832-1891), a *Meirokusha* member who attempted, especially in his later years, to combine Christianity with Confucianism. He also translated another popular book, *On Liberty* by J. S. Mill. Nakamura's educational activity was centered around the emancipation and education of Japanese women. From 1875 to 1880 he served as director of the Tokyo Women's Normal School[a], an institute in which Christian influences were very strong. From 1881 on, he was professor of Chinese Classics *(Kangaku)*[b] at Tokyo University. His career indicates his efforts to combine Christianity with Confucianism. Another book on ethics used at this time was Mark Hopkin's *Lectures on Moral Science.*

Among the first professors to teach philosophy in Japan was James Summer, who gave lectures on Logic at the Kaisei School in 1875. The textbooks used were Fowler's *Deductive Logic* and Mill's *System of Logic.* In 1876 W. Stanley Jevon's *Pure Logic* was used by Toyama Masakazu.

The first foreign professor to teach logic at the newly established Tokyo University came from England in 1877. He was named Syle; his textbooks were Mark Hopkins's *Study of Man* and Haven's *Mental Philosophy.* The latter, as mentioned was

a. 東京女子師範学校   b. 漢学

translated into Japanese by Nishi Amane. A. Bain's *Psychology* and Spencer's *Principles of Psychology* were used by Toyama Masakazu[a] (Shōichi, 1848-1900), who was noted as the propagator of Spencer's ideas. Toyama went to England in 1865, and then to the University of Michigan in 1872. After having studied natural sciences and philosophy, he returned to Japan in 1876, a confirmed Spencerian. Rather than as a professor of psychology, Toyama was known as the founder of the first chair of sociology at Tokyo Imperial University, in 1893.

Spencer's sociology was developed fully by a former philosophy student, Ariga Nagao[b], who published three volumes in the years 1883 to 1894 titled *Sociology*. It was due to Toyama and Katō, who was president of the University in 1897 and Minister of Education in 1898, that the first years of Tokyo University were known as the time of *Daigaku Shinkaron*[c] (lit. University Evolutionism), so much was this institution a center of diffusion of ideas on evolution.

The bio-zoological side of evolutionism was introduced to Japan by Edward S. Morse, an American appointed as professor of zoology in 1877. Another Darwinist was Yatabe Ryōkichi[d], a botanist who studied at Cornell University and held Haeckel's monism. Morse left Japan in 1879, and persuaded Ernest F. Fenollosa to come from Harvard. Fenollosa stayed in Japan from 1878 to 1885, teaching the history of philosophy. He followed an English edition of Schwegler's *History of Philosophy*, his lectures covering the period from Descartes to Hegel. Bowen's *Modern Philosophy* was also used as a textbook.

Fenollosa, known abroad for his pioneer work on Oriental

a. 外山正一   b. 有賀長雄   b. 大学進化論   d. 矢田部良吉

art, was a follower of Spencer, especially of the theory of the evolution of society and religion. As Inoue Tetsujirō protested with disgust in 1880, Spencer had become the "god of the time." Lectures given by Dr. Joseph Clark attacking the theories of Darwin and Spencer were of no avail. Clark, on a world tour, gave several lectures in Japan, where he was questioned avidly, and was even requested to answer such queries as the advantages cf inter-marriages, a concept which Japanese zealots favored in hope of improving the national stock by selection of the fittest.

Miyake Yūjirō[a] reported that Fenollosa was more eloquent than deep, and that he supported the introduction of *Hegel's Logic*. This book, written by Wallace, balanced the prevailing empirical logic of Mill. Around 1890, an Englishman, Professor Cooper, lectured on Kant's critics. However, German philosophy was not formally studied until 1887, when L. Busse, a disciple of Lotze, used Kant's *Critic of Pure Reason* as a reading text. This, though, belonged to a new phase of Japanese Western philosophy, one which will be considered in the following chapter.

In 1884 the *Tetsugaku-kai*[b], the first Philosophical Society, was founded. There were twenty-nine members; the leading figures were Katō, Nishi, Nishimura Shigeki, Toyama and several young first graduates from the philosophy department of Tokyo University, as well as from private schools, such as Inoue Tetsujirō, Ariga Nagao, Miyake, Inoue Enryō[c]. These young men played a leading role in the second decade of the Meiji period.

The Philosophical Society reached a membership of sixty-

a. 三宅雄二郎（雪嶺）   b. 哲学界   c. 井上円了

six by 1886, and in February of 1887 the first issue of the Society's journal *Tetsugaku-kai zasshi*[a] appeared. Besides articles on philosophy in general, this magazine contained writings of Motora Yūjirō on *Seishin butsurigaku*,[b] now called *Jikken shinrigaku*[c] or experimental psychology. Motora's term for it was "Spiritual Physics"; as this branch of learning had just begun, no precise terminology had been formed.

Although he studied in the United States, Motora, too, was under the influence of Anglo-German philosophy. Others, such as Inoue, went to Germany, and, on their return, began a trend favoring German or Anglo-German idealism. This trend was to succeed the early French-English positivism and empiricism.[16]

---

a. 哲学会雑誌　　b. 精神物理学　　c. 実験心理学

16) See especially *Kindai Nihon shisō-shi* 近代日本思想史 (History of Recent Japanese Thought), ed. by Tōyama Shigeki 遠山茂樹 and Others, Aoki Shoten, 1960, vol. I, pp. 219-56; Miyanishi Kazumi 宮西一積, *Kindai shisō no nihonteki tenkai* 近代思想の日本的展開 (The Japanese Development of Recent Thought), Fukumura Shoten, 1960, pp. 153-56. Short surveys in English are: Miyake Yūjirō, *The Introduction of Western Philosophy*, in *Fifty Years of New Japan*, ed. by Okuma Sh., London 1910, vol. II, pp. 226-41 Kaneko Umaji, *A Survey of Philosophy in Japan, 1870-1929*, in *Western Influences in Modern Japan*, ed. by Nitobe and Others, Chicago 1931, pp. 56-69

Chapter II

CONSERVATISM AND ANGLO-GERMAN IDEALISM
1886-1900

The Reaction Against the Westernization of Japan

I have purposely avoided discussion of the cultural and social background which brought forth the Meiji Restoration about which volumes have already been written. In this chapter as in the previous one, I shall attempt to by-pass involved discussion about the causes of the so-called reaction against Western ideas and customs. This reaction started, if a date can be set for cultural phenomena, approximately in 1866, and lasted until around 1900. The reader is invited to investigate Western works listed in the notes and the bibliographical references to Japanese historians, if he has any interest in this fascinating subject.[1]

Here I shall state the platitude that the fad and frenzy for things western, characteristic of the first decade of the Meiji times, was bound to have a healthy reaction. However, the problem is rather to determine the extent of Japan's fadism, to note which strata of society were permeated by enthusiasm for western learning, and to observe the impact made upon the guid-

---

1) See Sansom G.B., *The Western World* . . ., o.c., pp. 362-72; Yanaga C., *Japan Since Perry* . . ., o.c., pp. 163-73; *Japanese Thought* . . . ed. by Kōsaka, o.c., pp. 134-269; *Outlines of Japanese History in the Meiji Era*, ed. by Fuji Jintarō. transl. by H. K. Colton & K. E. Colton, Ōbunsha, Tokyo 1958, pp. 226-313

ing personalities of the time. The conservatism of the reaction must be deeply considered; it should be decided whether, given the background of Japanese pre-Meiji history, a middle course could have been possible. It would only be fair to warn that within so short a survey as this, the extreme complexity of the problem can only be hinted at while its solution must be found in an analysis of sources which treat the topic extensively. In view of this, the following pages should be accepted with caution and some reserve.[2]

The wave of anti-foreign feeling mounted from the year 1887. It was initiated by Japan's failure to persuade the Western nations to abrogate the "unequal treaties" granted forcibly at the time of the opening of Japan. A number of associations sprang up for the propagation of the *Kokusui*[a] (National Essence) In a sense, the battle cry of the pre-Restoration fanatic groups: "Revere the Emperor and expel the barbarians," never died out. In 1881, the advisor to the Emperor, Confucianist Motoda Eifu[b] (1818-1919), proposed the adoption of the essentials of *Shūshin*[c] the nationalistic ethical training for the youth of Japan. This was summarized in the words of the edu-

---

a. 国粋   b. 元田永学   c. 修身

2) On the thorny problem of the Meiji Restoration see bibliographical indication in John W. Hall, *Japanese History*, Publication N. 34 of the Service Center for Teachers of History, Washington 1961, pp. 43-48. For Japanese books see: John W. Hall, *Japanese History, A Guide to Japanese Reference and Research Materials*, Ann Arbor 1954, pp. 94-100. I must add here for their novelty of interpretation the articles by J. Siemes, *H. Roesler und die Rezeption des deutschen Staatsrechts in Japan*, in *Nippon*, 1961 n. 1, pp. 1-7, Japanische-Deutsche Gesellschaft E. V., Tokyo; and his four articles in Japanese on "The Social Development and Constitutionalism in the Theory of Constitution of H. Roesler" in the *Kokka gakkai zasshi* 国家学会雑誌 1962, Nn. 1-8

cational policy of Fukuoka[a] as being the "native doctrines of the Empire, and the principles of Confucianism."

Emphasis was placed on the "native doctrine of the Empire." Confucianism, though quite different from that practiced in China, was previously used in Japan for the political aims of the Tokugawa Shōguns, and at this time, by the ideologists of the "New Imperial Way." Western theories also were used to support the new autocracy, as seen in the case of Katō Hiroyuki's materialistic evolutionism. In 1889, the Minister of Education, Western-minded *Meirokusha* Mori Arinori, paid with his life for an alleged lack of reverence to the Ise Shrine,[b] the sacred place of Japanese national mythology. As Sansom and others have pointed out, Mori's new school and university regulations brought him nearer to the position of the *Kokugakusha*, or National Scholars, who emphasized Japanese learning, and to such Confucianists as Motoda. While stressing the importance of Western studies, Mori stated that schools were intended for the good of the country, and not for the students. Tokyo University was reorganized and called Tokyo Imperial University, in order to give it a more official stamp; this was a necessary move against the excessively liberal private schools which were flowering at that time. Mori's four ordinances between March and April, 1886, covered primary and middle schools, the Imperial University and the Normal school. These ordinances laid the foundations for the modern Japanese school system.

To avoid over-simplification of a very complex problem, it must be recalled that this spirit of education was proposed as early as 1879, by the *Kyōgaku Taishi*[c] or "The Great Purpose

a. 福岡孝弟   b. 伊勢神宮   c.教学大旨

of Education," of Emperor Meiji. The pros and cons of the problems of nationalism and Confucianism versus Western ideas were debated by Motoda and Nishimura Shigeki, another *Meirokusha*. Both of these men were for nationalism; their opponents were Fukuzawa and Mori, who took the problem to a higher level, the Imperial House. However, the Confucianist trend finally prevailed. Mori, a victim of fanaticism, was succeeded by Yoshikawa who, in 1890, promulgated the famous *Kyōiku Chokugo*,[a] the Imperial Rescript on Education.

The refusal of Christians (the case of Uchimura Kanzō[b] became especially famous), to bow in front of a copy of the Rescript which was kept in a shrine in all schools with the Emperor's picture, caused a national uproar. One of the most zealous defenders of the Rescript, Inoue Tetsujirō, started a campaign concerning *Shūkyō to kyōiku no shōtotsu*[c], the Conflict between Religion and Education. From 1892 he wrote several articles in which he extolled the Rescript and criticized cosmopolitan religions, such as Christianity, which, in his opinion, erred in placing Christ above the Emperor.

Before analyzing Inoue and other philosophers of this period, it must be added that Shintoism even more than Confucianism, played a leading role in the first years after the Meiji Restoration. National mythology was so strongly enforced and inculcated that fanatical movements like the *Haibutsu Kishaku*[d], the Extermination of Buddhism, destroyed Buddhist temples and statues taking the lead from the governmental policy of eliminating the long standing (since the Nara period,

a. 教育勅語   b. 内村鑑三   c. 宗教と教育の衝突   d. 廃仏毀釈

710-794) Buddhist-Shinto syncretism.[3]

The importance of the Rescript was apparent in the new Constitution, which was promulgated in February, 1889. This was said to have been drafted on the basis of more than twenty Western constitutions, a curious example of Eastern versus Western influence! The period of frenzied discussion over civil rights and democratic institutions had ended. The second decade of the Meiji period, which displayed such fervor for human rights, had given way to a period of more conservative trends. Yet, this period was one of transition as illustrated by the evolving thought of the leading thinkers of the times.

Old Thought and New Categories in Nishimura, Inoue Enryō, and Miyake

Nishimura Shigeki (1828-1902), mentioned as favoring Confucian ethics, was, nevertheless, a pioneer in opening Japan to the West. He, together with Mori Arinori, founded the *Meirokusha* group. As Sansom, Kōsaka and others have stressed, Nishimura was not a fanatical Confucianist. Although author of *Shūshin chikoku wa nito ni arazu no ron*[a] (The Indissolubility of Ethical Training and Government), a work in which he stressed, in oposition to Nishi Amane's *Hyakuichi shinron*, the identity of national ethics as the sole method of governing the

---

a. 修身治国非二途論
3) For Motoda Eifu's 元田永孚 role see: W. W. Smith Jr., *Confucianism in Modern Japan*, Tokyo 1959, pp. 68-88. See also:
Kaigo Tokiomi 海後宗臣, *Motoda Eifu* 元田永孚, Kunkyō Shoin. 1942, which is a study of his thought and also a collection of his essays. For Buddhism, Christianity, etc. see: *Japanese Religion in the Meiji Era*, ed. by K. Kishimoto, transl. by J. F. Howes, Ōbunsha, 1956, pp. 111-24; 251-76

country, he not only aimed at the masses, but even more strongly did he criticize the moral behaviour of the leading officials of the times. He also lectured to the Emperor on Western learning. In his early years when he founded the *Nihon Kōdōkai*[a], the Society for the Japanese Way, or when he wrote *Nihon dōtokuron* (On Japanese Morality), the nationalistic ethical code which he originally proposed then had not yet taken the form of the fanatical patriotism it was to become in later years. He was quite critical of many points of Confucianism, which, according to him, lacked precise formulation, was excessively conservative, stressed rights, not duties, denigrated women, etc.

Nishimura's lectures on Japanese morality given at Tokyo University, upon which the book of the same title was based, were so filled with criticism of Western ethics and proposed such a vague eclecticism as an alternative, that his philosophical position was not sustained. It became, in the hands of others, much more nationalistic than Nishimura had intended.[4]

Inoue Enryō (1859-1919) was another thinker who attempted to combine and reform an oriental religion, Buddhism, as opposed to Confucianism in Nishimura's case, with Western categories. Inoue was brought up in a family of Buddhist priests. From youth he was well versed in English as well as in the Chi-

---

a. 日本弘道会

4) *Hakuō Nishimura Shigeki den* 泊翁西村茂樹伝 (Hakuō [pen name] Nishi- mura Shigeki's Biography), ed. by Nishimura Sensei Denki Hensan-kai, 1933, 2 vols. Nishimura's complete works are: *Hakuō zensho* 泊翁全書 ed. by Nihon Kōdōkai Nishimurabe Toshobu, 1903, 3 vols. Nishimura Shigeki, *Nihon dōtokuron* 日本道徳論 (On Japanese Morality), ed. by Yoshida Kumaji 吉田熊次, Iwanami Shoten, 1935. The *Nihon dōtokuron* is to be found also in *Nihon tetsugaku zensho* . . ., vol. 14, pp. 269-354

nese Classics. In 1873 he applied himself to Western learning
with all the fervor of a novice. The Honganji Temple sent him
to study philosophy at Tokyo University, where he graduated in
1885. He went to Europe twice, in 1888 and again in 1902. He
founded the Tetsugakukan,[a] the Philosophical Institute, which
was the predecessor of Tōyō University,[b] a Buddhist influenced
institution. Inoue strongly criticized Christianity in his *Bukkyō katsuron joron*[c] (Introduction to the Vitality of Buddhism)
and in other writings such as *Shinri kinshin*[d] (The Essence of
Truth). Christianity was rejected because of antiscientific
tenets, such as Christ as the Son of God, or his resurrection.
Yet, Inoue considered Hinduism and Buddhism, especially the
two Mahāyāna Buddhist sects Kegon[e] and Tendai,[f] with their
emphasis on *Ritai,*[g] Pure Reason, as being close to Hegel's
"panlogism" or "pan-rationalism," as well as near to modern
evolutionary theories of Western science. This "pure-reason",
as the fundamental structure of the universe, transcended materialism and idealism. Ostwald's "energetism," too, was not very
distant from the Buddhist concepts of reality.

More philosophical in the Western sense than the above mentioned works was Inoue's *Tetsugaku isseki-wa*[h] (Brief Talks on
Philosophy.) Inoue was foremost as an apologist of Buddhism, as
indicated by his *Shingaku kōgi*[i] (Lectures on Theology), and on
Shūkyō shinron[j] (The New Theory of Religion). His eclecticism
was evident in the relativist position which he took pertaining to

a. 哲学館   b. 東洋大学   c. 仏教活論序論   d. 真理金針
e. 華厳宗   f. 天台宗   g. 理体   h. 哲学一夕話   i. 神学講義
j. 宗教新論

the essence of the universe and God. Depending on the point of view, there are four different interlocutors, the fifth being Enryō himself. God was presented as being undifferentiated matter, mind, transcendent and immanent. For Inoue, God was everything and anything, a substance and not a substance, matter or spirit, according to the position taken. This kind of dialectic, even impressing Nishida Kitarō[a], who read *Tetsugaku issekiwa* with interest, was strongly criticized by Ōnishi Hajime.[5]

The third thinker, actually a philosopher even though also considered a critic and a journalist for his activity as founder of the conservative magazine *Nihonjin*[b] (Japanese People), was Miyake Yūjirō (Setsurei, 1860-1945). He graduated from the philosophy section of Tokyo University in 1883. He remained in the University for a time, and in 1887 become a lecturer at the Tokyo Semmon Gakkō[c], the future Waseda University[d]. He combined the teaching of logic there and at another school, the Tetsugakukan, with the history of Western philosophy. While at the latter school he founded with the support of Inoue Enryō and other thinkers, the *Seikyō-sha*[e], a Society for Political and Moral Education. In 1889 Miyake published his first philosophical work, *Tetsugaku kenteki*[f] (Philosophical Trifles). This was a sketchy history of Western philosophy, from Descartes to Hegel. Around 1891 his articles on the Japanese

a. 西田幾多郎   b. 日本人   c. 東京専門学校   d. 早稲田大学
e. 政教社   f. 哲学涓滴

5) For Inoue Enryō's 井上円了, *Rinri shinsetsu* 倫理新説 (A New Theory on Ethics) see *Kindai Nihon shisō-shi* . . ., o.c., vol. 1, pp. 212-19; *Japanese Thought* . . . ed by Kōsaka, oc., pp. 242-45. *Inoue Enryō sensei* 井上円了先生 ed. by Tōyō Daigaku Gakuyū-kai, 1919 *Inoue sensei kiju kinen bunshū* 井上先生喜寿記念文集 (Festschrift on the seventy-seventh birthday of Inoue), ed. by Senken-kai, Fuzambō, 1931

people were published. These writings were a frank, truthful discussion of both the good and bad qualities of the Japanese, indicative of his moderate nationalism as compared with other ultra-nationalists of the time.

Miyake's socio-political views were influenced by Spencer's organic theory of the state, as well as by the hero worship of Carlyle. His work *Gakan shōkei*[a] (Personal Views), published in 1892, was, philosophically speaking, of great importance. This work followed Hartmann and Schopenhauer in stressing the illusory nature of consciousness, portrayed as a dream of reality; it begins with a fantasy and ends in nothingness. His flowery style and his extravagant use of metaphors resulted in a wide circle of readers, but also in sharp criticism. Kōsaka calls Miyake's thought "poetical philosophy," and says that his "infatuation" with the after-death, where liberty, equality, truth, beauty, and other virtues are acquired, showed his tendency toward the type of absolute non-existence. This concept recurred frequently in the writings of religious thinkers such as Nishida and others. Yet, Miyake's system contained little religious mysticism; he appeared to be a middle-way liberal thinker. To his credit, it must be noted that, in later years, he grew more critical of conservative trends, and aware of social problems. Already in his *Nihonjin* of 1888, he proposed new regulations to alleviate the inhuman treatment of miners who were on strike in the northern Kyūshu mines. In 1890, aided by Katayama Sen[b] and the Rev. C. E. Garst, he organized a society for the study of social problems.

a. 我観小景   b. 片山潜

Tsuchida Kyōson described Miyake, as well as Tokutomi Sohō[a], the founder of the *Min-Yūsha*[b] (Friend of the People Society), as a good representative of common sense in Japan, taking a middle of the way position. This appraisal was an accurate one, especially in the year 1925, when Tsuchida wrote. Tokutomi though, changed from liberal into conservative.[6]

The Thought and Influence of Inoue Tetsujirō

Inoue Tetsujirō (1855-1944) was previously mentioned as a leading figure in the controversy against Christianity as well as in the fight for national education. His life was long and his activity was prolific. His role spanned three eras of Japanese history covering the Meiji period and lasting into that of the Taishō and of Shōwa. He was the first Japanese to be appointed professor of philosophy at Tokyo University. Although his early Spencerianism turned into Japanese Confucianism, his intellectual stature as well as his position deserve special mention.

He was born in Dazaifu,[c] in the prefecture of Fukuoka,[d] of a physician's family. He had early training in the Chinese Classics and also mastered English. He entered the Kaisei

a. 徳富蘇峰   b. 民友社   c. 大宰府   d. 福岡

6) For Miyake Yūjirō (Setsurei)'s 三宅雄二郎 (雪嶺), *Nihonjin* 日本人 (Japanese People) see *Meiji bunka zenshū* 明治文化全集 (Collected on Meiji Culture), ed. by Yoshino Sakuzō 吉野作造, Nihon Hyōronsha, 1928-30, 24 vols. vol. 15, pp. 431-523. Extracts of *Tetsugaku kenteki* 哲学涓滴 are in *Nihon tetsugaku shisō zensho* . . .. o.c., vol. 1, pp. 135-99. **Yanagida Izumi**柳田泉, *Tetsujin Miyake Setsurei sensei* 哲人三宅雪嶺先生 **(The Philosopher Miyake S.),** Jitsugyō no Sekaisha, 1956. See also: *Kindai Nihon shisō-shi* . . ., o.c. vol. 2, pp. 279-89; Japanese Thought . . . ed. by Kōsaka, oc., pp. 245-48; Tsuchida K., *Contemporary Thought* . . . o.c., pp. 30-31: 173

School in 1875, and went afterwards to the philosophical department of the newly established Tokyo University. He graduated in 1880, afterwards becoming assistant professor. He went abroad to study in Germany in 1884. There he heard the lectures of K. Fischer, Zeller and Wundt. He came into contact with E. von Hartmann and other philosophers such as Fechner and Otto Lipmann. On his return in 1890, he became ordinary professor of philosophy, and from 1897 until 1904 was dean of the literature department. He was elected president of the Philosophical Society in 1916. In 1925 Inoue became the leading intellectual figure of the Daitō Bunka Gakuin,[a] the Academy for the Great Oriental Culture. This institution had evident nationalistic purposes. In 1926 Inoue ran into difficulty because he was not sufficiently cautious in speaking about the *Kokutai* or the National Polity. In the previous year he had written *Waga kokutai to kokumin dōtoku*[b] (Our National Polity and National Morality). This work was a source book approved by the Ministry of Education. It dealt with *Shūshin* or National Morality, identifying morality with ancestor and emperor worship. However, Inoue's interpretation of the three symbols expressing the divine nature of the National Polity (*Kokutai*) was considered as lacking respect. In order to avoid further criticism, he resigned from his official position.

Inoue favored, as did the fanatical nationalist, Hozumi Yatsuka,[c] the ethical textbooks of 1908-11 and the later ones on moral education. This favoritism, which he expressed in the *Kokumin dōtoku gairon*[d] (Outline of National Morality), publ-

a. 大東文化学院   b. 我国体と国民道徳   c. 穂積八束   d. 国民
道徳概論

ished in 1911, was not much endangered by the incident related above. According to W. W. Smith, in 1932 Inoue tried to justify the Japanese policy in Manchukuo and China by a far fetched explanation of Confucian texts. This occurred at the time when the Confucian *Wang-tao* (The Way of the True Kinship), was becoming increasingly identified with the *Kōdō*[a] or the Imperial Way. Inoue's nationalism grew more tendentious with the approach of the war. In 1939, his *Tōyō bunka to Shina no shōrai*[b] (Oriental Culture and the Future of China) proposed the notion that Japan was the leading nation in a Culture of the New East Asia (*Shin Tōa no bunka.*)[c]

The clearest expression of Inoue's nationalism was found in his *Nihon seishin no honshitsu*[d] (The Essence of the Japanese Spirit) published in 1934. This work analyzed Shinto, the national spirit and the spiritual culture of Japan.

Inoue's most authoritative books were on the subject of Oriental thought; they were both great collections of writings and original works. To the first category belonged *Nihon rinri ihen*[e], a collection of 77 works from the Confucianists of the Tokugawa time and the two other collections, one on *Bushidō*[f], the ethical code of the Japanese warrior class. The writings on *Bushidō* were published during the war. Inoue also edited a Buddhist dictionary. His works on the Japanese form of Confucianism of the Yōmei School (Wang Yang-min) were more original. Thinkers such as Nakae Tōju[g], Kumazawa Banzan[h], Ōshio Chūsai[i] and others up to the end of the Tokugawa time

a. 皇道   b. 東洋文化と支那の将来   c. 新東亜の文化   d. 日本
精神の本質   e. 日本倫理彙編   f. 武士道   g. 中江藤樹
h. 熊沢蕃山   i. 大塩平八郎（中斎）

were discussed. The philosophy of Shushi (Chu Hsi) School was taken up in another book which became the standard work on this branch of Japanese Confucianism. Inoue started his discussion with Fujiwara Seika[a], and Hayashi Razan[b], giving consideration to Yamazaki Ansai[c] and the Mito School.[d] Another volume was dedicated to the *Kogakusha*[e], the Ancient School of Confucianism; that is, to the Confucianism previous to the Chu Hsi Sung's interpretation of ancient texts. In this important work, philologist thinkers like Yamaga Sokō[f], Ito Jinsai[g], Ogyū Sorai[h] and others were dealt with. His intention, as stated in the preface of the book on the Yōmei School, was to contrast Confucianist ethics with the then prevalent utilitarian and individualistic ethics. The influence of German idealism was quite apparent in these books, which were published shortly after Inoue's return from Germany.

Inoue's scholarly reputation was based on the above mentioned works. He also lectured on Western philosophy, although his main field, after his return from abroad, was Confucianism and Chinese thought in general. During his early "illuminist" phase Inoue wrote *Shinri shin-setsu*[i] (A New Theory on Psychology, published in 1882. In the following year came out his *Seiyō tetsugaku kōgi*[j] (Lectures on Western Philosophy) and *Rinri shin-setsu*[k] (A New Theory on Ethics), a work in which he followed to some extent Henry Sidgwick's *Methods of Ethics*. Kōsaka is critical of this last writing, primarily because of the eclecticism included. Inoue's eclecticism attempted a combina-

---

a. 藤原惺窩   b. 林羅山   c. 山崎闇斎   d. 水戸学派   e. 古学者   f. 山鹿素行   g. 伊藤仁斎   h. 荻生徂徠   i. 心理新説   j. 西洋哲学講義   k. 倫理新説

tion of Sidgwick's theory of happiness, Spencer's evolutionism and Oriental ethics contained in the "sage" (*seijin*)ᵃ, the ideal man in pursuit of happiness. Spencer entered the picture because Inoue believed that, in order to comprehend the nature of ethics, the essence of the universe (*uchū no hontai*)ᵇ must be known. This was an unknowable "universal existence" (*banyū seiritsu*)ᶜ comprising space, time and force.

For the *Journal of Philosophy* in 1897 Inoue wrote an article on *"Genshō sunawachi jitsuzairon,"*ᵈ Phenomenon as Realism. This title was Inoue's rendering of the German *Identitaetsrealismus*. Inoue desired to overcome the naive realism of Haeckel and Katō Hiroyuki, which identified external experiences or phenomena with reality, a theory which is actually based on internal and immediate intuition. He also believed that Kant and E. von Hartmann were wrong in their attempts to separate the phenomenal world from reality. Accordingly, neither monism à la Haeckel nor Kant's theory of dualism were correct. What was needed was a realism identifying one with the other, or even transcending both elements. However, Inoue did not explain the nature of the new epistemological theory which he hoped would solve the dilemma. On the contrary, he introduced Buddhist concepts which, according to some critics, made matters even more confusing.

In the field of Western philosophy Inoue has to his merit the publication of a *Tetsugaku jii*ᵉ (Philosophical Dictionary). This was prepared in 1881. Due to the efforts of Ariga Nagao, a revised edition appeared in 1882. Ariga, Inoue's main collaborator, took over the publication during Inoue's trip to Ger-

a. 聖人　　b. 宇宙の本体　　c. 万有成立　　d. 現象即ち実在論
e. 哲学字彙

many. A completely new edition of this work came out in 1912, bearing the English subtitle *Dictionary of English, German and French Philosophical Terms*. Inoue compiled this work with the assistance of Motora Yūjirō and Nakajima Rikizō[a]. Critics, none the less, were quite severe. The Jesuit Fr. Tsuchihashi,[b] the learned professor of Sophia University, well versed in scholastic philosophy and even more capable in the field of Sino-Japanese characters, wrote a full-page article in the Yomiuri Newspaper pointing out the mistakes and incompetent rendering of much scholastic terminology. However, Inoue was sufficiently broadminded to admit his errors. Until his death he consulted Fr. Tsuchihashi on various problems with Chinese characters, a field in which the Jesuit professor had few equals. Inoue advised Morohashi Tetsuji,[c] the compiler of the greatest dictionary of Sino-Japanese characters, a thirteen volume work titled *Morohashi kanwa jiten*,[d] to utilize the knowledge of the modest priest, who reluctantly told me this story and gave me his article criticizing Inoue's philosophical dictionary.

It is both impossible and unnecessary to cover all the writings and academic activity of Inoue. He was a distinguished poet, trying in his "illuminist" phase to renew traditional style *Haiku* and *Waka* in a Western form. Later he was one of the few people who still composed in the Chinese classical manner.[7]

---

a. 中島力造   b. 土橋八千太   c. 諸橋轍次   d. 諸橋漢和辞典

7) Inoue Tetsujirō 井上哲次郎, *Tetsugaku to shūkyō* 哲学と宗教 (Philosophy and Religion), Kōdōkan, 1915. This book, a collection of articles, is very important as a presentation of Inoue's views on philosophy, religion, national ethics etc. Even more systematic is Inoue in the last part of his *Meiji tetsugaku-kai no kaiko* 明治哲学界の回顧 (Meiji Philosophy in Retrospect), *Iwanami Kōza Tetsugaku* 岩波講座哲学 (Iwanami's Lectures: Philosophy), Iwanami Shoten, 1932, pp. 72-86: *"Jibun no tachiba"*

A Critically Minded Ethician: Ōnishi Hajime

Ōnishi Hajime was an outstanding exception to the political conformism of many intellectuals of his time. In contrast to both Inoue and Miyake, he strove for clear thought and well defined positions in the socio-political field as well as in the realm of philosophy. Ōnishi did not enjoy the national recognition of Inoue Tetsujirō; going against the current was not in his favor, and his early death at only thirty-six prevented him from

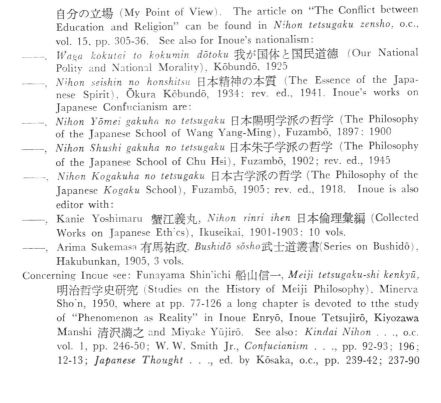

自分の立場 (My Point of View). The article on "The Conflict between Education and Religion" can be found in *Nihon tetsugaku zensho*, o.c., vol. 15, pp. 305-36. See also for Inoue's nationalism:

——. *Waga kokutai to kokumin dōtoku* 我が国体と国民道徳 (Our National Polity and National Morality), Kōbundō, 1925

——. *Nihon seishin no honshitsu* 日本精神の本質 (The Essence of the Japanese Spirit), Ōkura Kōbundō, 1934; rev. ed., 1941. Inoue's works on Japanese Confucianism are:

——. *Nihon Yōmei gakuha no tetsugaku* 日本陽明学派の哲学 (The Philosophy of the Japanese School of Wang Yang-Ming), Fuzambō, 1897; 1900

——, *Nihon Shushi gakuha no tetsugaku* 日本朱子学派の哲学 (The Philosophy of the Japanese School of Chu Hsi), Fuzambō, 1902; rev. ed., 1945

——. *Nihon Kogakuha no tetsugaku* 日本古学派の哲学 (The Philosophy of the Japanese *Kogaku* School), Fuzambō, 1905; rev. ed., 1918. Inoue is also editor with:

——, Kanie Yoshimaru 蟹江義丸, *Nihon rinri ihen* 日本倫理彙編 (Collected Works on Japanese Ethics), Ikuseikai, 1901-1903; 10 vols.

——, Arima Sukemasa 有馬祐政, *Bushidō sōsho* 武士道叢書(Series on Bushidō), Hakubunkan, 1905, 3 vols.

Concerning Inoue see: Funayama Shin'ichi 船山信一, *Meiji tetsugaku-shi kenkyū*, 明治哲学史研究 (Studies on the History of Meiji Philosophy), Minerva Sho'n, 1950, where at pp. 77-126 a long chapter is devoted to tthe study of "Phenomenon as Reality" in Inoue Enryō, Inoue Tetsujirō, Kiyozawa Manshi 清沢満之 and Miyake Yūjirō. See also: *Kindai Nihon* . . ., o.c. vol. 1, pp. 246-50; W. W. Smith Jr., *Confucianism* . . ., pp. 92-93; 196; 12-13; *Japanese Thought* . . ., ed. by Kōsaka, o.c., pp. 239-42; 237-90

forming a school of thought.

Modern historians of Japanese philosophy, left wingers and materialists, as well as men like Kōsaka, rank Ōnishi very high, above Inoue Tetsujirō and, as an historian of Western philosophy, even higher than Hatano Seiichi,[a] who will be discussed later. Onishi's understanding of Western philosophy was extraordinarily deep. His sharp, critical mind, trained in the best tradition of Kant's criticism, was a healthy contrast to the vague eclecticism in vogue at the time.

Ōnishi had an intellectual attitude on socio-political questions, supporting neither Westernism nor Japanese nationalism, neither radicalism nor conservatism. He favored instead a doctrine which rose above all these one-sided views. He compared, judged and criticized all trends. While readily admitting good and bad points in current theories, he never followed empty or abstract slogans like radicalism or conservatism.

The same was true for his philosophy. He believed that philosophy involved a duty to clarify and define certain concepts which popular usage and party interests had confused, reducing intellectual debates to a battle of words.

Ōnishi was born in Okayama prefecture. He attended the Dōshisha Christian school and in 1885 he entered the philosophy department of Tokyo University, where he graduated in 1888. He taught the history of philosophy, logic, ethics and aesthetics in Tokyo Semmon Gakkō (Waseda University.) In 1898 he traveled to Germany for further studies. Upon his return he was invited to Kyoto University, which was in the process of

a. 波多野精一

reorganizing its literature department. His death came too soon; if he had lived longer, in all probability Kyoto University would have developed quite a different philosophy. Before going abroad, he had a position on the editorial staff of the *Rikugō zasshi*,[a] a magazine started in 1880 by Kozaki Hiromichi.[b] This publication with Christian overtones was the opponent of the *Tōkyō gakugei zasshi*,[c] a conservative journal edited by men belonging to the circle of the Tokyo Imperial University and which featured the articles of Inoue Tetsujirō and others.

Onishi's qualifications as educator and teacher were reported to be superb because of his moderation and lack of bias. His methods of research were described as careful, thorough and undogmatic. He was impressive as a speaker, if we can rely on the vivid appraisal made by the famous novelist Shimazaki Tōson[d]. Onishi's merits as a critically-minded philosopher were, first, that he did not, in contrast to most of his contemporaries, go in for "flowery allegories" smacking of metaphysics, and secondly, that he proposed an ethical idealism which, although not completed, was a serious effort to build up a philosophy of ethics which would transcend East and West.

Kōsaka's discussion of Ōnishi indicates that Ōnishi was strongly influenced by his Christian background. Still, during this time, there were many Christians whose ideas were muddled on political questions. In his more positive work *Ryōshin kigenron*[e] (On the Origin of Conscience) the influence of T. H. Green's teleological evolution and, later, of Kant's criticism was evident.

a. 六合雑誌　　b. 小崎弘道　　c. 東京学芸雑誌　　d. 島崎藤村
e. 良心起源論

Working at the negative task of dismantling Inoue Enryō's God, termed by Ōnishi as the "Enryō substance", Ōnishi easily pointed out that such an eclectic dialectic was as much of an impossibility as mixing "oil and water." He added that Inoue's appeal to the "obscurity" or difficulty of philosophical problems was not a solution. Instead, he said, such a concept was rather the end of philosophy and not a characteristic of it, no obscure doctrine being possible of evaluation. Dealing with Miyake's abuse of allegories, he asked what kind of consciousness the universe possessed, since the world, quite likely, did not dream nor have a state of unconsciousness. Although Ōnishi was strongly in favor of progress and evolutionism, concerning Katō Hiroyuki's mechanicist evolutionism he said that, in the realm of history, standards must be present which are neither of the material world solely, nor simply historical, but which transcend both history and evolution.

Inoue Tetsujirō's utterances against Christianity and Motora Yūjirō's tenets on state and Christian relationship underwent Ōnishi's criticism. Christianity, he felt, was not anti-state nor anti-Japanese, but was "non-statist" in the sense that it was not of this world and proposed to give benefits to all mankind. Kōsaka, speaking out of personal experience in a comment on Ōnishi's position on national problems, said: "We feel, and we are not alone in this, that, had Ōnishi's ideas become dominant in Japan, they would have been able to exercise some restraint" on later nationalism and statism.

Ōnishi's positive task was the introduction of Western philosophy. For him, it was an academic pursuit, made with a full knowledge of the sources and increasingly exact renderings of alien ideas. This task was initiated by Nishi Amane and, after a delay brought about by Ōnishi's early death, it was taken up again on an extensive scale in 1910. Ōnishi's ethical views were evident in his *Origin of Conscience*. This writing was actually the thesis for his graduate work, and was published posthumously. Conscience, he held, was derived from the human tendency to fulfill our ideal. This ideal must be realized to conform with the totality of which people were part. The goal of man's life was his ideal; it must be constantly pursued, yet it can never be fully realized. To Ōnishi, conscience was the stimulating force toward the ideal.

In later articles and books Kant's influence was felt, both in the epistemological field and on moral problems. Ōnishi sensed that the "ideal" of idealists was not sufficiently clear, and that naturalists could not explain moral consciousness. Therefore, his position was not fully elaborated. He discarded incorrect theories, but he did not form his own. He could not finish his task and died, so to say, pointing out his own deficiency. His ethical bent was manifested in the foundation of the *Teiyū Rinri-kai*[a], Society for Ethical Studies, in his book *Rinrigaku* (Ethics) and in many articles.[8]

---

a. 丁西倫理会 (懇話会)

8) *Ōnishi Hajime zenshū* 大西祝全集 (The Complete Works of Ōnish' Hajime), Keiseisha, 1927, 7 vol. Vol. 1: *Rinrigaku* 倫理学 (Ethics) vol. 2: *Ronrigaku* 論理学 (Logic); vols. 3-4: *Seiyō tetsugaku-shi* 西洋哲学史 (History of Western Philosophy); vol. 5: Ryōshin kigenron 良心起源論 (On the Origin of Conscience); vol. 6: *Shichō hyōron* 思潮評論 Critic of Intellectual Trends); vol. 7: *Rombun oyobi kashū* 論文および歌集 (Essays and Tanka). Concerning Ōnishi see: *Japanese Thought* . . .. ed. by ⬚⬚⬚⬚, o.c., pp. 248-61; *Kindai Nihon* . . ., o.c., pp. 251-56

Experimental Psychology; Koeber Sensei

The philosopher usually credited with the introduction of experimental psychology into Japan was Motora Yūjirō (1858-1912). He graduated from Dōshisha and went to John Hopkins University to study psychology and sociology. Upon his return in 1887 he was appointed to Tokyo University. He wrote two introductions to psychology and, as mentioned, *Seishin Butsuri-gaku* (Spiritual Physics), so termed because experimental psychology in the East as in the West was conceived of as a type of physics of the spirit. Motora, incidentally, was not a materialist but a Christian. He tried to unify the multiplicity of spiritual phenomena with the regular recurrence of psychical relations which gradually formed the human being. He called this theory the "circular activity of the mind," an activity which could be tested and measured by statistical methods. On moral problems he stood with Ōnishi against Katō Hiroyuki's materialism. He reasoned that ethics could not be based on mores or customs alone, for those elements manifested only what "is" not what "ought" to be. Motora was rather conservative on the question concerning the Imperial Rescript on Education. On that point he was at variance with Ōnishi, by whom he was criticized. A more specialized psychologist was Matsumoto Matatarō[a] (1865-1943), who studied psychology at Yale and afterwards in Leipzig under W. Wundt. Matsumoto taught at the Tokyo Normal School, at Kyoto University, becoming finally the successor to Motora at the Imperial University of Tokyo.

Wundt's psychology introduced by Matsumoto was not much known during the years we are dealing with. Other foreign

a. 松本亦太郎

psychologists were more influential. Among the foremost was Harald Hoeflding's *Outlines of Psychology*, translated and read in Japan at the turn of the century. In 1900 George Trumbull Ladd came to Japan from Yale University. His *Philosophy of Knowledge* and *Philosophy of Conduct* were made known and later translated.[9]

Other foreign professors who came to Japan were George W. Knox, in 1885, followed by the German, Ludwig Busse, in 1887. The arrival of Busse marked the beginning of the study of Kant's two *Critiques* and Lotze's ideas. Inoue Tetsujirō was quite outspoken in his criticism of Lotze's philosophy, saying that the German philosopher did not understand what he was talking about. Inoue instead gave his support to E. von Hartmann's metaphysics and Hegel's dialectic. Toward the end of the century the thought of Paulsen also became known.

At that time German idealism, in contrast to the Anglo-Saxon type of German philosophy, was not very wide-spread in academic circles. The latter trend was represented by Thomas Hill Green, an English philosopher and a convinced neo-Hegelian who proposed self-realization as the ethical standard of life.

Upon the suggestion of Hartmann, Raphael von Koeber (1848-1923) came to Japan in 1893 to take the place of Busse. Koeber, who remained in Japan until his death, prevented as he was from leaving by the first World War, left on his numerous pupils an impression that few other foreigners can hope to match. Outstanding among the many examples are testimonials

9) P. Lüth, *Die japanische Philosophie*, Tübingen, 1944, pp. 93-96. For a survey on the "Origin of Japanese psychology and its development" see the article by Mantarō Kido in *Psychologia*, vol. IV n. 1 (March 1961), pp. 1-10, Kyoto.

by Natsume Sōseki,[a] Abe Jirō,[b] Watsuji Tetsurō.[c] Kubo Masaru's[d] collection of *"omoide"*[e] or memoires on Koeber, ran through five editions.

What impressed his students so greatly was not so much his philosophy (he had no real system), nor his wide erudition, but his arresting manner. He was an artistic type of sage-philosopher, who incarnated the almost mystical ideal of a tutor.

Koeber was called "sensei," the customary term for teacher but which in respect to him possessed the distinctly Oriental connotation of sage tutor. He was born in Nizhni-Novgorod, the present Gorki, a Russian of German and Swedish extraction. From 1879 he studied under Tchaykovsky at the Moscow Academy of Music. Naturally, while in Japan he taught piano at the Ueno School of Arts, as well as philosophy. In 1873 he went to the University of Jena and afterwards to Heidelberg. His doctor's thesis in 1881 was on the subject of Schopenhauer, whose *Parerga und Paralipomena* he edited and about whom he published a study in 1888 titled *Die Philosophie A. Schopenhauers*. While teaching in Munich, his *Repetitorium* of the history of philosophy appeared. In this he completed Schwegler's work, following Zeller and especially Kuno Fischer. This *Repetitorium* was the basis for his *Lectures on the History of Philosophy*, his text in Japan, which was printed in two volumes in the years 1896 and 1897. Although Koeber taught in German, English was the language most widely understood by the students. Consequently, he was obliged to explain many terms in English. Some of his pupils prepared a translation of his lectures which

a. 夏目漱石   b. 阿部次郎   c. 和辻哲郎   d. 久保勉   e. 想
出

was circulated privately among themselves.

Schopenhauer was discussed in his textbook and Plato's conception of philosophy as "pathos" was proposed. In 1918 Koeber's *Kleine Schriften* was printed in Japanese as well as in German. This work contained several essays, aphorisms and noteworthy letters to the Dean of the Faculty of Philosophy of the Tokyo Imperial University, in which Koeber recommended that students limit their ambition of studying all things and, instead, concentrate on a few important problems. Class attendance, complicated by the useless college dissertation assigned, was a problem even then; the lack of real knowledge of foreign languages plagued Koeber, as it does today's foreign teachers.

Besides introducing German philosophy, mostly Schopenhauer's, Koeber played a significant part in making Medieval thought as well as Greek philosophy known to Japanese students. At his home he taught Latin and Greek to dedicated students in order to foster a knowledge of the sources in them.[10]

Concluding this discussion which covered a period of great political and social changes in Japan, it should be noted that, out-

10) Raphael von Koeber, *Repetitorium der Geschichte der Philosophie,* Stuttgart, 1890
———. *Lectures on History of Philosophy,* 2 vols. 1897, vol. 2, pp. 382 ff.
———, *Kleine Schriften,* Iwanami Shoten, 1918, pp. 268-72. The Japanese edition is: *Shōhin-shū* 小品集, Iwanami Shoten, 1919
Kubo Masaru 久保勉, *Koeber sensei to tomo ni* ケーベル先生とともに (With Koeber sensei), Iwanami Shoten, 1951, 1952 fifth ed.
Watsuji Tetsurō 和辻哲郎, *Koeber sensei* ケーベル先生, Atene Bunko, 1948
In almost all the *zenshū* or complete works of leading thinkers, like Natsume Sōseki, Nishida Kitarō, Hatano Seiichi, Abe Jirō, Miki Kiyoshi, there are short memoires on Koeber.

side of Tokyo University, German idealism and German philosophy in general was not known at that time. It was occasionally identified with the growing reactionary trend. A tendency toward the new idealism and individualism prevalent in the next decade was already apparent. This tendency mainly consisted of the Anglo-German idealism of the Neo-Hegelian Green, which was an antidote to earlier utilitarian ethical trends. The new idealism of Eucken was introduced as indicated by Inoue Tetsujirō's work *Tetsugaku to shūkyō*[a], (Philosophy and Religion). This work, a collection of essays, reflected in part the spirit of the times.

Early Socialist Thought and Materialism

As a supplement to the matter presented above, a survey of socialist thought and materialism is presented here, covering a period exceeding the limits of the chapter. As socialist thought and materialism were very important trends in the history of contemporary Japanese philosophy, an explanation is required of their origins.

It is difficult to associate materialism with socialism during the period 1870-1911, primarily because early socialist thought in Japan was connected with a humanistic and Christian view of social problems. As pointed out in the first chapter, Nishi when dealing with socialism referred to French socialism, and D.W. Learned, the American Protestant missionary of Dōshisha, discussed socialism from the viewpoint of political economy, which he taught from 1879 on. Learned was critical of capitalism and socialism. He proposed a Christian, humanistic solution of social questions. Katō Hiroyuki too, in his

a. 哲学と宗教

Shinsei-tai-i[a] (Principles of True Government), published in 1870, criticized socialism and communism.

Newspapers, featuring reports on the European social movement and worker strikes, were the major sources of information about socialism for the Japanese. Marx apparently was introduced in 1881 by Kozaki Hiromichi. In 1882 Thomas More's *Utopia* and T. D. Wolsey's *Communism and Socialism* were translated. The first Oriental Socialist Party was organized in May 1882, but was dissolved in the following July even though Japan was experiencing a liberal period at the time.

The popularly read magazines of the time, *Kokumin no tomo*[b] (Nation's Friend) and *Nihonjin* (Japanese People), discussed social theories and practical problems. The former, founded by the already mentioned Tokutomi Sōhō, advocated a kind of populism in which the cult of the ordinary man, vague socialism and clear nationalism were happily mixed. The Christian Wadagaki Kenzō[c] and Motora Yūjirō, both wrote critical articles in the *Nihonjin* on socialism. They proposed concrete ways to alleviate the deplorable conditions of the Kyūshu miners. Tokutomi introduced H. George's writings, and later, Edward Carpenter's *Present Day Socialism*.

The first study group of social problems was organized in 1890. The leaders were Miyake Yūjirō, Katayama Sen and the Rev. Charles E. Garst, an ardent follower of H. George and a supporter of a special tax system. Katayama became the leader of socialism in Japan. Later he went to Soviet Russia, where he remained until his death. He was originally a Christian, although he later renounced his Christian beliefs. There were

a.真政大意　　b. 国民の友　　c. 和田垣謙三

other Christians among the early promoters of the Union of Railway Workers (*Kyōseikai*)[a], which was organized in 1898. About this time regular meetings under the leadership of Katayama were held in the Unitarian Church of Tokyo to discuss socialism. Another famous member was the Christian Abe Isoo[b]. Abe graduated from Dōshisha and the Hartford Theological Seminary. He was later professor at Waseda University and titular head of the Socialist Mass Party. Abe was always a moderate type of socialist. Another attending the meetings was Kōtoku Shūsui (Denjirō)[c], certainly no Christian.

The meetings resulted in the formation of the *Shakaishugi Kenkyūkai*[d], the Association for the Study of Socialism. This group was formed in the spring of 1901. But after several splits where the more liberal members, such as Motora, left, the Social Democratic Party came about; this party survived a mere three hours because Katayama was ordered by the police to dissolve it at once.

The Russo-Japanese War (1904-05) was another occasion which united the socialists and Christians in anti-war meetings. These were held at the Y.M.C.A. headquarters in Tokyo. The *Heimin shimbun*[e] (the Commoners' Newspaper), a radical weekly started by Kōtoku and Sakai Toshihiko[f], was the most vehement voice against capitalistic war and the existing social order. The noted Christian leader, Uchimura Kanzō, also favoured peaceful movements, and did not hesitate to write a preface to Kōtoku's *Imperialism*. On November 13, 1904, the *Heimin shimbun* printed Marx-Engel's "Communist Manifesto," although the

a. 日本鉄道矯正会   b. 安部磯雄   c. 幸徳秋水   d. 社会主義研究会   e. 平民新聞   f. 堺利彦

prevailing trend was toward Tolstoi's pacifism and Kropotkin's anarchism.

In 1905 the National Socialist Party (*Kokka Shakaitō*)[a] and afterwards, the Japan Socialist Party were organized by Katayama, Sakai and Nishikawa Kōjirō.[b] Riots of miners and farmers served as excuses for the government to adopt stricter measures against social movements. In 1900 the so-called Law for the Preservation of Public Peace was passed. Its application became increasingly stiff, thwarting the efforts to channel progressive trends into legal party movements. Kinoshita Naoe[c], a Christian socialist, was obliged to resort to novels such as his famous *Hi no hashira*[d] (Pillar of Fire) to discuss socialism. Others took to a more theoretical plane. The extremists, such as Kōtoku discarded any sort of parliamentarianism in favor of direct and revolutionary action. In 1911 Kōtoku and eleven others, including his wife, were hanged for an alleged plot against the life of the emperor. This was a fatal blow to all social progressive movements in Japan. More and more people were obliged to limit their interests in socialism to purely critical academic studies of the social ideas. Even social novels were forbidden.

The reasons for socialism's early connection with Christianity in Japan were not too difficult to discover. Traditional thought, even of the Buddhist or Confucianist form, let alone nationalistic Shintoism, did not offer too many progressive ideas, and even less a basis for the international spirit of a common worker front. Marxist socialism and to a greater degree com-

a. 国家社会党　　b. 西川光二郎　　c. 木下尚江　　d. 火の柱

munism, were instrumental in changing the Christian aspect of early Japanese socialism.[11]

Before briefly introducing the thought of Kōtoku, his master, Nakae Tokusuke (Chōmin, 1847-1901)[a] must be mentioned. Nakae Chōmin, as he is called according to his pen name, was an influential political thinker of a clear materialistic bent. Nakae, who went to France in 1871, became famous for his translation of Rousseau's *Social Contract*. He was a liberal of constitutional monarchist views and a supporter, at the end of his life, of Japanese nationalism. He had a strong well-defined attitude toward Russia. Among his best known works on political problems was the *Sansuijin keirin mondō*[b], a fairly long dialogue between Three Intoxicated Men, with one of them, Nankai, representing Chōmin's political ideas. Of a more philosophical nature was the shorter tract *Ichinen yūhan*[c] (One Year and a Half). This was followed by the *Zoku ichinen yūhan*[d] (The Continuation of One year and a Half). These works were written while Nakae awaited death from cancer, which he faced with remarkable stoicism. Nakae's materialism was nearer to the 18th century French materialism, physiology and psychology being one thing in man, and the spirit being a form of fuel which evanesces once the body is gone. In the second chapter of *Zoku ichinen yūhan* entitled *"Mushin mureikon"*[e] (No God, No Soul) Nakae forcefully expressed his stand on atheism and anti-spiritualism. His criticism of theism, which he identified with panthe-

---

a. 中江篤介 （兆民）　　b. 三酔人経綸問答　　c. 一年有半　　d. 続一年有半　　e. 無神無霊魂

11) Abe Isoo, *Socialism in Japan*, in *Fifty Years of New Japan*, o.c., vol. 2, pp. 393-512; *Japanese Thought . . .*, ed. by Kōsaka, o.c., pp. 332-60

ism and termed *Shimbutsu dōtaisetsu*,[a] was really too simple.
The simplicity of this explanation, even admitted by Saigusa,
was also true of his denial of the existence of any real philosophy in Japan. Although he was not a socialist, because of his
influence upon Kōtoku, Nakae was listed among the forerunners
of Marxist philosophy in Japan. Perhaps he should rather be
classified with another materialist or early Meiji thinker, Katō
Hiroyuki. As Katō was excessively nationalistic and a supporter of autocracy, he was not considered a precursor of later
Marxist thought.[12]

Kōtoku was no doubt a materialist; at least, he clearly stated
that he was so in his last days in prison. However, his early
socialism was strongly influenced by humanistic and idealistic
notions, which made possible the prefacing by a Christian
Uchimura Kanzō, of Kōtoku's *Teikokushugi*[b] (Imperialism),
published in 1910. The same spirit pervaded the *Shakaishugi shinzui*[c] (The Quintessence of Socialism) published in
1903. In this book, Kōtoku followed R. Ely's *Socialism and
Social Reforms*. He proposed that the hatred which forms
the base of.... imperialism, using nationalism and militarism

---

a. 神物同体説   b. 帝国主義   c. 社会主義神髄

12)   Hijikata Kazuo 土方和雄 *Nakae Chōmin* 中江兆民, Tokyo Daigaku Shup-
      pankai, 1958, with bibliography, pp. 224-29; Sakisaka Itsurō ed. 向坂
      逸郎編, *Kindai Nihon no shisōka* 近代日本の思想家 (Modern Japanese
      Thinkers), Wakōsha, 1954, pp. 60-77; Saigusa Hiroto 三枝博音, *Nihon
      no yuibutsuronsha* 日本の唯物論者 (Japanese Materialists), Eiōsha, 1956,
      pp. 207-33; Also: *Japanese Thought* ..., ed. by Kōsaka, o.c., pp. 330-
      44; Nobutaka Ike, *The Beginning of Political Democracy in Japan*,
      Baltimore, 1950, pp. 124-29

as means, was formulated by the animal instincts of man. Kōtoku was an evolutionist. He held that the struggle for life was in the realm of animal instincts, to be eventually superseded by an ideal society dominated by spiritual forces. The contradictions of capitalism were not of the Marx's type, but rather of the French socialism and Lassalle blend, both full of humanistic and romantic elements. Kōtoku also invoked Bushidō, the warrior's code of fighting and loyalty, in order to eliminate capitalism from Japan.

Kōtoku's anarchist phase began in November 1905, when he went to the United States, where he came in contact with many American anarchists. His numerous translations of Kropotkin's works were printed in San Francisco. When he returned to Japan, he plunged headlong into direct action methods. Kōtoku's newly acquired views were expressed in *Heiminshugi*[a] (Commonerism) published in 1910, while his extreme views against Christianity were apparent in his *Kirisuto massatsuron*[b] (On the Destruction of Christ), also published in 1910. This work, written in prison, was a testament parallel to Nakae Chōmin's last work. However, in Kōtoku the materialism of Chōmin became a hatred directed against the historical person of Christ, whose existence he attempted to deny. According to Kōtoku, this work had no pretension of originality, nor under the conditions in which it was written, was it the result of much research. It was a passionate attempt to shock the many Christian-minded socialists into breaking away from Christ, who was for them a social redeemer. Actually, he denied the existence

a. 平民主義   b. 基督抹殺論

of the basis of their belief.[13]

From this time on, socialist thought became more and more tied to Marxist philosophy. However, a current of Christian socialism still, and has always, existed in Japan.

13) *Kōtoku Shūsui senshū* 幸徳秋水選集 (Selected Works of Kōtoku Shūsui), ed. by Hirano Gitarō 平野義太郎, Sekai Hyōronsha, 1948-50, 3 vols.; Itoya Hisao 糸屋寿雄, *Kōtoku Shūsui den* 幸徳秋水伝 (A Biography of Kōtoku Shūsui), San-ichi Shobō, 1950, which is not only a biography of Kōtoku, but has good material on Nakae, early socialism and pragmatism. *Kōtoku Shūsui hyōden* 幸徳秋水評伝 (A Critical Biography of Kōtoku Shūsui), ed. by Shakai Keizai Undō Kenkyū-sho, Ito Shoten, 1947, with bibliography, pp. 171-81

Chapter III

INDIVIDUALISM, PRAGMATISM, AND
NEO-KANTIANISM 1901—1925

Individualism and Japanism

The turn of the nineteenth century and the beginning of the twentieth saw the upsurge of nationalism and individualism in Japan, as well as the formation of a pragmatist trend. The latter continued throughout the Taishō period until about 1925. Neo-Kantianism and philosophical studies, in general, became increasingly academic; they passed from what might be called a period of popularization to the point of refined scientific investigation.

Japanism or nationalism, which became more emotional after the Sino-Japanese (1894-1895) and the Russo-Japanese (1904-1905) wars, was not exactly a problem of philosophy. However, it was so connected with philosophers like Tanaka Ōdō[a], Takayama and others, that it must be mentioned. On account of the two victorious wars, a new national conscience had developed.

To follow the chronological order, Takayama Rinjirō (Chogyū)[b] must be mentioned first. He was born in 1871 in the prefecture of Yamagata and died in Tokyo in 1902. He was known more for his critical essays and his novels than for his work as a philosopher. Nevertheless, Takayama had formal philosophical training, and wrote books on ethics, logic and

a. 田中王堂　　b. 高山林次郎 (樗牛)

aesthetics. He graduated from the Tokyo Imperial University in 1896, together with Anesaki Masaharu[a] (Chōfū), who became a great scholar on the science of religion, and the future Kantian, Kuwaki Gen'yoku. Takayama's ethics advocated the realization of self as the ideal of man, following, like Ōnishi, T.H. Green's *Prolegomena to Ethics*. Green's neo-Hegelianism was influential in Takayama's "reification" of the state. For his views on *Nihonshugi*[b] (Japanism) Hartmann was invoked. Takayama held that the state was only the *"Mittelzweck"*, the means, and not the final goal, the *"Endzweck"*. Kōsaka, on the other hand, states that Takayama's "adoration" of the Imperial Rescript on Education and the emphasis he placed on the Japanese polity of the unity of the Emperor and his subjects in a family relationship classed him among the earlier ideologists of nationalism. In his last phase, Takayama turned to individualism, inspired by Nietzsche. Takayama's changing phases can easily be seen from the angle of his literary career. As a student he won literary prizes. At heart, he was a romantic, and translated, among other works, Goethe's *The Sorrow of Young Werther*.

Nietzsche's *Birth of Tragedy* influenced his aesthetic views, which were the main spring of his individualism. He believed that individualism was best expressed in aesthetical emotion, which was also the greatest force in the formation of human personality. His connection with literary naturalism was due to the belief that individualism was also instinctivism, and that sexual love was one of the forms of its expression, if not the most important. Nietzsche's *Uebermensch* he found to a great degree in Nichiren[c] (1222-82), the founder of a Buddhist sect.

a. 姉崎正治（嘲風）　　b. 日本主義　　c. 日蓮

Takayama extolled Nichiren as the best incarnation of Japanism. He scorned the ordinary man, saying: "Give me one Nichiren. I shall still give ten million men in exchange!" Later his preference changed from greats such as Nichiren and Buddha to heroes like Napoleon and Nietzsche. He came to favor the way of will and power rather than the way of abnegation and sacrifice.

Takayama was also noted for his criticism of civilization, a genre of philosophical writing which was developed primarily in the period of the twenties and thirties.[1]

Pragmatism in Japan

Before presenting Tanaka Ōdō, an advocate of individualism and nationalism, and a critic of culture, pragmatism in Japan must be discussed, for Tanaka's philosophical inspiration was Dewey's instrumentalism.

Already in 1888 Motora Yūjirō presented the psychology of Dewey and James' pragmatism in the journal *Rikugō zasshi*. The Yale professor G.T. Ladd, who visited Japan three times, was instrumental in spreading the psychology of James. Another who called attention to James was the Kantian, Kuwaki Gen'-yoku, who discussed the *Will to Believe*. Translations began to appear: in 1902, James' *Principles of Psychology* was translated

---

1) Takayama Rinjirō (Chogyū)'s 高山林次郎 (樗牛) philosophical works are: *Rinri kyōkasho* 倫理教科書 (A Textbook on Ethics), Hakubunkan, 1897; *Ronrigaku* 論理学 (Logic), Hakubunkan, 1898; *Kinsei bigaku* 近世美学 (Recent Aesthetics), Hakubunkan, 1899; *Nihonshugi* 日本主義 (Japanism) was printed in the magazine *Taiyō* 太陽, 1897. His complete works are: *Chogyū zenshū* 樗牛全集, Hakubunkan, 1925, 7 vols. Concerning Takayama. see: *Japanese Thought* . . ., ed. by Kōsaka, o.c., pp. 292-312 Tsuchida K., *Contemporary Thought* . . ., o.c., pp. 59-60; 152

by Motora and Fukumoto Kazuo[a], and in 1910 *Pragmatism* was rendered into Japanese. In 1903 Anesaki Masaharu (Chōfū) introduceed the *Varieties of Religious Experience,* a book which had great influence upon the Christian poet Tsunajima Ryōsen[b] (1873-1897), who wrote a *History of Western Ethics.* This work was published by the Tokyo Semmon Gakkō (Waseda University). On account of the activities of Tanaka, Hoashi Riichirō[c] and Sugimori Kōjirō,[d] Waseda became the center of pragmatism.

Besides Kuwaki, who was first professor at Kyoto and later went to Tokyo University, Nakajima Rikizō, also of Tokyo University, introduced Dewey's *Outlines of Critical Theory of Ethics.* In 1900 this was translated into a shorter form. Nishida's "pure experience" concept was influenced by James' as well as by Bergson's philosophy, the latter being in vogue during the first decade of this century. Other traces of pragmatic ideas upon non-pragmatic philosophers were apparent in works such as Nishida's *Gendai ni okeru risōshugi*[e] (Idealism in Contemporary Thought), published in 1917, Tanabe Hajime's[f] *Ninshikiron ni okeru ronrishugi no genkai*[g] (The Limits of Rationalism in Epistemology), published in 1914 and Ide Takashi's[h] *Tetsugaku izen*[i] (Before Philosophy), published in 1921. Apparently pragmatism was a widely talked-about subject in the philosophical circles of the late Meiji and Taishō periods, until the early twenties of this century.

Waseda University seems to have been the main focal point of pragmatism. This was because literary movements and, to

a. 福本和夫　　b. 綱島梁川　　c. 帆足理一郎　　d. 杉森孝次郎
e. 現代における理想主義　　f. 田辺元　　g. 認識論における論理主
義の限界　　h. 出隆　　i. 哲学以前

a greater degree, liberal political ideas were formed in this private institution. The *Waseda bungaku*[a], the Journal of Literature of Waseda, in opposition to *Teikoku bungaku*[b], which represented the literary trend of Tokyo Imperial University, discussed naturalism, a literary movement which was quite popular during the late Meiji and early Taishō periods. According to Hasegawa Nyozekan[c], a well-known social critic and thinker who wrote on the subject of "The Philosophy of Naturalism", pragmatism, rightly or wrongly, was frequently connected with naturalism. Nevertheless, Tanaka Ōdō, as well as other Waseda men, was not in favor of naturalism because his idealistic view of artistic work did not permit him to be a naturalist.

A further reason for Waseda's connection with pragmatism was that the university was the center of the "Taishō democracy," a democratic movement which flourished before the Shōwa period (1926). The Shōwa period was climaxed by the rise of military nationalism. Here an exception to the rule must be made, because democracy, in its political aspects, was especially proposed by Yoshino Sakuzō[d] (1878-1933), professor of political science at the Tokyo Imperial University. Ideas, not possessing the static quality of institutions, are difficult to localize. On the whole, however, some credit must be given to Waseda because, as a private university, it was less under the influence of the governmental policies prevalent in the pre-war years. However, this belongs to a more recent history of Japanese thought. It must not be forgotten that, in 1906, the Ministry of Education published a translation of Dewey's *School and*

a. 早稲田文学   b. 帝国文学   c. 長谷川如是閑（万次郎）
d. 吉野作造

Society, and that the most representative philosophical journal *Tetsugaku zasshi*[a], before and after the Russo-Japanese War, presented pragmatic views. Exponents of Japanism, like Kihira Masami[b], wrote about T.C.S. Schiller, pointing out his differences and variations from Confucianist thought. Later, the influence of Dewey's pedagogical theories was felt. His *Democracy and Education* was the basic book for all democratic educators. The Taishō period witnessed the establishment of schools like the Jiyū Gakuen[c] and the Seijō Shōgakkō[d] in which the new pedagogical methods were tried.

Upon completion of this description of the phases of Japanese pragmatism, the reader is perhaps curious to know why it did not become the predominant trend, a fact which is stressed by all historians of Japanese thought. The explanation for those who believe in the national spirit was that pragmatism did not suit the Japanese mentality. They believe that a mythical national soul is not really a man-made cultural reality, but a racial or instinctive product. Lüth was one of those believers; he thought that *"der Geist"* of Japan did not suit the nature of empiricism, utilitarianism, or pragmatism, these being too practically oriented trends, and not deep enough. Kōsaka's answer is more scientific, although it is based on the "national character." Kōsaka says that the Japanese could be considered even "excessively utilitarian and practical", because they possess a character which runs to the extremes of passion and coldness. Japan, he holds, is a nation which can be easily aroused and just as easily pacified; therefore, an ordinary philosophy like empiricism or pragmatism is not capable of duration. If a few socio-

a. 哲学雑誌   b. 紀平正美   c. 自由学園   d. 成城小学校

political reasons are added, such as the years of feudal oppression which brought about as a dialectical result the tendency toward rapid progress, and the following reaction to blind conservatism, the explanation appears more "scientific." Yet, this kind of solution actually explains very little. It seems to be a *post factum* reconstruction, based too frequently on the fallacy *post hoc, propter hoc.* At any rate, empiricism and utilitarianism as well as pragmatism took quite a hold upon the Japanese "intelligentsia" at different times in its philosophical history. The rise of materialism and Marxism will, in the future, no doubt lead to many other down-to-earth "isms." However, I shall deal with this at the conclusion of this book, if not completely, then at least by showing a wider approach than the usual simplification of Eastern mysticism and Western pragmatism.[2]

The Instrumentalism of Tanaka Ōdō

In 1890, upon completion of his studies at the Tokyo Semmon Gakkō, Tanaka Ōdō (Kiichi, 1867-1932) went to the United States. In this he was following in the footsteps of others like Nakajima who helped introduce pragmatism into Japan. Tanaka stayed abroad nine years and graduated from Chicago University. While studying there, he felt the impact of Dewey's ideas. Upon his return, he taught at Waseda, his alma mater, and

2) For Pragmatism in Japan see: Ōi Tadashi 大井正 *Nihon kindai shisō no ronri* 日本近代思想の論理 (The Logic of Modern Japanese Thought), Gōdō Shuppansha, 1958, pp. 86-147; *Gendai no tetsugaku kōza, V Nihon no gendai shisō* 現代の哲学講座 V 日本の現代思想 (Contemporary Philosophy-Lectures V Contemporary Japanese Thought), ed. by Yamazaki Masakazu 山崎正一 and others, Yūhikaku, 1958, pp. 93-97; Lüth P., *Die japanische . . .*, o.c., pp. 68-69

also, among other places, at Rikkyō (St. Paul's) University[a]. In spite of his teaching work, the main part of his time was spent in writing for magazines. From these contributions to magazines came his books, which were mostly collections of essays. Only at the end of his career did he concentrate on a more systematic work, *Tetsugaku gairon*[b] (Introduction to Philosophy). His death, at 66, barred completion of this treatise. His style of writing similar to Carlyle, Emerson and Walter Pater, made Tsuchida Kyōson exclaim that Tanaka deserved translation into foreign languages for he could have been easily understood.

The first writings of Tanaka, which came out in book form, were *Shosui yori gaitō e*[c] (From the Study-Room to the Street), published in 1911, and *Tetsujinshugi*[d] (Philosopher-ism). His pragmatic bend was evident, not only from the titles of his books, but also from the fact that his efforts to unify theory and practice brought him, more than any pragmatist in England or America, to a combination of philosophy with social and political purposefulness. To be a "patriot with the attitude of a scholar" was his main intent. Considering the multitude of interests in which he was involved, Tanaka's pragmatism had many phases. This can be confirmed by glancing at the different titles of his books, included in the notes. His "philosopher-ism" became "non-philosophy" and his "radical individualism", stemming from James' radical empiricism, became "philosophy as interpretation". His democratic thought was based on a romantic utilitarianism or idealistic experimentalism, pregnant with nationalism, and on a worship for the "philosopher-king" and

a. 立教大学   b. 哲学概論   c. 書斎より街頭へ   d. 哲人主義

"representative personalities".

Although milder than in Takayama, hero-worship was nonetheless present in Tanaka, who developed his "Philosopher-ism" into "Radical individualism" (*Tettei kojinshugi*)[a], an essay published in 1918. However, even in Yoshio Sakuzō, the promoter of democracy in Japan, geniuses were overstressed. The nature of this survey bars the treatment of Tanaka's views on history and civilization, in which he followed E. Burke and W. Bagehot, another English Victorian.

Tanaka's instrumentalism was expressed as *Jikken risō-shugi*[b] (Experimental Idealism or Idealistic Experimentalism). He defined his attitude in the following English terms: "natural" or naturalistic in opposition to any metaphysical and mystical conception of life. Life, in turn, must be lived experimentally, that is, it must be based on daily social life. Secondly, it was a "developmental" conception, because, contrary to animal tendencies which are a determined and "fixed datum", human tendencies are indeterminate and tend toward an ideal. Thirdly, the experience of life was "organic" in the sense that, notwithstanding all strife and suffering, man progresses toward a higher and better unity of the self. Finally, it was "functional", as all ideals must possess social efficiency, which will make possible an adjustment to society. From these and other statements, Tanaka's instrumentalism appeared to be derived from Dewey's position. His originality consisted in his other views, and in his philosophy of culture.

Tsuchida Kyōson praised Tanaka's thoughts on culture as found in his *Shōchōshugi no bunka*[c] (Toward Culture of

---

a. 徹底個人主義   b. 実験理想主義   c. 象徴主義の文化

Symbolism) This book declared that civilization was inclined to symbolize, in potential form, any actual manifestation of the future. Therefore, before reconstruction could begin, re-interpretation was needed to appreciate and distinguish the latest symbol. Tanaka being a radical actualist, his appraisal of the practical identity between the ideal and the real gave little stimulus to transcend the present.

Mention should be given to Hoashi Riichirō, who taught with Tanaka at Waseda University, not because of his great importance as a philosopher, but on account of his *Tetsugaku gairon*[a] (Outlines of Philosophy), a book printed in 1921. In a few years this work had eighteen editions printed. In the preface, he bluntly stated that the philosophy of the Imperial Universities was merely doing service to Prussian autocracy. Another Waseda professor, who, according to Tsuchida, was comparable to Tanaka is Sugimori Kōjirō (1881-   ). Sugimori reduced philosophy to social philosophy, and was known for his work *Shakaigaku*[b] (Sociology). His ultra-pragmatism did not prevent him from becoming president of the Japan Publicists Association and a member of the East Asian Cultural Council. These two offices, both held during the Second World War, the most critical period for independent thought, showed his blend of pragmatic nationalism. At any rate, today he is

a. 哲学概論   b. 社会学

remembered as a journalist more than anything else[3].

The Ethical Personalism of Abe Jirō 1883-1959

Before passing to the more academic philosophers, the proponents of systematic German philosophy, Abe Jirō, the influential thinker of the Taishō and early Shōwa period, must be discussed. His *Santarō no nikki*[a], published in 1914, was a best-seller among the youth of pre-war times, and is still read. At present, his complete works are in the proceses of being published. In a sense Abe could be dealt with later on, yet his most important philosophical works appeared during the time surveyed here. He was also connected with the trends of individualism and personalism prevalent from 1912 until 1923.

Abe was born in 1883 at Kamisato, in Yamagata[b] prefecture and graduated in 1907 from the Tokyo Imperial University. His professors were, among others, Koeber and Hatano Seiichi, both of whom left a deep impression upon the young Abe. He was a religious person, given a strict Confucian training at his home and otherwise influenced by his Catholic grandmother. His

---

a. 三太郎の日記   b. 山形

3) Tanaka Ōdō's 田中王堂 philosophical works are: *Shosai yori gaitō e* 書斎よ
    り街頭へ (From the Study-room to the Street), Kōbundō, 1911: *Tetsu-
    jinshugi* 哲人主義 (Philosopherism). Kōbundō, 1912, 2 vols.; *Waga hi-
    tetsugaku* 我が非哲学 (My Non-philosophy), Ke'bundō, 1913, *Sōzo to
    Kyōraku* 創造と享楽 (Creativity and Hedonism), Ten-yūsha, 1921; *Shō-
    chōshugi no bunka e* 象徴主義の文化へ (Toward a Culture of Symbol-
    ism), Hakubunkan, 1924; *Kaishaku no tetsugaku* 解釈の哲学 (Philoso-
    phy as Interpretation), Shūhōkaku, 1925; *Carlyle, Emerson*, Tōho Bunka
    Shuppambu, 1926. Concerning Tanaka's pragmatism see: Ōi T., *Nihon
    o.c.*, pp. 111-27; *Gendai no tetsugaku* . . ., vol. c., pp. 97-116; Miyanishi
    K., *Kindai shisō* . . ., o.c., pp. 269-70; *Japanese Thought* . . ., ed. by Kō-
    saka, o.c., pp. 477-84; Tsuchida K., *Contemporary Thought* . . ., o.c., pp.
    61-63; 153-59; 159-163

literary talents appeared early in his life; as a student he won praises and, after graduation, he assumed a position in the editorial staff of the literary section of the influential *Tōkyō Asahi* newspaper[a]. His senior writer was none other than Natsume Sōseki, who postulated critical individualism in his philosophical essays.

Abe's interest in philosophy was manifested in his slightly rearranged translation of T. Lipps's *Die ethischen Grundfragen* (*Rinrigaku no kompon mondai*[b],) or Fundamental Problems of Ethics) published in 1916; his collaboration in the translation of Plato's works, and in his *Jinkakushugi*[c] or Personalism, which came out in 1920 and 1922. The majority of his works were dedicated to the philosophy of art. *Bigaku*[d] (Aesthetics) was printed in 1917. He later published *Art and Society* and *Art in the Tokugawa Times*. This was done from 1921 on, while he was professor in the Tōhoku University[e] of Sendai[f]. He went to Europe in 1922 and studied philosophy at the University of Munich. The works of Dante and Goethe were of great interest to him. In 1919, Abe published a critical study of Nietzsche's *Zarathustra*.

His ethical and religious personalism was evident in his *Santarō no nikki*, a collection of philosophical reflections written in a diary (*nikki*) form. Abe called the author of this diary "Santarō", an ordinary man who symbolized Abe's views. This work was not an autobiography, but a kind of philosophical journal, such as today's existentialist philosophers write. It defies any summary since there is no order in the reflections, which cover a multitude of subjects. The only unifying trend

a. 東京朝日新聞　　b. 倫理学の根本問題　　c. 人格主義　　d. 美学
e. 東北大学　　f. 仙台

was Abe's personalistic quest for an Absolute, (the reality toward which he aspired, but did not attain), through a way of absolute freedom and salvation.

The semi-religious asceticism and moralism found in *Santarō* changed to social personalism in his *Jinkakushugi* (Personalism). In this work Abe was greatly influenced by T. Lipps. The book opened with statements concerning the need of an ideal standard for human practical life; a moral idea, "*Die schoene Seele*" borrowed from Goethe and M. Scheler. Abe identified the beautiful with the moral; by personality he meant, not a psychological description of character, but the distinctive and individual intellectual self which is at the bottom of all human experiences. He felt that personalism developed the selfhood to the highest degree, passing from *Sklavennatur* to *Herrennatur;* that is, man was king of nature and of himself. Although these concepts were borrowed from Lipps, Abe's emphasis on freedom and love (Dante's *amor della sfera suprema*) was his own. He conceived of love in a mystical manner. The second part of his book considered concepts of society as an organic being; and even social problems such as labor relations appeared abstract and utopian to the more practically minded social thinkers, who at this time were fighting for social justice.

His personalism found in another major work, *Sekai bunka to Nihon bunka*[a] (World Culture and Japanese Culture, 1933), became, under the impact of Dilthey, a world view which had a more sophisticated epistemological foundation than that which was expressed in his earlier works. This book, too, was

a. 世界文化と日本文化

a collection of long essays, written at different times, in which noteworthy studies were made on Nietzsche, Goethe, and comparative literature. The studies were mostly based on Dilthey's *Der Aufbau der geschichtlichen Welt in den Geisteswissenschaften.*

In explaining the difficult terms of Dilthey's *Verstehen und Auslegen* (*Rikai to kaishaku* or Understanding and Interpretation) for a collection of philosophical studies published by Iwanami, Ame proved his capability in doing strictly critical studies. Abe Jirō's wide reputation was due to his simpler ethical works in which his passionate and persuasive style delighted his young readers[4].

4) Abe Jirō's 阿部次郎 philosophical works are: *Santarō no nikki* 三太郎の日記 (The Diary of Santarō), Tōundō, 1914; the most recent and complete edition is in the Kadokawa Bunko, 1960 (32 ed.); *Rinrigaku no kompon mondai* 倫理学の根本問題 (Fundamental Problems of Ethics), Iwanami Shoten, 1916; *Jinkakushugi* 人格主義 (Personalism), Iwanami Shoten, 1922, pp. 45; 56-57; 107; 134-37; *Nietzsche no Zaratustra kaishaku narabi ni hihyō* ニイチェのツァラツゥストラ解釈ならびに批評 (Explanation and Critic of Nietzsche's Zarathustra), Shinchōsha, 1919; *Sekai bunka to Nihon bunka* 世界文化と日本文化 (World Culture and Japanese Culture), Iwanami Shoten, 1933, pp. 216 ff. In this volume there is also *Rikai to kaishaku* 理解と解釈 (Understanding and Interpretation), pp. 443-516, formerly published in the *Iwanami Collection Tetsugaku sōsho* 哲学叢書 (Iwanami Philosophical Series); *Bigaku* 美学 (Aesthetics), Iwanami Shoten, 1917; *Tokugawa jidai no geijutsu to shakai* 徳川時代の芸術と社会 (Art and Society in Tokugawa Time), Kaizōsha, 1931, Abe Jirō complete works: *Abe Jirō zenshū* 阿部次郎全集 are in course of publication in 15 vols., Kadokawa Shoten. Concerning Abe see: Takeuchi Yoshitomo ed. ed. 竹内良知, *Shōwa shisō-shi* 昭和思想史 (History of Thought in Shōwa Time), Minerva Shoin, 1958, pp. 238-67; Tsuchida K., *Contemporary Thought* . . ., o.c., pp. 153-64

Studies in Kantian and Neo-Kantian Philosophy

German philosophy in Japan began with the efforts of men like Katō Hiroyuki, Inoue Tetsujirō, and Ōnishi Hajime, who was called the "Japanese Kant", as well as with the work of the foreign professors mentioned in previous chapters. There was a prevalence of Anglo-German idealism and neo-Hegelianism advocated by Green which lasted until the end of the century. Japanism, Philosopherism and Personalism were a search for a philosophy of life, if not a basis for a national policy. More technical philosophy was needed; this need was fulfilled, to a great extent, during the second decade of this century by the so-called Southwestern and Marburg schools of neo-Kantianism which had exponents not only in the Imperial Universities of Tokyo and Kyoto, but also in Waseda and other private institutions. A great majority of the philosophy students who went abroad during this period went to Germany rather than to the United States. Therefore, upon their return, they introduced the thought of their German teachers.

Before considering a few of the main followers of German philosophy of the neo-Kantian type, authors like Eucken and Bergson must be mentioned on account of their wide popularity. The former proposed an "ideal spiritual kingdom", to use the words of Kaneko Umaji[a], which was considered a god-send "after the deluge of naturalism." The latter, translated by Kaneko, was widely read because the proposed intuitionistic and spiritualistic philosophy was a good antidote to positivistic and pragmatistic trends. Bergson offered an approach, (which

---

a. 金子馬治 （筑水）

many felt to be quite Oriental), to those who were in search of a Weltanschauung. His influence was reflected in the *Zen no kenkyū*[a] (A Study of Good), Nishida Kitarō's first work. The new-Idealism movement, which, in Germany, had Eucken as its best representative, in France took the form of Bergson's anti-positivism and vitalistic intuitionism. The new-Idealism movement had its counterpart in Japan. Inoue's work *Tetsugaku to shūkyō* (Philosophy and Religion) was a testimony to this trend as were the works of other authors treated in this chapter.

Knowledge of Schopenhauer in Japan was due to the work of Inoue and Koeber. Anesaki Masaharu was a leading member of the Schopenhauer Society, founded in 1911. During this time Schopenhauer's masterpiece *Die Welt als Wille und Vorstellung* (The World as Will and Representation) was translated. Nietzsche's impact on Takayama and Abe has already been discussed; more could be said, however, if the fields of the history of ideas and of culture in general were entered into.

The Marburg school of neo-Kantianism was known through the works of P. Natorp, while the Southwestern (Baden) branch was known mostly through the influence which Rickert had upon his many Japanese pupils. On the occasion of the translation of his *Gegenstand der Erkenntnis* (The Object of Knowledge), Rickert remarked that he was more read in Japan than in Germany. This translation was prefaced by Nishida Kitarō, the greatest Japanese philosopher, who said that when he went to Kyoto in 1910, the University was a center of neo-

---

a. 善の研究

Kantianism. Nishida's *Intelligible World* stemmed from Rickert's *Die Erkenntnis der intelligibelen Welt*.

Among the best pupils of Rickert was Sōda Kiichirō[a] (1881-1927). He wrote, in both Japanese and German, on the philosophy of economics, being the first to do so in a systematic way. He was also a critic of culture, as Tsuchida explained profusely. Later, as his economic pursuits became more and more successful, he succeeded his father as head of the Sōda Bank. His commercial achievements did not eclipse his philosophical name, which is reported in every book on Japanese thought.

Other neo-Kantian works which were widely read were W. Windelband's *Praeluden* and E. Lask's *Feldtheorie* (Theory of Place), which had direct influence upon Nishida's analogue concept. Tanabe Hajime, another outstanding Japanese philosopher, was indebted to the influence of neo-Kantianism for his philosophy of science and mathematics. Abe Yoshishige[b], a philosopher, who, for reasons of systematic rather than chronological order, will be discussed later, was an exponent of Kant under the influence of neo-Kantianism. Another philosopher heavily influenced by this trend was Kuwaki Genyoku.

According to Kaneko, the book which was the main reference text, and which Kuwaki, Nishida, and even Watsuji Tetsurō relied upon to explain the fundamentals of philosophy to almost three generations of Japanese students was Windelband's *Einleitung in die Philosophie* (Introduction to Philosophy).

a. 左右田喜一郎   b. 安部能成

The preponderance of neo-Kantianism during the Taishō period can be seen in the published works on philosophy at that time. In 1915 the well-known publisher Iwanami printed the collection *Tetsugaku sōsho*[a] (Philosophical Library). This consisted of twelve volumes, which, with the exception of one or two, represented the above mentioned trend. That the popularity of German philosophy, in general, was to last was evident from later collections all by the same publisher, such as *Tetsugaku ronsō*[b] and *Iwanami kōza tetsugaku-gaisetsu*[c], published respectively, from 1928-1932 and from 1931. The same was true for the leading philosophical journals such as the *Tetsugaku zasshi* and, from 1910 on, Kyoto University's *Tetsugaku kenkyū*[d] (Philosophical Studies). In 1921 the publisher Iwanami started *Shisō*[e] (Thought).

From 1920 Husserl's phenomenalism, Heidegger's existentialism and Hegel's dialectic became more and more prevalent. However, during the Shōwa period (1926 on) Hegel became the topic of the day, particularly on account of the debate against Marxist dialectic. What made neo-Kantianism the leading philosophy of the Taishō times was the fact that, until then, Anglo-American thought, from Mill to Dewey, was too much involved in politico-social problems, to the exclusion of critical epistemology and metaphysical questions. For academic philosophers, epistemology and metaphysics were becoming important. Early Meiji thinkers, pressed as they were by political problems, thought that every philosopher like Mill was supposed to write on governmental policies or on human rights. This teaching was carried to such an extent that,

a. 哲学叢書   b. 哲学論争   c. 岩波講座哲学概説   d. 哲学研究
e. 思想

notwithstanding the pioneer work of Nishi Amane and Ōnishi Hajime, "pure" philosophy (called literally *Junsui tetsugaku*[a]) and metaphysical problems were totally neglected, as there was not a real epistemology. Because of their many interests, and their writing for general magazines, Takayama, Abe, Tanaka and many others belonging to the *Zaiya*[b], non-official academic line, continued to study culture and life from a broad point of view. The need for a more speculative basis was fulfilled later by neo-Kantianism and Kantian studies.[5]

We must not think though, that only German philosophy was studied from an academic point of view. The Taishō period was the beginning of academic philosophical studies in general. Although Kuwaki was primarily a Kantian expert, he was also well informed on the thought of Descartes. Another Kantian scholar, Tomonaga Sanjūrō[c], was famous for his two books on Descartes. Hatano Seiichi, chiefly a philosopher of religion, was a good historian of philosophy and wrote an important book on Spinoza. During this time translations of classical works of ancient as well as modern philosophy were begun, although the complete works, of Plato and others, appeared later.

---

a. 純粋哲学   b. 在野   c. 朝永三十郎

5) For Kantian studies and neo-Kantianism see: Itō Kichinosuke *hen* (ed.) 伊藤吉之助編 *Kanto to sono shūhen no tetsugaku* カントとその周辺の哲学 (Kant and the Philosophy around him), in the third vol. of *Kuwaki Gen'yoku chosaku-shū* 桑木厳翼著作集, Shunjūsha, 1949; Saigusa Hiroto 三枝博音, *Nihon ni okeru tetsugakuteki kannenron no hattatsu-shi* 日本における哲学的観念論の発達史 (History of the Development of Philosophical Idealism in Japan), Bunshōdō, 1934, pp, 115-81; *Kindai Nihon . . .*, o.c., vol. 2, pp. 437-44; Miyanishi K., *Kindai shisō . . .* o.c., pp. 207-10. The article "Rickerts Bedeutung für die japanische Philosophie" by Miki Kiyoshi 三木清 is in his *Chosaku-shū* 著作集 (Collected Works), vol. XI, pp. 1-9, Iwanami Shoten, 1946-1951

The academic philosophical activity at the end of the Meiji period and during the Taishō times was directed at compiling philosophical dictionaries, a tool necessary for any kind of precise rendering of Western concepts into Sino-Japanese characters. Not all of these dictionaries were perfect. Some had gross errors, such as that previously mentioned which came out in 1912, edited by Inoue, Motora and Nakajima. Another, edited by Miyake Yūjirō (Setsurei) and Tokutani[a], was called *Futsū jutsugo jii*[b], a general dictionary of philosophical terms. In the same year, 1905, Tomonaga Sanjurō's *Tetsugaku jiten*[c] (Philosophical Dictionary) was published. This work was quite accurate, and went through several editions.

The *Tetsugaku daijiten*[d] was truly an opus magnum. It had the German subtitle *Enzyklopaedisches Woerterbuch der Philosophie*, and was a philosophical encyclopedia in seven large volumes, published during the years 1909-1912. The leading philosophers of the time were listed as editors or were in charge of special sections; for example, at the head for logic were Kuwaki and Kihira; Motora and Matsumoto were in charge for psychology, while Tokunō Fumi[e] and Nakajima were responsible for the section dealing with ethics. The work can be used as a kind of "who's who" for philosophy, where familiar names such as Tomonaga, Hatano, Anesaki, Abe Jirō and others are listed.

A much better philosophical dictionary came out in 1922. It was published by Iwanami and edited by Tomiyama Wakichi[f] and others. The most standard dictionary was the smaller

a. 徳谷豊之助　　b. 普通術語辞彙　　c. 哲学辞典　　d. 哲学大辞典
e. 得能文　　f. 富山和吉

Tetsugaku shōjiten[a], published by Itō Kichinosuke[b] in 1930. It has been continuously reprinted, in a slightly revised edition.

Leading Professors: Kuwaki and Tomonaga

Although he did not belong to the Imperial Universities of Tokyo or Kyoto, Kaneko Umaji is among the oldest of the pioneers in the field of philosophy teaching in Japan. Kaneko Umaji (Chikusui, 1870-1930) graduated from the Tokyo Semmon Gakkō (Waseda), where he later became a lecturer in 1894. He went abroad to Germany and studied at Leipzig, Berlin, and Heidelberg Universities. He received his Ph.D. in philosophy. He was previously mentioned as the translator of Bergson's *Creative Evolution,* but his several books on modern philosophy and introductions to philosophy show marked influence of neo-Kantianism. He stressed the point of philosophy as the esence of culture. He had no definite system, nor specific point of view. Traces of pragmatism, too, can be found in his work. He was also responsible for the introduction of Husserl into Japan.[6]

Kita Reikichi (1885-   ) was also from Waseda, and he, too, was under the influence of Windelband and Rickert. He was a politically-minded man: he became a member of the *Nihon Minshutō*[c] (Japanese Democratic Party) and was elected eight

---

a. 哲学小辞典   b. 伊藤吉之助   c. 日本民主党

6)   Kaneko Umaji's 金子馬治 main works are: *Ōshū shisō taikan* 欧洲思想大観 (General View of European Thought), Tōkyōdō, 1920, *Gendai tetsugaku gairon* 現代哲学概論 Outline of Contemporary Philosophy), Tōkyōdō, 1922; *Tetsugaku gairon* 哲学概論 (Outline of Philosophy), Waseda Shuppambu, 1927. His selected works are: *Kaneko Umaji Hakase senshū* 金子馬治博士選集 Risōsha, 1939-1940, 2 vols. Concerning Kaneko see: Ueda Seiji 植田清次 in *Risō* 理想, 1961, n.2., pp. 1-5; Tsuchida K., *Contemporary Thought* ..., o.c., pp. 165-66, where also Kita Reikichi 北玲吉, pp. 164-65, and Nakajima Rikizō 中島力造 p. 62 are mentioned.

times to the Diet. Here, however, the real centers of Kantian studies in Japan must be examined, namely, the Universities of Tokyo and Kyoto.

Before speaking of Kuwaki Gen'yoku, Nakajima Rikizō (1858-1918) deserves mention, although he was not a representative of German philosophy. He graduated from Dōshisha school and went to Yale University for further study, as well as to England and Germany. Upon his return, in 1890, he became professor at Tokyo University. He belonged to the old generation of exponents of T.H. Green's neo-Hegelianism, who were fighting for idealistic ethics against the lingering positivism and utilitarianism. He collaborated with Inoue and Motora Yūjirō for the publication of the *Tetsugaku jii* (Dictionary of Philosophical Terms). Perhaps his American background is a partial explanation for his translations of Dewey's book on ethical theories in 1900.

The main Kantian of Japan was Kuwaki Gen'yoku (1874-1946). Nevertheless, according to his pupil Ide Takashi, Kuwaki did not like to be identified with neo-Kantianism; he rather wanted to be near the position of Aloisius Rihel, a Kantian of a realistic ontological orientation. He was primarily a dispassionate and critically minded investigator, who had been brought up when positivism and Spencerian influence was still great in Japan. He did not want to be associated with the form of idealism, which was also being used for less academic purposes by nationalist thinkers. Ide reports that Kuwaki emphasized in his writings the Cartesian methodological doubt. In fact, he did this to such an extent that his young students, such as Ide, were dispairingly unable to reach any certainty by his critical method.

Kuwaki was born in Tokyo, and graduated from Tokyo University in 1896. He continued his graduate studies while teaching at the best High School of Tokyo (Daiichi Kōtōgakkō)[a]; he was later called to Kyoto University. In 1907-1909 he went to Europe and the United States for further studies. In 1914 he returned to his Alma Mater, where he took the position held by Inoue Tetsujirō, who had reached the age of retirement. He served as professor until 1935. After quitting Tokyo University, he continued his academic activities in several capacities, also teaching at Waseda University.

It is unnecessary to give a survey of Kuwaki's philosophical production, which was extensive, for he made no pretence of originality. The characteristics can be summarized easily: while studying mainly Kant, he tried, in all fields of philosophy and of social problems, to go to the exact meaning of the question in order to specify the real issue. He was a kind of precursor of analytical philosophy. In his early work *Tetsugaku kōyō*[b] (Outline of Philosophy) published in 1912, and in his later studies such as *Tetsugaku oyobi tetsugaku-shi kenkyū*[c] (Studies on Philosophy and the History of Philosophy) published in 1936, his painstaking efforts to clarify philosophical problems by studying the meaning and content was obvious and praiseworthy. Typically, in his first book, he analyzed "Norm and Normative Science" in relation to the socio-cultural problems discussed in Japan at the time. In the second, he discussed *Gengo to tetsugaku*[d] (Language and Philosophy) as seen in Western philosophers, who also had their semantic difficulties,

a. 第一高等学校   b. 哲学綱要   c. 哲学および哲学史研究
d. 言語と哲学

given the long history and changing meaning of concepts which expressed, by the same word, totally different meanings in different ages.

Kuwaki's *Gendai shichō jukkō*[a] (Ten Lectures on Modern Trends), published in 1913, criticized pragmatism and the new realism of Perry and Russell. However, his main works, written in a clear and witty style, were studies of Kant's philosophy; for example, *Kant and Present Philosophy*, published in 1917, and *Considerations on Kant*. The latter work dealt with many problems, and not solely with Kant. Kant's methods were related to Japanese problems discussed at that time in and out of academic circles. Out of these works, Kuwaki's "subjectivism" was developed, this being the last position of Kant's *Critiques*, or rather Rihel's interpretation of Kant.[7]

Another famous professor of Kyoto University was Tomonaga Sanjūrō (1871-1951). Like Kuwaki, Tomonaga graduated from Tokyo University, but did not return there, preferring to

a. 現代思潮十講

7) Kuwaki Gen'yoku's 桑木厳翼 extracts from *Tetsugaku kōyō* 哲学綱要 (Outline of Philosophy) in *Nihon tetsugaku shisō zensho* . . . , o.c., pp. 201-48; *Gengo to tetsugaku* 言語と哲学 (Language and Philosophy), is in *Tetsugaku oyobi tetsugaku-shi kenkyū*哲学および哲学史研究(Studies on Philosophy and History of Philosophy), Iwanami Shoten, 1936, pp. 26-54. Among his many other works published by Iwanami such as *Kant and Contemporary Philosophy, Kant, Philosophical Method in Science*, there is *Seiyō kinsei tetsugaku-shi Rōmaji-kaki* 西洋近世哲学史ローマ字書き (History of Recent Western Philosophy, written in Romaji). Romaji is the Latin alphabet used as transliteration of Sino-Japanese characters. Concerning Kuwaki see: Funayama Shin'ichi 船山信一 *Nihon no kannenronsha* 日本の観念論者 (Japanese Idealists), Eiōsha, 1956, pp. 198-204; Ide Takashi 出隆 in *Risō* 理想, 1961, n.2, pp. 15-20; Tsuchida K., *Contemporary Thought* . . . o.c., pp. 73-74

remain at Kyoto until the end. He was noted for his work *Kinsei ni okeru ga no jikaku-shi*,[a] (A History of Self-Consciousness in Modern Times), published in 1916. This work analyzes the passage of man from self-awareness of the neo-Hegelian type of Green and Bradley prevalent twenty years earlier to a neo-Kantian formulation, as the subtitle of the book also states. Tomonaga was also associated with Kuwaki because of his pioneer work on *junsui*, "pure" philosophy, which he mentions in the introduction to his philosophical dictionary. His academic spirit was evident in all his many works, and especially in his books on the history of philosophy and his scholarly works on Descartes. Because of his many articles on Kant, he was considered one of the earliest Kantians in Japan; the others being Kuwaki, Abe Yoshishige, Amano Teiyū,[b] (for chronological reasons to be dealt with later). Yet, the critical spirit, rather than real Kantianism, was planted during this period. The Taishō period saw the rise of Japanese academic, scholarly philosophy, which continued, with abundance and quality to surprise every student of Japanese Western philosophy. Before concluding this chapter, two Kyoto University professors, the philosopher of aesthetics, Fukada Yasukazu,[c] and the ethician, Fujii Kenjirō[d] should be mentioned. Both were influenced by neo-Kantianism. The latter is especially remembered for his *Shukanteki dōtoku yōshi*[e] (Outline of Subjective Morality, 1910), and for his later works, *Rinri to kyōiku*[f] (Ethics and Educa-

---

a. 近世における我の自覚史   b. 天野貞祐   c. 深田康算   d. 藤井健治郎   e. 主観的道徳要旨   f. 倫理と教育

tion), published in 1932 and *Kokumin dōtokuron*[a] (National Morality), which opposed the nationalistic studies of Inoue.[8]

Chapter IV

THE PHILOSOPHY OF NISHIDA KITARŌ

1870—1945

The Significance of Nishida's Thought

A halt to the chronological sequence of this survey must be made here in order to study the thought of the leading philosophers of Japan. I have chosen four of them, cramming my material into two crowded chapters. No one will object to the fact that the first place is given to Nishida Kitarō and that a full chapter is devoted to him. He is the only Japanese philosopher of recent times around whom a philosophical school has been formed. This is the so-called *Kyōto-ha*[b] or the school of the University of Kyoto. Furthermore, as we shall see below, he is credited with having developed the typical oriental "logic of nothingness", and therefore with being a philosopher spanning the East and the West. More debatable is my choice in the following chapter, although there is little question about Tanabe Hajime being second in importance to Nishida. Watsuji

---

a. 国民道徳論   b. 京都派

8) Tomonaga Sanjūrō's 朝永三十郎 main works are: *Kinsei ni okeru ga no jikaku-shi-Doitsu shisō to sono haikei* 近世における我の自覚史　ドイツ思想とその背景 (History of Self-Consciousness in Modern Times—German Thought and its Background), Hōbunkan, 1916. On Kant, besides many articles: *Kanto no eien heiwaron* カントの永遠平和論 (The Theory of Kant's Eternal Peace), Kaizōsha, 1922; *Tetsugaku-shi shōhin* 哲学史小品 (Excerpts on History of Philosophy), Reimeishobō, 1948

Tetsurō who ranks third is considered to have a system of his own, while Hatano Seiichi, in the field of philosophy of religion, has some claims to original thought. Hatano, being older than Watsuji and Tanabe, has, for chronological reasons, been inserted before the former two.

My choice can be supported also by a fact which I did not know when I started writing these pages: namely, that besides the works of Nishida, those of Hatano, Watsuji, and Tanabe are being translated into English by the Japanese Commission of UNESCO, to acquaint Western readers with the thought of leading Japanese philosophers.

Nishida Kitarō's life does not present any singular incident or events worthy of special mention. He was born near the city of Kanazawa[a] in 1870, and died in Kamakura,[b] near Tokyo, on June 7, 1945. His youth was highlighted by his entering Tokyo University in 1891, as a special student, where Busse, Inoue Tetsujirō, and later Koeber were teaching. He did not attract the attention of his professors particularly, nor after graduation did he teach at the better known high schools. He was, it seems, resigned to remain a middle school teacher in a remote place all his life. It was during this period that he showed an interest in Zen Buddhism.

That he remained intellectually alive is clear from the fact that from 1906 on he was engaged in his first work, *A Study of Good*, which was published in January, 1911. In 1909 he was teaching German and philosophy at the Peers' College (Gakushūin)[c] of Tokyo, and the following year he was called to the University of Kyoto, where a place had been left vacant by

a. 金沢   b. 鎌倉   c. 学習院

the departure for Tokyo of Kuwaki Gen'yoku. The unassuming and modest Nishida gave no indication at first that it would be because of him that Kyoto University would become the center of a new philosophical school which would create a tradition surpassing its rival, Tokyo University.

It was his books more than his lectures that created Nishida's reputation. Among these should be singled out *A Study of Good*, which was and still is the most widely read philosophical book written by a Japanese. Mutai Risaku[a] recalls that he quit teaching in order to enter Kyoto University and study under Nishida, who around 1915, was becoming famous for his publications. Nishida, according to Mutai, was then lecturing on the introduction to philosophy, following Windelband's *Outline of Philosophy*, and in special lectures he was explaining Bolzano, Brentano, Meinong and Husserl. Mutai, who followed Nishida's special lectures for eleven years, testifies that he never heard the master utter a single word concerning political problems, although the world situation, let alone social changes in Japan, could have given more than a pretext for extra-curricular comments. I mention this detail because the post-war critics of Nishida have tried to blackball him as a supporter of nationalism. According to Mutai, the only one who showed an interest in political matters at Kyoto University then was Tomonaga Sanjūrō, Nishida and the other professors of philosophy being solely concerned with academic work.

Nishida retired from the University in 1928, but his philosophical production continued in many books and lectures. He was of continuous help to his former pupils, who were to become

a. 務台理作

leading professors of philosophy in the best schools of Japan, with the exception of Tokyo University which never showed much inclination for the type of philosophy characteristic of the Kyoto school. Nishida's private life was darkened by the death of his first wife in 1925 (he married again in 1931) as well as the death of his eldest son and four daughters. Although his fame increased with the years and honors were bestowed upon him, family tragedies, the mounting tide of national militarism, and, finally, the war, were to be a great trial to this retired and scholarly man. He died two months before the Japanese surrender.[1]

The significance of Nishida's philosophy consists in the fact that he was the first Japanese who discarded the work of being only a popularizer of Western philosophy and tried to build up a system of his own. This system, though including the method of Western philosophy, is still thoroughly Oriental in its theme and fundamental approach. It was Sōda Kiichirō who in 1925 first spoke of "Nishida's philosophy," meaning that Japan had at last found a new original thinker. Since then many studies have been devoted to explaining the difficult thought of the master. Naturally, Nishida is not the only one who aspired to be more than a purveyor of Western philosophy, nor is he unique

---

1) On Nishida Kitarō's 西田幾多郎 life see: Shimomura Toratarō 下村寅太郎 *Wakaki Nishida Kitarō sensei* 若き西田幾多郎先生 (The Young Nishida Kitarō sensei), Jimbun Shorin, 1947. It covers the life, and also the thought, of Nishida up to "A Study of Good"; Kōsaka Masaaki 高坂正顕 *Nishida Kitarō sensei no shōgai to shisō* 西田幾多郎先生の生涯と思想 (The Life and Thought of Nishida K. sensei), Kōbundō Shobō, 1947. A standard work. Nishida's *Nikki* 日記 (Diary) is the XIII vol. of the Complete works, (*Bekkan I*) His letters in the XVII-XVIII vols. (*Bekkan V-VI*)

in his Oriental approach. Nevertheless, he must be singled out for his perseverance in the task and his positive accomplishment.

In the Meiji period and after, Inoue Enryō tried to blend Buddhist philosophy with Western categories, while Inoue Tetsu-jirō showed a combination of Confucianism, Buddhism and German neo-idealism in his identity theory of phenomenon with reality. Neither one, though, had a real grasp of the problems he was facing in this kind of superficial eclecticism. Inoue Tetsujirō, by far the best of the old philosophers, in his *Soku*[a] or "identity" logic does not make a real effort to incorporate German logic, which nevertheless he knew well. Nishida, however, at least from the time of his work, *Hataraku mono kara miru mono e*[b] (From the Acting to the Seeing, 1927), was working systematically to build up what he called the "logic of place." Nishida also tried to use this logic to give a basis upon which Oriental culture could be founded, as Greek logic was the basis of Western culture. Typical of Mahāyāna Buddhism is his emphasis on the contradictory aspect of phenomenological reality, which is finally "nothingness" or "voidness." Nishida took up these concepts in his "logic of place," giving a new philosophical content to them. Everyone who is familiar with Indian and Buddhist philosophy knows the difficulty of rendering into Western terms and concepts those Oriental views which are ascetical ways of approaching salvation rather than philosophical concepts and therefore defy analytical examination. Nishida, though, tried with the help of Western philosophy to find a new logic which would also incorporate such views. No wonder, then, the difficulty in understanding him, and his constant com-

a. 即　　b. 働くものから見るものへ

plaint that he was never understood even by his best pupils, Orientals though they were, familiar with his cultural background.

I say this because Nishida is difficult for others besides Western readers who are not so familiar with Oriental thought. What makes it hard to understand him is neither his use of common concepts like nothingness, nor his intuitive approach, nor his dialectic, but rather his specific "logic of place", or the qualification he gives to nothingness. He surely does not repeat what there is in Mahāyāna Buddhism, nor is his nothingness the same as that of Takahashi Satomi,[a] Tanabe Hajime, Kihira Masami and other Japanese philosophers, who before and after him, used the same concept or approach.

Daisetsu T. Suzuki,[b] who wrote a preface for a translation of Nishida's A *Study of Good*, seems to tell us in his "How to read Nishida," that no less than an initiation in Zen Buddhism is necessary to grasp Nishida's thought. Suzuki, who is fond of repeating that Orientals have no need for the speculative and rational thinking common to Western philosophers, seems to forget how much Nishida was a debtor, in the good sense of the word, to Western philosophy. To exaggerations like that of Suzuki, another which was occasionally heard in the immediate post-war years might be counterposed, namely that Nishida's ability consisted in scanning, faster than any other, the German philosophical magazine *Logos*, in order to create his own system. Some Japanese critics even speak of the logic of nothingness as the nothingness of logic!

But leaving aside these extreme views, the fact remains that

a. 高橋里美   b. 鈴木大拙

Nishida is the most demanding thinker Japan ever produced. To understand him the reader must bring, in addition to a competent knowledge of Western and Eastern philosophy, a willingness to try to see "the beyond" which is Nishida himself. The crux of the matter is, I think, that Nishida wants to be a universal thinker. To put it better, though Nishida wants indeed to give his logic to Oriental culture, his aim is also to place it in a world culture, to make it universal. It is this bold attempt much more than his poetical style or his over-repetitious accumulation of dialectical negations, which gives rise to the complexity of Nishida's thought and the reader's difficulties.

His way of writing has been compared to that of Hegel and Heidegger. This comparison has validity for his later and most involved works but is hardly applicable to his *A Study of Good,* and other earlier works which are not so difficult. The task of understanding Nishida has been made easier for Western readers today by the translation of the above book *A Study of Good* by V. H. Viglielmo, and especially by the translation and introduction of R. Schinzinger, who tackled more difficult aspects of Nishida's philosophy than those considered in *A Study of Good.* A remarkable article by Noda Matao[a] in *Philosophy East and West* on Nishida must also be mentioned. Studies in the Japanese language have been numerous and they are continuing to come out. A survey of these works is given in the notes. I am indebted for the interpretation of specific points of Nishida's mature thought, as seen, for example, in *From the Acting to the Seeing,* to Professor Mutai Risaku, who was a pupil of Nishida, and who knows, as few today know, the philosophy of his

a. 野田又夫

master.[2]

2) Studies on Nishida's philosophy, besides the above by Kōsaka: Takizawa Katsumi 滝沢克己, *Nishida tetsugaku no Kompon mondai* 西田哲学の根本問題 (The Basic Problems of Nishida's Philosophy), Tōkō Shoin, 1936; new edit. Shimizu Shobō, 1946. A good study of the dialectic of identity (*soku*) of Nishida beginning from *Hataraku mono kara* . . . to the early essays of "Acting Intuition" Takahashi Satomi's criticism is included.

Kōyama Iwao 高山岩男, *Nishida tetsugaku* 西田哲学 (The Philosophy of Nishida), Iwanami Shoten, 1935; *Zoku Nishida tetsugaku* (The Philosophy of Nishida, Continuation), Iwanami Shoten, 1940. It is considered the best study on Nishida, although it may be too systematic, following Hegel's Phenomenology of the Spirit. The world of nature, (Kōyama too starts from *Hataraku mono kara* . . .), of consciousness, of reality, of personality, and the historical dialectical world are considered in the first volume. The second (*Zoku* or continuation) deals with the later development of Nishida, i.e., especially the third vol. of *Tetsugaku rombunshū* An appendix is added on the relation of Nishida and Japanese philosophy.

Yanagida Kenjūrō 柳田謙十郎 *Jissen tetsugaku toshite no Nishida tetsugaku* 実践哲学としての西田哲学(Nishida's Philosophy as Philosophy of Praxis), Kōbundō Shobō, 1939; *Nishida tetsugaku taikei* 西田哲学体系 (The System of Nishida's Philosophy), Daitōsha, 1946. The first volume deals with the framework of Nishida's ethical thought (*jissen*), beginning from "A Study of Good" up to the historical world of the philosophical essays. The second study, as the title indicates, is more general and systematic.

Shimomura Toratarō 下村寅太郎, *Nishida tetsugaku* 西田哲学 (The Philosophy of Nishida), Hakujitsu Shoin, 1947. A short introduction by a well known expert on Nishida, the result of two lectures.

Ueda Seiji 植田清次. *Nishida tetsugaku to Dyū-i tetsugaku* 西田哲学とデュ ーイ哲学 (Nishida's Philosophy and Dewey's Philosophy), Hikari no Shobō, 1947. *A Study of Good* is considered in relation to Dewey; to the latter, the second part is devoted.

Kōsaka Masaaki 高坂正顕. *Nishida tetsugaku to Tanabe tetsugaku* 西田哲学と田辺哲学 (Nishida's Philosophy and Tanabe's Philosophy), Reimei Shobō, 1949. A comparative study of the two founders of the Kyoto school of philosophy.

Mutai Risaku 務台理作, *Nishida tetsugaku* 西田哲学 (The Philosophy of Nishida), Kōbundō, Atene Bunko, 1949. In Mutai Risaku, *Bunka to*

shūkyō 文化と宗教. (Culture and Religion), Kōbundō Shobō, 1947, two chapters are dedicated to the meaning of *"basho"*, pp. 96-136. Also *Risō,* 1961, 2, pp. 5-10.

Nagao Michitaka 長尾訓孝, *Nishida tetsugaku no kaishaku* 西田哲学の解釈 (Explanation of Nishida's Philosophy), Risōsha, 1958. After a few preliminary chapters, the logic of place, the intelligible world, acting intuition, and the religious view of Nishida are studied.

For a Marxist critic of Nishida and his school see:

Hayashi Naomichi 林直道, *Nishida tetsugaku hihan* 西田哲学批判 (A Criticism of Nishida's Philosophy), Kaihōsha, 1948. Also many other recent works like Takeuchi Yoshitomo, ed. *Shōwa shisō-shi* 昭和思想史, (History of Shōwa Thought), Minerva Shoin, 1958, pp. 86-137. An important work on the social and cultural background of Nishida's thought up to the time of *A Study of Good* is:

Miyajima Hajime 宮島肇, *Meijiteki shisōka-zō no keisei* 明治的思想家像の 形成 (The Formation of the Meiji Type of Thinkers), Miraisha, 1960. Another work which came out while this book was at the press is:

Yamada Munemutsu 山田宗睦, *Nihongata shisō no genzō* 日本型思想の原像 (The Prototype of Japanese Thought), San-ichi Shobō, 1961.

In Western languages:

Kitarō Nishida, *Intelligibility and the Philosophy of Nothingness. Three Philosophical Essays,* transl. and introduced by R. Schinzinger, Maruzen Tokyo, 1958. This translation is the adaptation of the previous German edition by Schinzinger titled K. Nishida, *Die intelligible Welt,* Berlin, 1943, The three essays translated are *Eichiteki sekai* 叡智的世界, (The Intelligible World); *Goethe no haikei* ゲーテの背景, (The Metaphysical Background of Goethe); *Zettai mujunteki jiko dōitsu* 絶対矛盾的自己同一 (The Unity of Opposites), respectively from the V, XII, IX volumes of the complete works of Nishida below indicated.

Nishida Kitarō, *A Study of Good,* transl. by V. H. Guglielmo, Tokyo, 1960. While the translation of Schinzinger has a very good introduction, this one has "How to Read Nishida" by D. T. Suzuki, and a study by Shimomura Toratarō.

Taketi T., Japanische Philosophie der Gegenwart, in: *Blätter für Deutsche Philosophie,* 1940, Heft 3, pp. 277-99.

Noda Matao, East-West Synthesis in K. Nishida, in: *Philosophy East and West,* 4, pp. 345-59 (1955); Noda M., Modern Japanese Philosophy and the Philosophy of Nishida K., in *Actes du XI Congrès Int. de Philosophie,* Bruxelles, 1953, pp. 263-67.

The Early "Pure Experience"

The fundamental concept of the maiden work of Nishida, *Zen no kenkyū* (A Study of Good, 1911) was called *junsui keiken*[a] or "pure experience," by which is meant the direct awarenesss of things as they are. In this "pure experience", thought and thinking are included. Thinking is considered not only as a cause of abstract universal concepts, but also as the source of the Hegelian universal which is the soul of concrete reality. "Pure experience" transcends also the individual or particular experience. It is, rather, a universal intentionality, not a mere passive perception, much less a subjective state of consciousness. Will too, is included, because it is the realization in the praxis of "pure experience", just as thoughts are a kind of desire toward objective facts. Manifestations of "pure experience" are many, going from the perception of colors, or the primitive experience of the infant to the direct *Erlebnis* of artistic and religious experiences. Schelling's *Identitaet* is a characteristic of "pure experience". That is to say, all oppositions like subject and object of truth and falsehood must be transcended in a unifying awareness, which alone opens the way to the knowledge of the reality considered in the second part of *A Study of Good.*

Reality must be a self-conscious phenomenon, the result of the self-contained activity of pure experience. The changing nature of consciousness is explained not through a mechanicist law of causality, but with the help of Hegel's *das Unendliche* (non-finite), which has no quantitative limitations of space or time. Therefore, even from nothing something can be experienced. All the distinctions are but partial views, required by

a. 純粋経験

our way of knowing things. Reality is in the whole and must be grasped through the animation or personification of everything. Nishida invokes here Greek anthropomorphism. Different stages of the conscious process can be distinguished, and Nishida uses many psychologists to support his views, mostly James, Wundt, and G. F. Stout. But just as such antinomies as those between the spiritual and the material, the active and the passive, nature and spirit must be overcome in a unified reality, so all the psychological stages of our awareness must finally reach the ultimate reality which is God. This reality cannot be reached by the classical proofs for the existence of God, nor by the even "weaker", because less metaphysical, argument of Kant, but through the direct experience of mystics like J. Boehme, who see God with an "open eye", or through the negative theology of Nicholas of Cusa.

The third part of *A Study of Good* considers, finally, the good, i.e., our activity, which in so far as it is willed and conscious can be called human activity and can have a moral connotation. Here again will and intellect are not really separated; knowledge and action are but one operation. Will, being the most unifying function of our consciousness, cannot originate from matter. This is not because the will and matter are fundamentally different, but because the will is prior to consciousness and therefore must be spiritual. On freedom of the will, Nishida does not seem satisfied either with the determinists or with the indeterminists, but holds that we are free because a manifold possibility of ideals is present in us. After scrutinizing many theories on good and evil, he proposes his *katsudō-setsu*[a] or

a. 活動説

"activist-theory", according to which the good is the realization of our internal desires, i.e., ideals, which must tend to the development and perfection of our wills. This position must be understood in the light of Nishida's basic idea, namely that the will is the most unifying element of our consciousness and, therefore, the a-priori or deepest stratum underlying all our actions. He quotes here Aristotle's concept of "Eudaimonia" as the moving factor of our will toward the good.

The consummation of the good, though, is to be seen in religion (treated in the fourth part of his book), which must be a "relationship of father and son". Christian terminology is freely used by Nishida. He is indeed very free in quotations of any number of views that will illustrate his point, namely that the oneness of God and man must be the basis for any true religion. Hence, his "panentheism" a theory not too different from the position of the German philosopher Krause is hinted at here. Namely, Nishida is not in favor of Spinoza's pantheism, nor does he accept the absolute transcendence of God. Rather, he opts for an immanent-transcendent phenomenon, which, in fact, we are unable to express. Only mystics like Eckhart or Boehme and their "obscure vision" may be of some help.

A Study of Good does not represent the final point of view of Nishida, since he later confessed to have indulged too much in psychology in his analysis of consciousness. Furthermore, his reliance on James' "pure experience" is more than a question of terminology. For James too, the immediate experience embraces not only the singular content of the terms, but also the relations between them. Also, the stricture of a famous critic of Nishida and a good philosopher in his own right, Takahashi Satomi, must be granted: namely, that *A Study of Good*, lacking

THE SELF-CONSCIOUSNESS 97

as it does an epistemological foundation, does not make clear the nature of the "pure experience". In other words, psychology is not enough to be the basis of such a well rounded Weltanschauung as Nishida wants to offer.

Still this work, imperfect as it may be, represents Nishida in his most characteristic aspects, which will be perfected and elaborated later on and will recur again and again in all his other phases. His main themes and main fields of interest were laid out in this first work.

The Self-Consciousness of the Absolute Free Will

The works of Nishida written between *A Study of Good* and *From the Acting to the Seeing* (1911-1927) are relevant for their emphasis on the self-consciousness and the absolute free will, two elements which must be grasped if we are to understand his "logic of place". The first work *Shisaku to taiken*[a] (Thinking and Experience, 1915) is of significance in explaining the philosophical atmosphere surrounding Nishida when he first went to Kyoto University, where Rickert's "pure logic", and Bergson's "pure duration" were widely discussed (I, 203-03).[3] Neo-Kanti-

---

a. 思索と体験

3) *The complete works of Nishida Kitarō* 西田幾多郎全集 published by Iwanami Shoten, 1947-1953, comprehends 12 volumes, plus 6 volumes (*Bekkan*) in which unpublished material, letters and the diary are included. A full index is to be found in the XVIII vol. (*Bekkan VI*), pp. 501-14. For brevity's sake in the text the Roman numerals indicate the volume, while the Arabic, the pages referred to. Two titles indicate that two books are included in one volume.

    I *Zen no kenkyū* 善の研究 (A Study of Good), 1911; *Shisaku to taiken* 思索と体験 (Thinking and Experience), 1915.

    II *Jikaku ni okeru chokkan to hansei* 自覚における直観と反省 (Intuition and Reflexion in Self-Consciousness), 1917.

    III *Ishiki no mondai* 意識の問題 (The Problem of Consciousness).

anism and Bergsonism were in full swing. Nishida's book clearly
reflects this trend. Rickert, Cohen, Bergson, Lotze, Poincaré and
many other thinkers are considered, with such problems as the
difference between natural and historical science being paramount (I, 208-09).

Much more important for an understanding of the development of Nishida's thought is *Jikaku ni okeru chokkan to hansei*[a]
(Intuition and Reflection in Self-Consciousness, 1917), which is
a systematic work not dissimilar in intent from *A Study of Good*.
Nishida was trying to revise his early position and to go beyond
the "pure experience" and neo-Kantian categories, as well as
Bergson's "pure duration", and this not only through epistemology, but with the help of a new and deeper philosophy or a
new metaphysics. The stimulus for this further step was the
"Supplementary Essay" of J. Royce's *The World and the Indi-*

---

a. 自覚における直観と反省
   1920; *Geijutsu to dōtoku* 芸術と道徳 (Art and Morality), 1923.
IV   *Hataraku mono kara miru mono e* 働くものから見るものへ (From
      the Acting to the Seeing), 1927.
V   *Ippansha no jikakuteki taikei* 一般者の自覚的体系 (The System of
      the Self-Consciousness of the Universal), 1930.
VI   *Mu no jikakuteki gentei* 無の自覚的限定 (The Self-Conscious
      Determination of Nothingness), 1932.
VII   *Tetsugaku no kompon mondai (Kōi no sekai)* 哲学の根本問題
      (行為の世界) (The Basic Problems of Philosophy: The World of
      Action), 1933; *Tetsugaku no kompon mondai zoku-hen (Benshōhō-
      teki sekai)* 哲学の根本問題続編 (弁証法的世界) (The Basic
      Problems of Philosophy, Continuation: The Dialectical World),
      1934
VIII-XI *Tetsugaku rombunshū* 哲学論文集 (Collection of Philosophical Es-
      says)
XII   *Zoku shisaku to taiken* 続思索と体験 (Thinking and Experience,
      Continuation), 1937
XIII-XVIII *Bekkan* 別巻 I-VI (Supplementary volumes)

vidual (II, 16-17). By *"jikaku*ᵃ*"* (consciousness or, better, self-consciousness), Nishida means not the psychological phenomenon of self-analysis, but rather Fichte's *Tathandlung,* or the self-consciousness of the transcendental a-priori (*senkenteki jiga*)ᵇ (II, 55-60).

In the first six introductory chapters of this work Nishida spells out the different meanings of consciousness and self-consciousness; he follows this with eighteen chapters on "Nature of the System of Experience", namely the nature of self-consciousness. Self-consciousness is at the root of logical principles, such as that of identity, because what gives "A" is "A" its value is the fact that we have the intuition of "I am I" (II, 68-69). Many other problems are treated here, such as the meaning of "ought" and "is", objectivity versus subjectivity, and Cohen's interpretation of the experience of intelligibility (II, 104-15). In the second part of the book (chapters 29-39) Nishida carries the initial intuition of self-identity through the identity of several aporias; the world of numbers and space; the three realms of the spirit, of matter, and finally of the will. His conclusion (chapter 41) is expressed in asserting the absolute primacy of the self-consciousness of the absolute free will where all aporias are solved. This "voluntarism" does not come as a surprise (see a similar development also in *A Study of Good*), because an analogous role is accomplished by Fichte's *Tathandlung,* which resolves all problems of knowledge and consciousness in the creative activity of the "transcendental ego". For Nishida pure experience is operational thinking (for Fichte too it was a form of action) which transcends every *psychisch fringe* (II, 92),

a. 自覚   b. 先見的自我

every limit or *Tangenten-Punkte* (II, 111).

Nishida, using Cohen's work on *Kant's Theory of Experience* as well as many other sources, emphasized that, in the last instance, we are always transcending the finite experience, looking as we are for the affirmation of the infinite. In this context he again quotes the mystics (II, 274-78). The world in which all aporias are solved is, in the last analysis, the world of the absolute beyond, a world which is not, however, very far away and must be realized in the manifestations of art and religious experience.

In *Ishiki no mondai*[a] (The Problem of Consciousness, 1920), Nishida tried to clarify the ultimate basis of consciousness, or, what comes to the same thing, that of the absolute freedom of the will. He is looking, in other terms, for the *"Grund"* or ultimate reason for, and substratum of the unification of the ego. In his search he availed himself of the findings of experimental psychology (III, 3), considering an analysis of the oneness of the object of self-transcendent consciousness, "sensation" (III, 28) and "feeling" (III, 59) in the manner of Wundt, Titchner and Stout. He appealed, too, to Husserl's phenomenology as well as Dilthey's descriptive psychology. Sensation and feeling, in their immanent tendency, are based upon an a-priori unity of the ego, manifested through thinking (III, 80-82). Will is the final stage of feeling which represents the subjective aspect of consciousness (III, 83-93). The ultimate place of realization of the will is seen in Fichte's "self-identity". The latter imports the *Aktualitäts-begriff,* or the conceptual actuality of all world realities, objectively and subjectively manifested (III, 148-51).

a. 意識の問題

Although dealing with different problems in *Geijutsu to dōtoku*[a] (Art and Morality, 1923), Nishida remained faithful to the way of thinking developed in *Ishiki no mondai*. This is clear especially in his insistence that the transcendental ego is the basis of the whole cultural world and that, therefore, there can be no opposition between art and morality. Nature, at its deepest layers, or "nature seen in itself" is culture. The absolute will, going deeper than the world of mathematics, logic, and natural phenomena, seeing nature in itself, realizes the world of art and religion by the force of its self-transcending tendency (III, 239-52). The world of art is a new a-priori, the manifestation of eternity in time, a pure consciousness totally different from other experiences. Its expression is the aesthetic feeling. After considering different theories of aesthetics (III, 261-87), Nishida examines the content of aesthetic consciousness (III, 288 ff.). In a chapter with the programmatic title "Unity of the True, the Beautiful, and the Good" and headed by the "Hymn of the Creature" to God of St. Francis of Assisi, Nishida more specifically explores the relationship between art and morality. In this context he concludes that the true, the beautiful, and the good are to be found in the personal activity of the artist rather than in the unity of the external world of nature (III, 355-58). The identity of the beautiful and the true is based upon the consciousness of the idea of good, which is always latent in us. The will enters the world of moral decision, "an a-priori of a-priori" to use Nishida's expression. This expression means that the will has a creative dynamism expanding into the infinite. Therefore, it is an "absolute will" (III, 396; 412). The same striving is to

a. 芸術と道徳

be seen in the acting subject (*kōiteki shukan*)[a] (III, 441-54). The conclusion is that even in art the ethical ideal of forming a personality must not be forgotten (III, 484).

I shall mention here a short essay of Nishida on art, written in 1931, some eight years after the appearance of *Geijutsu to dōtoku*, and published in the volume entitled *Zoku shisaku to taiken*[b] (Thinking and Experience, Continuation, 1937). This essay translated by R. Schinzinger under the title "Goethe's Metaphysical Background", though really not related to the book discussed above, is important because in it, Nishida hints that Oriental art is a formless, impersonal expression. To this topic he was to give a form and a logic in his next phase. This essay, written after the concept of "place" had been evolved and echoing what he had written in the preface of *From the Acting to the Seeing*, stresses the point that every artistic manifestation must have eternity as a background, and that the historical forms of art are more or less rooted in this infinity. Greek art is, in its concrete forms, too far apart from such an eternal setting while Oriental art is almost immersed in it. Early Christian art uses infinity as a background without, however, personality being totally absorbed in its eternal depths. Goethe has some "formless" aspects, but even his pantheism sees forms and individuality everywhere. Art, the temporal apparition of the eternal in time is in Greek civilization almost lost in the eternal past, while Christian civilization and its art face the eternal future. In the East, the kingdom of the eternal present, neither whence nor where is considered; instead, only a formless, endless, voiceless echo of the eternal present is felt.

a. 行為的主観   b. 続思索と体験

The Logic of Place and Nothingness

The importance of the next work of Nishida, *Hataraku mono kara miru mono e* (From the Acting to the Seeing, 1927), stems in large measure from the fact that it presents an elaboration of the idea of "place" (*basho*) in an essay of the same title (IV, 207-89). The concept of "place" or "field" though treated explicitly in this essay, is evolved throughout the whole book as well as in subsequent works. In the preface to the book Nishida states the purpose of this new phase of his thought, namely (as has been said at the beginning of this chapter), to give to Oriental culture its logical foundation, or to see "a form in the formless, hear a voice in the voiceless". Nishida himself explains to us how he came to the formation of the concept of "place". After having tried, with the help of Fichte's *Tathandlung,* to overcome Rickert, and the neo-Kantian position in general, he had tentatively concluded that the ground or basis of the will was to be found in a kind of Plotinian intuition. Not satisfied with this conclusion, however, he began (IV, 3-4) again to look for the ultimate basis of the absolute will, considering next A. Meinong's ideas on the foundation of knowledge (IV, 76 ff.). Another spur to his thinking was his realization that Aristotle's stress on the importance of the individual substance must be taken account of. Like Aristotle's *hypokeimenon,* the final subject of predication and the starting point of the syllogism (IV, 109;315), Nishida's "place" has both logical and ontological significance. Aristotle's "substance" and Lask's *Feldtheorie* (field theory), not to mention Plato's *"topos"* and world of ideas, are the immediate inspiration of Nishida's idea of "place".

The reference to Aristotelian and Platonic influence on

Nishida may come as a surprise to some, but, as Noda Matao explains, it was an influence mediated chiefly by Husserl after the first world war. Husserl's role in the formation of Nishida's "logic of place" cannot be overlooked in any full study of the question. According to Noda, Nishida was looking for a principle of individuation of the true being, i.e., of the existing individual itself, which could not be defined in logical terms. Therefore, its specification must be found elsewhere in a kind of universal, much like the concrete universal of Hegel, which was supposed to include the individuality of things. In order to understand why this universal and individuating factor came to be called "place", and finally "nothingness" by Nishida, it will be very helpful to keep in mind the analogous concept of the principle of individuation in classical philosophy.

Aristotle's *hyle* or prime matter is a pure potentiality lacking all positive characteristics, which come from the form. Though in Scholastic philosophy prime matter is not the principle of individuation, still the potentiality inherent in matter, with all its privative elements, may serve as an indication why Nishida thought of the individuating "place" of things as "nothingness" (IV, 223-24). Lask's *Gebietskategorie* or the field and sphere of categories, to which Nishida made reference earlier in the book under discussion, must be understood as different "places" which determine the universal into individual realities.

It is true that the concept of nothingness is suggested more by Mahāyāna Buddhism and Taoism than by any other type of thought. In these systems though, as Noda observes, nothingness often means "non-egocentricity", a concept similar to the Christian notion of absolute poverty, or the total spoliation of the self. Nishida, however, has in view something else- "a sort of

material field wherein forms emerge"-, as forms emerge from the potentiality of matter in Aristotle. Nevertheless, the reader must not forget that for the elaboration of the concept of place and its logic other works of Nishida besides *From the Acting to the Seeing* must be kept in mind. These are *Ippansha no jikaku-teki taikei*[a] (The System of Self-Consciousness of the Universal, 1930), *Mu no jikakuteki gentei*[b] (The Self-Conscious Determination of Nothingness, 1932), and one of his last essays entitled *Bashoteki ronri to shūkyōteki sekai*[c] (The Logic of Place and the Religious World, 1945). This last work (XI, 371-464) shows how religiously oriented was his logic of place, which was an attempt to locate the ultimate place of everything, and was therefore bound to reach the bottomless depths of absolute negation and absolute nothingness. The "dazzling obscurity" mentioned in *From the Acting to the Seeing* has become in his last essay more and more religious in content, while the logic of space itself has been transformed into negative dialectics.

Let us at this point return to *From the Acting to the Seeing*, and try to follow Nishida in as orderly a way as possible. In this work, it is clear that his epistemological quest is rather negative, showing as it does the insufficiency of Kant's *Bewusstsein überhaupt* (Consciousness in general) to serve as the valid basis or place of cognition in general. Nishida's main argument is that there are in man such subjective phenomena as will, emotions, and religious experiences, all of which require another foundation. In his efforts to find a replacement for Kant's *Bewusstsein überhaupt*, Nishida introduces his "predica-

---

a. 一般者の自覚的体系   b. 無の自覚的限定   c. 場所的論理と宗教
　的世界

tive" or transcendental logic as well as the three main fields or "places", especially as was mentioned earlier in the essay *Basho* (Place) (IV, 232; 236). These three "places" are: the physical world, the world or field of human realities (relative nothingness).

A discussion of these three "places" was reserved for the next work which we will consider *The System of Self-Consciousness of the Universal*. He states in the third chapter of this work that it is only through "a transcendental predicate that the universal judgement becomes a transcendental universal self-consciousness" and therefore the place of things (V. 116). In general, the logic of Nishida (see the two first chapters of this work) considers a special predicate (the transcendental) to grasp the individuality of things. In Aristotelian logic, the individual is the subject about which anything can be affirmed or denied but which cannot itself become a predicate in statements about other things. For Aristotle though, the individual can never be fully expressed; it is truly "ineffable". Nishida, taking as a starting point the judgement of subsumption, in which the subject is a concrete individual, made the transcendental predicate a kind of universal which alone can give general knowledge of things. Of individuals as such there can be no science, no universally valid knowledge. The predicate called "transcendental" is so called in order to distinguish it from the ordinary predicate, which has no concrete universality, and also to indicate that the subject is mirrored or transferred in the predicate in its objective actuality. In other words, the subjective-objective duality is transcended through this predicate.

It is precisely at this point that the transcendental self-consciousness of the universal begins to take on meaning, and

the reader is able to see why Nishida entitled his book as he did. Self-consciousness, a constant *motif* in the philosophy of Nishida, has a prominent place in this and in later works, but with the important difference that in order to avoid giving the impression that "self-consciousness" is merely a psychological "self-awareness", Nishida prefers to speak of "place" as a much better rendering of the substratum or matrix where every form comes to actuality. The universal or general concept (*ippan gainen*)ᵃ must be specified and limited by many logical constructions in the physical world. Even the usual predicate can be considered as a kind of individuating factor. But in the world of human realities, where the underlying factor is the self-consciousness more clearly actuated than before, the subject becomes a transcendental predicate, since it can intuitively grasp itself both as subject and as predicate. In "The Intelligible World" (*Eichiteki sekai*)ᵇ or world of values, the self-awareness of the subject becomes even more pronounced (V. 123-85). In the physical world it is the predicate, either alone or cumulatively, that determines the place of individual reality. In the world of human reality it is the inner self which becomes the place of the individual subject. In the intelligible world self-consciousness is determined by the vision of the true, the good, and the beautiful. Obviously, we are here in a transcendental world which defies definitions, and through religious experience we enter into "absolute nothingness", the final determination and field of everything (V, 180-82; 410-12).

The religious orientation of Nishida's logic, apparent in the essay "The Intelligible World" is manifested too in the last chap-

a. 一般概念　　b. 叡智的世界

ter of this work (V, 419-81). Among other mystics or religious thinkers whom he mentions in this essay, we might single out Plotinus (V, 471), for his religious philosophy can well serve as an illustration of Nishida's logical process. Plotinus, it will be recalled, works down from the One or eternal source of all being through the Nous (Nishida's universal judgement) and Psyche (Nishida's Self-Consciousness), reaching finally the realm of intelligibility or the divine sphere. It must be added though, that when Nishida reaches this last sphere or "place" every philosophical consideration seems to become secondary. Although he has a long analysis of the religious experience (V, 173-82), he tells us that these philosophical considerations, necessary as they are, have nothing to do with the religious experience itself, which is really beyond description; and therefore he makes allusions to Western and Oriental mystics. No doubt, to Nishida, the "absolute nothingness" is a much more profound expression of religious experience than Western formulations, because there the universe is swallowed up and the ego too has disappeared, only however, to emerge again in another instant of this dazzling obscurity, in a kind of Zen Buddhistic enlightenment. Mahā-yāna Buddhism too says that "the concrete reality is the void, and the void concrete reality".

What is characteristic of Nishida, however, is his critical construction of three realms or worlds and of different forms of nothingness, as well as his entire philosophical system of the self-consciousness of the universal. This, to repeat, is a "universal of judgment" first, becoming subsequently a "universal of self-consciousness" and finally a consciousness of absolute nothingness.

In any full treatment of Nishida's thought, attention should

be given to his use of Husserl's categories of *noema*, the idea or intelligibility of things, and *noesis*, the intentionality, or the tendency of consciousness towards the object.   Both *noema* and *noesis*, Nishida maintains, are required for the full understanding of reality, which is arrived at in the last world, the world of values, i.e., of art, morality and religion.   While it would be profitable to linger and consider the relation between Nishida and Husserl, I must leave such a discussion for another time and briefly consider now Nishida's next work *Mu no jikaku-teki gentei* (The Self-Conscious Determination of Nothingness, 1932).

In this study Nishida gives another nuance to his analysis of place and nothingness by stressing that the eternal present becomes an important negative limit of place.   In chapters such as those on "The Self-Limit of the Eternal Present" and "Temporal and Non-Temporal Things", as well as in other essays, Nishida gives great prominence to the *zettai genzai*[a] or "absolute present", while at the same time he begins to develop his social philosophy.   This stress gives to nothingness a qualification which in its identity of past and present conveys a sense of the immediacy of actual intuition of dialectical reality.   Absolute nothingness is also the absolute place of every contradiction, because without such negations no individual reality is ever established.

Summing up Nishida's logic of place, we may select the following points as particularly helpful.   For Nishida two ways of knowing things are possible: one being the direct apperception of the object, the other the knowledge which we can have

a. 絶対現在

through self-consciousness. Whereas before he had stressed the consciousness of the transcendental ego (Fichte's *Tathandlung*), he now insists on the self-consciousness of the place. Place is preferred to self-consciousness because it is a neutral term without psychological connotations and because it is all-inclusive. Its justification depends on the transcendentality and nothingness element which is in the predicate. The subject, on the other hand, is not universal enough and is too closely related to being. The predicate in its self-determination constitutes the subject, or the concrete universal. In order to avoid any kind of judgment which could leave opposition between subject and object, or too much "being" in the judgment, Nishida thinks of the predicate, as having nothing of the entitative nature of the subject. Therefore, it is a transcendental predicate which precisely as applicable to subjects without distinction can be called nothingness.

This type of dialectic, then, equips Nishida with a logic able to express the meaning of Oriental culture, based as it is upon the voidness of reality. This voidness, it must be insisted upon, is not the ontological nothingness of Western philosophy, which is usually rendered in Japanese by *kyomu*.[a] It is, rather, what is called *mu*[b] in Japanese, the absolute present with all its inclusive processes and contradictions, which even in its most religious nuances has nothing to do with a Christian conception of God as a transcendent and personal being.

The Acting Intuition and the Historical World

The last phase of Nishida's philosophy covers the so-called philosophical essays: *Tetsugaku rombun-shū*[c] (VIII-XI), some

---

a. 虚無　　b. 無　　c. 哲学論文集

of which are small treatises in themselves. This phase is characterized by "place" becoming the historical world, through the mediation of new concepts like "the acting intuition" and "the historical body", where the contradictory or dialectical aspects of reality are paramount. As a matter of fact, Nishida's interest in the historical world began with the two parts of *The Basic Problems of Philosophy*, which came out in 1934, and are respectively subtitled: *The World of Action*, and *The Dialectical World* (VII). Hegel's dialectic and historicism, not to speak of nationalism, were predominant or about to become predominant in Japan and their influence on Nishida is obvious. In effect, Nishida was trying to create a philosophy of history, a field of research he had not yet cultivated.

The first chapter of *Tetsugaku no kompon mondai*[a] (Basic Problems of Philosophy, first part) starts with a long analysis of classical and modern metaphysics. Nishida, of course, included his own thought as "modern" inasmuch as he counterposes his own metaphysics of the "Acting-Self" (*Hataraku mono, hataraku jiko*)[b]. to the Aristotelian metaphysics of being. Nishida considers this "Acting-Self" or historical being as the basis for a new metaphysics because it is his intent to grasp the ultimate reality of the world. In "I and the World" (*Watakushi to sekai*[c], VII, 85-172) he gives voice to his social dialectic and criticizes the philosophy of praxis of Marxism (VII, 173-75). It is however, in the second part of *The Basic Problems . . .* (*Zoku* or Continuation), that the world is considered not only from the side of the acting individual, but in itself, with its limits and contradictions. The world, in other

a. 哲学の根本問題   b. 働くもの働く自己   c. 私と世界

words, must be seen as the dialectical universal (VII, 203). In an entire chapter called *Benshōhōteki ippansha toshite no sekai*[a] or "The World as a Dialectical Universal", Nishida develops this theme, advancing the reason that, though individual things have their own self-determination, a truer and more universal self-determination cannot be discovered, unless they are considered in the whole historical world. Individual things, confronting one another as the acting monads of the world, limit themselves not through the abstract universal but through a dialectical universal which alone is capable of preserving their originality. This dialectical universal is obviously the historical setting of the individuals themselves, but for Nishida it becomes an absolute dialectical universal, so many and complex are the dialectical oppositions in the historical world. A parallel might be drawn here between the absolute nothingness and the absolute dialectical universal, but it is more important to consider the logical justification of this whole phase of Nishida's thought. Our consideration can start with some observations on a new term, *kōiteki chokkan*[b] (acting intuition) which is introduced in two studies of his *Philosophical Essays* (VIII, 107-218; 541-71). "Acting-intuition" means that no action is possible without intuition and, conversely, that no intuition is possible without action. This is especially true of creative and artistic action, or historical action. This conception, discussed also in another essay entitled *Jissenteki tetsugaku joron*[c] (Preface to Practical Philosophy, X, 7-123), was brought to perfection in an essay with the resounding title of *Zettai mujunteki jiko dōitsu*[d] (The Absolute Contradictory Self-Identity, IX, 142-222).

a. 弁証法的一般者としての世界論   b. 行為的直観   c. 実践的哲学序論   d. 絶対矛盾的自己同一

Nishida observed that his concept of "Acting-intuition" had been the occasion of many misunderstandings (X, 32). He had earlier defined it as the point of view from which "we see things (i.e., the concrete individual reality) through action, things which while determining and limiting themselves, are, at the same time, limited and determined by other-selves" (XIII, 131). Evidently the dialectical nature of "Acting-intuition" had not been clearly expressed in these terms, and therefore Nishida wrote the essay above mentioned, the title of which has been simplified by R. Schinzinger into the "Oneness of Opposites".

This "oneness" arises from the emphasis on the identity of contradictions which Nishida sees everywhere. This dialectic, it should be emphasized, differs from the Hegelian, for not only is stress laid upon the identity and even simultaneity of oppositions but also all the individual things are seen as a unified mutual interaction which is an eternal self-limitation or negation (IX, 147-48). Everything is moving by itself from the already formed thing to a new determination, but for Nishida the process as such is not as important as the present now, which is the crossroad of the past and the future. In this process, considered apart from action, there is a determination, but not a qualifying factor. We may recall here, that "place" also had become the absolute present, i.e., the actual reality dialectically limited and qualified. The present limits itself, not only because of, or in relation to the past and the future, but because, as the actual "now", it transcends time's limits and is thus the most qualified reality. It is action which brings fulfillment to the present and "Acting-intuition" which grasps the flowing "now" in its contemporaneity which

serves as the final determining factor.

Another reason for the evolution of "Acting-intuition" into the semi-final phase of dialectics of the absolute has been pointed out by Mutai Risaku. "Acting-intuition" in its threefold negation, he points out, evolves itself into "the absolute contradictory self-identity". "Acting-intuition" inasmuch as it is self-reflection, has relation to the continuing self, which is not lost in the process of acting and seeing but tends toward the place and thus sets up a second relation. The third relation is produced in the creation of the historical world. All these three relations must limit and negate themselves to be operative at all. Therefore, we move in this process of mutual negation into a total dialectic: the absolute dialectic or the absolute self-identity of contradictories. Specifically historical action is brought about by the *hyōgenteki risei*[a] (reason as expression), and especially by the *hyōgenteki ippansha*[b] (universal expression). This means that the historical world is not made in a mechanicist way of cause-effect relationship, or only in accordance with a biological pattern; rather it must be an expression, a symbol, of our own personality. Personality in its turn is strongly limited by and related to the *shu*[c] or species, which is the society and nation. For Nishida the acme of dialectical opposition is to be found in the "historical-body" (*rekishiteki shintai*)[d], where the self must continuously negate itself to conform to the substance, i.e., the Hegelian moral substance, which the state is supposed to be (IX, 186-87).

An important role in the self-contradicting process in the "universal expression" is reserved for the will, which, as will

a. 表現的理性   b. 表現的一般者   c. 種   d. 歴史的身体

be recalled, is a recurring theme in all the works of Nishida. Its actual presence in the "universal expression", constantly shifting as it does from potentiality to actuality, is not only the pivotal center of action, but also the source of perennial contradictions. For this reason, will is called by Nishida the "absolute paradox". To understand what Nishida means here, one or two illustrations may help. "Acting-intuition", for example, moves in two directions quite different, namely the direction toward the general as manifested in the *hyōgenteki sekai*[a] or world as expression, and the direction toward the individual or world where the free will plays the most important part. Again, while "reason as expression" creates those general laws which are at the base of moral and social life, the individual tends to deny completely these general expressions and laws. Thus, the individual, through his absolute will, seems to be in perennial contradiction to the generalizing reason.

The final aspect of the dialectic of the absolute contradictory is the "self-identity" (*jiko dōitsu*)[b]. All the dialectical aspects of the self, as well as the negation of it in relation to others, evolve into a fundamental oneness, which is also knowledge of one's self. Through this identity in the dialectic of the absolute we come, once more, to the absolute nothingness and its religious implication.

Nishida's Religious and Cultural Views

The last essay written by Nishida was *Bashoteki ronri to shūkyōteki sekaikan* (The Logic of Space and the Religious World View, XI, 371-464), a real testament in which the great

a. 表現的世界   b. 自己同一

philosopher wanted to give a final view of his thought.   It would, of course, be too much to expect to find in this essay a final and perfect exposition of Nishida's logic, if only for the reason that it is mostly on his last point of view about religion.   It seems that death took him while he was preparing another essay on his logic.   As far as his religious views are concerned, it is clear that Nishida preferred panentheism to pantheism and to the Christian understanding of God as transcendent (XI, 309).   In this last phase of his life Nishida, according to Noda Matao, was more inspired by dialectical theology or by the Christian existentialism of Kirkegaard than by Zen Buddhism or Oriental thought.   While it is true that many existentialist thinkers are quoted in this last essay, there is no lack of quotations from Buddhist sources.   Far more important, however, are the main concepts of Nishida, like "the absolute present" and "the self-identity of absolute contradiction", which occur over and over again.   For this reason, I think we should look at quotations from or allusions to other thinkers and thought rather as illustrations than as his own real view, which appears most clearly when he remarks, for example, that if God must be absolute love, immanent and transcendent as panentheism wants, God must also be the "absolute self-limit" and the "absolute nothingness".   He hopes that Christianity as well as Buddhism will try to create a new civilization in order to give a new moral backbone to society, but he is not quite sure that this will be done (XI, 462).   On this note of cautious hope he concludes the essay, which had opened with an exhortation to become more religious minded.

Nishida's cultural views, a very important aspect of his thought, are expressed in two works, which while written at different times and under different circumstances reveal his position on Oriental and world culture. The first belongs to the early phase of his studies on the historical world. The second was written when nationalism was rampant in Japan, but, in a sense, it is less emphatic than the first in stressing the peculiarity of the Japanese spirit. The first study was completed in 1934, and under the title of "The Form of Ancient Oriental Culture Considered from the Metaphysical Point of View". It was included in the second volume, or continuation (*zoku*) of *Basic Problems of Philosophy* (VII, 429-53), a work we have already noted. The second work, the result of a series of lectures which he gave at Kyoto University in 1938, is called "Problems of Japanese Culture" (XVIII, 35-142).

In the first work Nishida was primarily concerned with a search for ultimate historical reality (metaphysics). His starting point is the fact that the Orient has a well defined Weltanschauung, and therefore must also have a deep metaphysics as basis. This basis is the conception of reality as nothingness, in sharp contrast to the basic Western notion that reality is to be considered as being (VII, 429-30). Nishida considers the Greek idea of reality, Roman civilization, and Christianity which gave the concept of personality to the Western world (VII, 423-33) and then contrasts the more religious Indian civilization to Chinese culture, which is neither philosophical like the Greek nor mystically minded like the Indian. It has a social ethos, which nevertheless alights the individual (VII, 434-37). Modern European civilization has developed the scientific spirit, which however, is an obstacle to idealistic and personalistic trends. Nishida sees in the depersonalization of Western civilizaton an element of nothingness, which though, has little to do with Buddhistic nothingness. Russia in Nishida's view has some Oriental characteristics (VII, 438-40).

After this review of some world cultures, Nishida turns to Japan and stresses the artistic features of her culture, features different from the Greek where art is a form of the eternal idea. Japanese art is a form of sensibility, and therefore Japanese culture is *jōteki bunka*[a] or a culture based upon sensibility and feeling which perceives reality as formless and voiceless (*katachi naki, koe naki*).[b] Japanese culture, although based on sensibility and feeling, is not erotic, nor is it religious or even specially ethical in the Chinese sense. Impersonal and arational elements are pointed out by Nishida, who here seems to approve of them. Japanese culture has at its goal "absolute negation". Buddhism, in its most rational or speculative forms, like Tendai Buddhism, has never taken deep root in Japan, a country which preserves its sensitive attitude toward nature and reality. Nishida concludes that Japanese culture, in order to be placed in a world-wide setting and at the same time preserve its originality, must through negation overcome its weak points, which he blandly hints at (VII, 440-45).

The second work of Nishida on Japanese culture does not require a summary, because by now the Western reader has seen long excerpts of it in the excellent volume, *Sources of Japanese Tradition*. The main idea is that notwithstanding all the *jōteki* and arational elements, there is in Japanese culture a fundamental trend toward "going to the truth of things". Nishida here advocates a scientific and rational spirit, which

a. 情的文化   b. 形なき声なき

was not emphasized in his earlier work. Admittedly, some of his statements about the Emperor have been taken by post-war critics as an appeasement of ultra-nationalism, but the true story is quite different. The fact is that Nishida delivered these lectures at a time when the pressure of military nation alists was at its worst. As we are told by Kōsaka, Nishida was called from his retirement in Kamakura, to give the lectures in Kyoto precisely because his personality could not be easily maneuvered into becoming an instrument of political propaganda. Militaristic nationalists were then canvassing all the academic circles to extol the uniqueness of everything Japanese and the superiority of Japanese culture. If we consider the times (just the year before the official book on Cardinal Principles of the National Entity of Japan (*Kokutai no hongi*) was published by the ultra-nationalists), we must admit that Nishida delivered his lectures in quite a scholarly way and that his moderation is obvious. He no doubt realized how the arational elements of the Japanese spirit were being stressed by the ultra-nationalists in order to enforce blind obedience to the Emperor's will. Under these circumstances he was anxious to modify what he wrote in his first work about Japanese culture, and hence it is that he spoke of the necessity of a more rational and scientific spirit.

I must confess, though, that some ambiguity is present in Nishida's last works, and other interpretations are possible. Noda Matao, for example, is quite critical of the transition of Nishida from his logic of space to the historical world, not to speak of what Noda calls the Christian inspiration of his last phase. Most Japanese critics, while they are pleased with Nishida's new logic, are highly puzzled by his emphasis on nothingness, which while very Oriental, is not so easy to explain. I do not mean here Marxist critics, but philosophers who believe in conceptual analysis of terms. We shall see in the next chapter how Tanabe Hajime, the greatest pupil of Nishida, criticized it. Here we can briefly recall Sōda Kiichirō who, while praising Nishida's thought in general, points out the weak points in his system, for instance, his failure to explain the role of the will in epistemological problems. Sōda has also raised the question why place must be thought of as nothingness. He concedes that Nishida thought of being as the determinate and objectified content of our thought, while what is not so is nothingness. Still, according to Sōda, indetermination in the non-objectified reality too easily produces a determinating limit and reality, which therefore can be called being. Another point not clear to Sōda is the graduation or distinction of nothingness into relative and absolute. Sōda insists that once relative nothingness is admitted, there is no way out of admitting several kinds of nothingness, with all the correlative ontological implications. Therefore, nothingness is but a name, covering a metaphysics of being. In this context it is interesting to note that another critic of Nishida, Takahashi Satomi, transformed "absolute nothingness" into "absolute being".

Students of Nishida's thought like R. Schinzinger explain well what nothingness is not. Positively, Schinzinger says both that it is "just nothingness", adding to this tautology a reference to Hegel's *gutes Unendliches* (true infinite), and that it is "the present in and with finite being". Kōyama thinks that while the Indian concept of nothingness is essentially emptied and other-worldly, the Japanese one is alive and fulfilled. This is, beyond a doubt, true of Nishida's meaning of nothingness. Logical difficulties obviously are not solved with the above explanations. They could be if such concepts could be kept in a religious sphere, from which they really originated; and as a way of salvation, nothingness can be explained. The effort to make it a philosophical outgrowth of a systematic process of thinking, is bound, as yet, to many inconsistencies. Nishida, though, must be credited with one of the best and most persevering attempts. As a final remark we may note with Noda Matao that liberal and socialist critics of Nishida tend to ignore "the fact that Japan is as yet full of situations needing *consolationem philosophiae*". Therefore the Japanese people even more than the philosophers have always showed a great interest in Nishida's thought, as being "an expression of the general Japanese, and perhaps Oriental mentality, which the liberal and socialist fronts are apt to neglect".[4]

I would add to these perceptive remarks of Noda that the Japanese people have found in Nishida a type of *consolatio religionis* and that, regrettably, both the religious *intent* of Nishida's work as well as his appeal to the religious side of the Japanese mind are too frequently overlooked by critics for whom such dimensions have no meaning.

It may be objected that Nishida did not write a philosophy

4) *Sources of Japanese Tradition*, compiled by R. Tsunoda, Wm. Th. de Bary, D. Keene, New York, 1958, pp. 857-72. For Sōda Kiichirō see: Funayama S., *Nihon . . .* , o.c., pp. 262-69. For Takahashi Satomi's 高橋里美 criticism as well as the answer by Nishitani Keiji 西谷啓治 see: *Shisō* 思想 n. 164 (Jan. 1936), pp. 1-41; 98-129
For a good study in English on "Oriental Nothingness" see the article by the Buddhist scholar Hisamatsu Shin'ichi in *Philosophical Studies of Japan*, compiled by the Japanese National Commission for Unesco, vol. II, 1960, pp. 65-97

of religion in the technical sense of the term. That is indeed
true, but anyone who has carefully examined Sunshin's *Nikki*
(The Diary of Sunshin), a work whose pseudonym does not
hide the fact that it is an expression of Nishida's own inner
thoughts, cannot escape the conclusion that religion is the alpha
and omega of his philosophizing. This intent of his thinking
was clearly attested to by those of Nishida's pupils whose
appraisals of their master I have sought for. It is confirmed
in one of the most recent studies on Nishida, in the dissertation
of Dr. Takeno Keisaku[a]. In the light of this evidence I can only
conclude that to neglect or to miss entirely this side of Nishida's
thinking is to lose sight of the wood for the trees.[5]

a. 岳野慶作
5)   Shimomura T., *Wakaki Nishida* . . . , o.c., pp. 68 ff.; Kōsaka M., *Nishida
      tetsugaku* . . . , o.c., pp.46-47; Keisaku Takeno, Pascal et la philosophie de
      Nishida. 1961, passim, (unpublished thesis) by kindness of the Author.

Chapter V

OTHER LEADING PHILOSOPHERS: HATANO, WATSUJI AND TANABE

The Philosophy of Religion of Hatano Seiichi (1877-1950)

Hatano Seiichi, historian of Western philosophy and philosopher of religion, deserves a special position in the history of modern Japanese thought. He cannot be ranked with Nishida nor with the two other philosophers considered in this chapter, but his influence as the first systematic thinker on the philosophy of religion is still in evidence today.

Hatano Seiichi was born in Nagano.[a] After graduating from the First High School, he entered Tokyo University. Here Hatano came under the strong influence of Koeber sensei, who guided him in his post-graduate work *Spinoza no kenkyū*[b] (A Study on Spinoza), a dissertation written first in German, then printed in Japanese in 1910. In 1901, Hatano published *Seiyō tetsugaku-shiyō*[c] (Outline of the History of Western Philosophy), which marked him as the outstanding historian of Western thought in Japan. Thus, Hatano added his own name to the list of such authors as Nakajima and Ōnishi (later, in 1917-18, to be joined by Abe Yoshishige), whose works on philosophy were widely read in Japan. Hatano still enjoyed wide popularity up to the last war. Making use of the best German and British-American sources available, Hatano started with the early Greek thinkers and ended with the philosophy of Spencer. At that time

a. 長野　　b. スピノザの研究　　c. 西洋哲学史要

he was teaching at Waseda University (then still called Tokyo
Semmon Gakkō), and it is of no small wonder that a book of
such scope was written by a young lecturer of only twenty-five
years old.

In 1904, the officials at Waseda University sent Hatano to
Germany. There he studied at Berlin and Heidelberg universities. In Berlin, Harnack and Otto Pfeiderer were lecturing,
and at Heidelberg he heard the lectures of Johannes Weiss, E.
Troeltsch and A. Deissmann. Although his interests in Christianity dated to a time much earlier than his studies abroad
(he was baptized about the year 1902), these interests increased
greatly because of the contacts and lectures found in the German
universities. Upon his return in 1906, he resumed teaching at
Waseda. In 1907, he was asked to serve as a temporary replacement for Anesaki Masaharu, who held the chair of science of
religion at Tokyo University. Anesaki, well-known for his book
on Japanese religion, went abroad for a short period. During
this time, Hatano published *Kirisutokyō no kigen*[a] (The Origins
of Christianity), which appeared in 1908. This work caused
quite a stir, because it was the first time that the German *text
kritik*, the historico-philological method of analyzing the Gos-
pels, of W. Bousset and K. Wiezsaecker was introduced into
Japan. It should be noted, however, that Hatano's view changed
in his later but similar book *Primitive Christianity*, which was
prepared in 1950. In this later work, Hatano tried to overcome
the historico-textual method with a deeper study of the essence
of Christianity. This, however, belonged to his later phase, in
which he cultivated the philosophy of religion more than its his-

a. キリスト教の起源

torical problems. He was then a cultural historian, a historian of ideas, seeing in Christianity a strict relation with Hellenism. The works of Windelband and of E. Troeltsch were his inspiration and guide. This type of historical study was also evident in his *Pauro*[a] (St. Paul), a work which came out originally in 1928 and appeared again in a new edition in 1947.

Hatano made other studies on Greek thought. Through his many disciples, in whom he fostered a love for Greek sources as well as for modern philosophers such as Hegel, Hatano could have become the foremost historian of philosophy that Japan ever produced. However, his interests were elsewhere. The turning point of his career was his sudden resignation from the staff of Waseda in 1917. He was immediately invited by Nishida and others to come to Kyoto. There he was offered the chair of the science of religion, a position which would free him from giving the routine courses on the introduction to philosophy and the history of philosophy, courses which were compulsory for first and second year students in Japanese universities. He could, therefore, study the religious phenomenon to which he dedicated the remainder of his life.[1]

Two studies, one on Plotinus and another on Kant's philosophy of religion, were the starting points for Hatano's new phase of philosophical activity, both men being the representa-

---

a. パウロ

1) *Shūkyō to tetsugaku no kompon ni aru mono-Hatano Seiichi hakase no gakugyō ni tsuite* 宗教と哲学の根本にあるもの 波多野精一博士の学業について (The Basic Element in Religion and Philosophy—Dr. Hatano Seiichi's scholarly Achievements), by Ishihara Ken 石原謙, Tanaka Michitarō 田中美知太郎. Katayama Masanao 片山正直, Iwanami Shoten. 1954, pp. 1-36; 145-253

tives of their respective cultures. The first work on the philosophy of religion in this period (1920) was *Shūkyō tetsugaku no
honshitsu oyobi sono kompon mondai* (The Essence and
Fundamental Problem of the Philosophy of Religion). This
work, however, was but a preparation for three other volumes,
considered to present Hatano's philosophy of religion in a more
systematic manner. He tended to refute the positivist bias of
the nineteenth century historians of religion. The influence of
Kant's critical method was clearly in evidence in this work, as
well as in the article which he wrote for *Iwanami's Great
Philosophical Dictionary* in 1922. Writing about the science
of religion, he said that this science, if it did not want to ignore
the best aspects of religion, must not limit itself to a purely
historical consideration. History was but a starting point for
the understanding of the religious experience which was the
paramount element in philosophy of religion.[2]

In 1925, the *Shūkyō tetsugaku*[a] (The Philosophy of Religion) appeared. In this, Hatano's starting point was Schleiermacher's *hoeherer Realismus* (higher realism), by which was
meant the personal contact of man with a higher transcending
reality which is God. God is manifested as power, as truth
and as love. Hatano's familiarity with the works of scholars of
the science of religion, such as Soederblom, Otto and Heiler, as

---

a. 宗教哲学

2) *Hatano Seiichi zenshū* 波多野精一全集 (The Complete Works of Hatano Seiichi), Iwanami Shoten, 1949, 5 vols. The last three volumes includes
Hatano's works on the philosophy of religion. I am not using this edition,
but the one indicated below. *Shūkyō tetsugaku no honshitsu oyobi sono
kompon mondai* 宗教哲学の本質及びその根本問題 (The Essence and
Fundamental Problem of Philosophy of Religion), Iwanami Shoten, 1920,
is, as stated in the preface, a result of a summer course of lectures and,
is to be completed later.

well as with the philosophers of religion like Scholz, not to speak of the more ancient ones, was the instrument by which he focused on the *ens realissimum et perfectissimum,* which for Hatano constituted God. He evidently tried to justify the Christian concept of the living God. For him, Kant's criticism of the classical proofs for the existence of God and the ontological argument of Anselm were but indirect or direct testimonials of the religious experience felt by those thinkers who tried in many ways to prove what really needs but to be experienced. In this regard, metaphysics was not much of an aid to revelation, another essential category of religion. Hatano contended, as he did in his first work, that the problem was not to prove the objectivity of religious concepts but to come in contact with the truth itself, which was God. For their neglect of the religious experience, positivists were felt not to be sufficiently empiricist. Kant's criticism was consdered too shallow, becoming lost in the critique of the reason, while religious intuition or "negative theology" was needed to grasp the ultimate reality.[3]

In *Shūkyō tetsugaku joron*[a] (Introduction to the Philosophy of Religion), published in 1940, Hatano's methodology was stated in a more systematic form in order to clarify his position in the face of erroneous views such as rationalism, supernaturalism and

---

a. 宗教哲学序論

3) Hatano Seiichi, *Shūkyō tetsugaku* 宗教哲学 (Philosophy of Religion), Iwanami Shoten, 1925, pp. 1-28. For a detailed explanation of Hatano"s system see: Hamada Yosuke 浜田與助, *Hatano Seiich: shūkyō tetsugaku* 波多野精一宗教哲学 (Hatano Seiichi's Philosophy of Religion), Tamagawa Daigaku Shuppambu, 1949, where Hatano's *hoehere Realismus,* pp. 33-62, personalism, pp. 63-104, etc., are treated with all the references to German philosophers. More concise is Katayama M., in the study above quoted: *Shūkyō to tetsugaku . . .* o.c., pp. 37-144

the Barth-Brunner theories. After a criticism of positivism and relativism, the rationalism of natural or, more properly termed, rational theology (*gōriteki shingaku*)[a] was considered. The aftermath of Kant's agnostic attitude toward the philosophy of religion was also discussed. Supernaturalism, meaning a ratioralistic explanation of the theological content of revelation, was a method of approaching religion not too different from that of naturalism. *Credo ut intelligam* was not enough for Hatano. Passing from Anselm and Thomas Aquinas to contemporaries like Barth and Brunner was not much better. Thomas Aquinas' scholastic systematization was at least more rational; theology, as such, requiring a rationalistic approach. Hatano proposed a religious experience based on auto-reflection,which was an ever growing self-understanding toward the totally different, which is God. He tried to give a typology of the religious experience, of which the first element was an experience tending toward the life of God. The second step was *der ganz Anders*, or God's absolute sanctity. The third element was a personalist religion, or religion of personality, by which was meant personal contact with the living God. This contact alone brings to life the abstract categories or typology of religion.

It must be mentioned that, for Hatano, reality was always the starting point, in so far as it was determined by the content of *Erlebnis*, or vital experience, which through reflection and self-denial realized the nothingness of the world and turned toward the totally different, God. The final consideration in his methodology was the anthropological aspects of religion, which were formed by the experience of living. This, to put

a. 合理的神学

it briefly, meant the "interiorization" of man in order to experience the religious phenomenon. In his concluding chapter, Hatano discussed Luther and Calvin, Kant and Schleiermacher, not so much their theological or philosophical points of view, but their manifestation, at moments, of the consciousness of the essence of religion. For example, Luther's *ex sola fide* was interpreted by Hatano in the following manner. Luther was in contact with the sacred in a unique way. For him the Reformation was to be not merely a cultural phenomenon but primarily a religious experience.

Miki Kiyoshi[a] rightly pointed out the systematic nature of *Shūkyō tetsugaku joron* when he noticed that it was based on Dilthey for the distinction of cultural phenomena, but nonetheless praised Hatano's original concept of the nature of the religious experience.[4]

The final touch to Hatano's philosophy of religion came in 1943 with the publication of *Toki to eien*[b] (Time and Eternity). After the completion of this work, Hatano stopped writing, with the exception of a short essay on Miki Kiyoshi and the editing of *Pauro* (St. Paul), the work above mentioned. After retiring from Kyoto University in 1947, Hatano became president of Tamagawa University. He died in 1950 at the age of seventy-four. As Hatano stopped writing after the publication of *Time and Eternity*, his many followers came to believe that he had said all that he intended to say on the

a. 三木清　　b. 時と永遠

4)　Hatano Seiichi, *Shūkyō tetsugaku joron* 宗教哲学序論 (Introduction to Philosophy of Religion), Iwanami Shoten, 1950, pp. 56-58; 90-94; 1-6; 125. *Miki Kiyoshi zenshū* 三木清全集 (Complete Works of Miki K.), Iwanami Shoten, 1946-51, vol. 15, pp. 471-76

philosophy of religion in this work. This last endeavor dealt
with death, immortality, eternity, love and life everlasting after
death.

Hatano's analysis of time, the most essential structure of
man, goes through three stages. In the first phase we have
natural time encompassing the world of nature. This time is
not the ordinary measured relationship connecting past, present
and future, but "experienced temporality". That is, it is the
experience of the instability and the changing aspects of man's
existence, where the future (*shōrai*)[a] is the mediating element
between past nothingness and present being. Hatano dis-
tinguishes between *mirai*,[b] a future which has yet to come, and
shōrai, a future which is already present or is about to come.
The latter activated by desire and hope goes beyond past and
present. The natural world, though, shows man only in the
effort of defending himself against others. The second
type of time is cultural time, characterized by "eros" or love
which absorbs others into the self. Man's contemplative power
shows the illusory quality of natural time as well as of cultural
time, the latter too having a spurious infinity as perishable as
the former. Cultural or historical permanency is but a fiction,
where the fragmentary nature of the present is always facing
death. The reality of death cannot be solved by the Buddhist
deliverance of one's self (*gedatsu*)[c], which is annihilation or
isolation of the self from the others. Eternity must be
a community of love, and therefore Hatano postulates the time
of "agape" or Christian religious love, as his third category
of time. This religious love has as its characteristic selflessness

a. 将来   b. 未来   c. 解脱

and generosity toward others, which is already an anticipation of the true eternity. Through agape man experiences the presence of the eternal which is God himself.

Occasionally Hatano's epistemological premises are not convincing to critically-minded readers. Still, in reading his books, written in a uniquely clear and logical style, one feels that Hatano truly portrayed his own philosophy or his own experience, so strong is the impression made on the reader. Hatano's philosophy of religion was really a religious philosophy, which, for its systematic nature, merited him a unique place in this field of inquiry.[5]

The Ethical System of Watsuji Tetsurō (1889-1960)

Watsuji Tetsurō, who has but recently passed away, is assured a position in the history of contemporary Japanese philosophy for his systematic treatment of ethical problems. He was also a historian of Japanese ethics and wrote many books on the history of ideas and culture, embracing the East and the West. If Nishida is considered the thinker who tried to express Oriental metaphysico-logical problems in Western categories, Watsuji may be called his counterpart in the field of ethics. According to Kaneko Takezō,[a] Watsuji was more systematic than Nishida, who left to his disciples the task of building up a system from his many written works. This systematic formulation may be due to the fact that Watsuji's field of inquiry was limited to ethical problems. Nonetheless, his ethics was a well-rounded general philosophy, the only

a. 金子武蔵

5) Hatano Seiichi, *Toki to eien* 時と永遠 (Time and Eternity), Iwanami Shoten, 1945, pp. 7-16; 27-35; 135-37; 218-20

philosophy of man, according to Watsuji. Watsuji's main systematic theme recurred in all of his works, either historico-cultural or the more systematic ones.

Watsuji was born in Himeji, Hyōgo[a] prefecture, and entered the philosophy department of Tokyo University in 1909, although he wavered between choosing the austere philosophical discipline and that of English literature. His original intention was to follow Byron's path in his youth, and as a matter of fact Watsuji's literary talents were manifested in all his works, his style meriting him a place in the collection of Shōwa period writers. At Tokyo University he was greatly impressed with Dr. Koeber, and wrote most vivid recollections of his master. Watsuji's early years of philosophico-literary activity were characterized by studies on Nietzsche in 1913, Kierkegaard in 1915, and by *Gūzō saikō*[b] (Revival of Idols), or the revival of the spirit of the past, in 1918.

This last work was also directed against the "platitudes" heaped on the modern democratic spirit. During this early period Watsuji strongly favored Nietzsche's *Will to Power* and the "élite" spirit as well as the poetical revival of the cult of nature as found in ancient Greece. He adopted an existential *Lebensphilosophie* mixed with Nietzschean stoicism, feeling that, in the world, the problem of suffering was paramount.[6]

a. 兵庫   b. 偶像再興

6) A chronological table of Watsuji's life and works is in *Watsuji Tetsurō-shū* 和辻哲郎集 (Selected Works of Watsuji T.) vol. 50, 1954, pp. 363-68 of *Shōwa bungaku zenshū* 昭和文学全集 (Collection of Shōwa Literature), Kadokawa Shoten. *Risō* 理想, 1961, 6, has a special issue on Watsuji, see pp. 84-87

Another survey on Watsuji, Takeuchi Y., *Shōwa shisō-shi . . .*, o.c., pp. 214-38

One of his more serious works was *Homerus hihan*[a] (A Critic of Homer), which, although published in 1946, dated back to the early twenties. The work was a critical study of the culture of ancient Greece based on European philological studies of the Homeric problem. The study was undertaken under the instigation of Koeber who introduced Watsuji to this type of work. Another book which dealt with cultural problems of the origins of Western culture was *Porisuteki ningen no rinri-gaku*[b] (The Ethics of the Man of the Polis, 1948). This too dated back to 1932, and was a manifestation of his later interest in ethical problems; an interest which is manifested especially in chapters dealing with the ethics of Socrates, Plato and Aristotle. His cultural interest in the development of the historical meaning of Western ideas was expressed in *Genshi Kiristokyō no bunkashiteki igi*[c] (The Culturo-Historical Significance of Primitive Christianity, 1926). This work contained the confession that his Nietzschean phase had given way to a wider view of the importance of Christianity for the development of religio-cultural ideas. Christians will be not satisfied with Watsuji's evaluation, which over-stressed the importance of Hellenism in relation to Christianity and reduced the latter to a historically important but culture-creating myth. His literary, more than historical, interest in the Virgin Mother of God was vividly revealed in the last chapter of the book, where the interpretation of the Virgin's role is given according to the above mythological explanation.

As a cultural historian Watsuji was more at home when dealing with Oriental history. In 1920, while lecturing at

a. ホーマー批判   b. ポリス的人間の倫理学   c. 原始キリスト教の
   文化史的意義

Tōyō University, he published *Nihon kodai bunka*[a] (Ancient Japanese Culture), a work examining the origins of the Japanese people, the introduction of Chinese writing, the art of *Kojiki*[b] (the oldest record of Japanese legends and events), and the religion and morality of ancient times. This book stressed the conventional patterns of Japanese life such as the family institution, together with an attitude which considered nature as a harmonic synthesis placing man beyond good and evil. The volumes dealing more directly with the Japanese spirit, *Nihon seishin-shi kenkyū*[c], were published respectively in 1926 and 1934; they dealt with the aesthetic and political thought of the time of Asuka[d] and Nara[e] as well as with Dōgen[f] (1200-1253), the founder of the Sōtō[g] sect of Buddhism.

Of greater importance for students of Japanese culture is no doubt the second volume, in which Watsuji tried to define the essence of the Japanese spirit, studying it as he did in relation to the adaptation of Buddhist thought and art. In the chapters on Japanese social history, which discussed topics like the development of capitalism in Japan, Watsuji followed Sombart more than Lenin for the analysis of the development of imperialism, insisting that Japan took a special course. The conclusive chapter dealt with the Japanese language characteristics in relation to philosophy. In analyzing Japanese grammar and terms, he stressed their indeterminate nature, the lack of logical construction, and the intuitive type of reasoning connected with words expressing emotion. Heidegger's influence is obvious in this book, many chapters of which were

a. 日本古代文化　　b. 古事記　　c. 日本精神史研究　　d. 飛鳥
e. 奈良　　f. 道元　　g. 曹洞宗

first published for a journal.[7]

A clear manifestation of his post-war feeling was his work *Sakoku Nihon no higeki* (National Seclusion, Japan's Tragedy), published in 1951. The period of seclusion referred to was the Tokugawa era. However, Watsuji did not deal with this period directly, neither its effects upon Japanese history nor the character of the policy of the Tokugawa Shōguns which had such tragic consequences according to post-war thinking. His concern was rather with the expansionist tendencies stemming from the past, the West toward the East (Marco Polo), the West toward the Americas (Columbus). He also covered in great detail the Christianity during the time of the first missionaries in Japan.[8]

His other works are of a quite different nature, all being concerned with Buddhist and Japanese ethical thought. A reason for Watsuji's new interest was perhaps his appointment to Kyoto University in 1925 as assistant professor of ethics, a development he never dreamed would occur. Sent to Germany in 1927, he studied the history of ethical thought. He was abroad for two years, traveling also in Italy and Greece, countries about which he wrote interesting reports.

7) Watsuji Tetsurō 和辻哲郎, *Nihon kodai bunka* 日本古代文化 (Ancient Japanese culture), The revised edition is: *Shinkō kodai bunka* 新興古代文化 Iwanami Shoten, 1951: *Nihon seishin-shi kenkyū* 日本精神史研究 (Studies on the History of Japanese Spirit), Iwanami Shoten, 1926; revised edit. 1940: *Zoku Nihon seishin-shi kenkyū* 続日本精神史研究 (Studies on the History of Japanese Spirit, continuation), Iwanami Shoten, 1934; pp. 3-24 on *Yamato Damashii* (Japanese Soul); pp. 246-383 on *Chōnin* (Townsmen class); Heidegger's influence pp. 385-90

8) Watsuji Tetsurō, *Sakoku Nihon no higeki* 鎖国日本の非劇 (National Seclusion, Japan's Tragedy), Chikuma Shobō, 1951; see the preface and his conclusive remarks on the effects of early Christian cultural contacts.

In *Genshi Bukkyō no jissen tetsugaku* (The Practical Philosophy of Primitive Buddhism, 1927), Watsuji stated that he was not a specialist of Buddhism, nor did he ever become one. Nonetheless, the critical method and scholarly knowledge employed in this volume were impressive (possibly because it constituted his doctoral dissertation), and are highly praised by the expert Nakamura Hajime[a] even today. Watsuji presented Hinayāna and Mahāyāna Buddhism as being practical philosophies of life, deserving the most careful attention not only of Orientalists but of philosophers at large. The introductory part was a detailed discussion of the sources, while the second stated in general the fundamental tenets of Buddhist philosophy. The latter is stated as the ordinary experience of *Hō*[b] (*Dharma*) which involves all practical knowledge of life and transcends subject and object as well as all epistemological problems. It forms a wisdom of life not inferior at all to formal philosophy.

Contrary to Oldenberg and other Orientalists, Watsuji believed that primitive Buddhism, owing to its Hindu heritage, was not as silent on metaphysical problems as is commonly held. Nonetheless, he laid the stress on practical philosophy as char-with the *engisetsu*[c] or theory of causality, and with *dōtai*[d] or the ways by which man is guided to the practical fulfillment of Buddhist ideals.[9]

a. 中村元   b. 法   c. 縁起説   d. 道諦

9) Watsuji Tetsurō, *Genshi Bukkyō no jissen tetsugaku* 原始仏教の実践哲学 (The Practical Philosophy of Primitive Buddhism), Iwanami Shoten. 1927, pp. 144-80. See also for Watsuji's conception of *"hō"* 法 (Dharma), and *"kū"* 空 (emptiness), his *Jinkaku to jinruisei* 人格と人類性 (Personality and Humanity), Iwanami Shoten, 1938, pp. 195-220 Nakamura Hajime 中村元 in *Risō*, 1961, 6, pp. 44-52

In 1952 the two-volume *Nihon rinri shisō-shi* (History of Japanese Ethical Thought) was published. This work defined ethics in a very broad social sense of manners and customs. Watsuji stressed social and communitarian life and showed evidence of being biased against individualistic ethics, which, he said, was a result of bourgeois egoism. Based upon these premises, he masterfully described the evolving pattern of Japanese morality from mythological times up to the early Meiji period. The volumes were composed of earlier studies but gave a more organic synthesis of the subject. At present they are the best general history of Japanese ethical thought as manifested through the ages. An expert historian, Ienaga Saburō, having to his credit besides many monographs a history of moral thought in Japan, states that Watsuji's work lacked objectivity. This can be granted if by objectivity is meant a tint of postwar social historiography. However, Watsuji's studies were quite an accomplishment if compared, as Furukawa Tetsushi compared them, with the works of Inoue Tesujirō, who frequently disregarded historical facts in order to emphasize and enhance the Emperor cult and the *bushidō* spirit.[10]

A work which shows to what extent Watsuji studied

10) Watsuji Tetsurō, *Nihon rinri shisō-shi* 日本倫理思想史 (History of Japan's Ethical Thought), Iwanami Shoten, 1952, 2 vol. See the long preface for his methodology, pp. 1-27. Ienaga Saburō 家永三郎, in *Le Japon au XI Congrès International des Science Historiques à Stockholm*, Nippon Gakujutsu Shinkōkai, 1960, p. 81. Furukawa Tetsushi 古川哲史 in *Risō*, 1961, 6, pp. 20-27

　　Watsuji's former work on Japanese ethics is: *Sonnō shisō to sono dentō— Nihon rinri shisō-shi I* 尊皇思想とその伝統日本倫理思想史　I (The Thought of the Reverence for the Emperor and its Tradition: History of Japanese Ethical Thought. vol. I), Iwanami Shoten, 1943

Oriental themes under the influence of Western philosophy is *Fūdo*. The Japanese word *"fūdo"* is usually translated "climate". In its original meaning, however, *"fūdo"*[a] carries with it the connotation of a natural geographical setting conditioned by climate which endows the people of the area with a particularly sensitive attitude toward their natural surroundings. Opposed to this is the Japanese word *"kikō"*[b] which means simply "climate". *"Fūdo"* denotes a special attitude conditioned by climate; it denotes almost a way of life.

Fūdo was published in 1935, but was written during the years 1928-29. The occasion of this work was his reading of Heidegger's *Being and Time* while in Berlin in 1927. As shown in the preface, Heidegger's temporality of man left a deep impression upon Watsuji. Nonetheless, the German existentialist did not sufficiently develop the concept of spatiality. To temporality and historicity of man, the natural living condition of man must be added. Space and geographical setting must be taken into account to study the social nature of human existence, which was already a basic problem of Watsuji's ethics. As he stated by the sub-title of the book, the work was intended to be an anthropological study of climate, and although geographical theories of human development are related, Watsuji's approach wants to be philosophical. As a matter of fact, into Watsuji's environment enters not only climate, but also the family, the community, and society in general. Man's individuality is shaped by all these elements.

The most theoretical part of this work is the first chapter where Watsuji stated his position taking as the structure of

a. 風土   b. 気候

human existence the *ex-sistere* of Heidegger or his own *aida-gara*,[a] that is, the relationship of man with external reality. It is not a question of the exteriorization of man, because man for Watsuji is a being totally set in the process of outward expression. In the last chapter, Watsuji compared his views with environmental theories of history from Hippocrates through Bodin, Montesquieu, Herder and Hegel, the last two being most influential on his thought. Geographers' theories, too, are discussed, but obviously Watsuji's interest is in Herder and Hegel and in modern philosophers like Heidegger. This does not prevent him from studying three types of climate in the two central chapters, and also in another the climate aspects of art. Few revolutionary concepts were contained in these considerations. Watsuji, unfortunately, was not acquainted with the most recent development of the French school of Vidal de la Blache, which could have given him some useful hints on "human geography". A sobering book like L. Febvre's *A Geographical Introduction to History* should be read while studying the generalizations of Watsuji.

At any rate the three main types of climate considered by Watsuji are the monsoon, the desert and the pastoral zones. India is the most typical zone of the monsoon climate which determined a passive-receptive form of culture, expressed also in the Buddhist doctrine of mercy and benevolence. The desert zone is represented by African and Muslim cultures and characterized by a combative spirit. The pastoral zone, or the region of the grass land, is represented by Greece and Europe, the home

a. 間柄

of Western culture, whose characteristics are the rational spirit and the conquest of nature.

The monsoon zone, and especially Japan, where changes of climate are continuous, has produced peoples who have the main traits of passivity and forbearance. Sensibility, lack of consistency, temperamental outbursts are characteristics common among monsoon people. Natural forces make man sentimental, intuitive and artistically minded, rather than scientifically inclined, while individuality in these countries is neglected for collective life. Other considerations are added by Watsuji in reference to Japanese feelings, to the house-home concept, and to Japanese *mezurashisa*[a] (novelty-wonder). The main philosophical theme, though, is the localization or spatiality of human existence, which is enveloped by the *fūdo*.[11]

Watsuji's ethical system was expressed in five works, the first two being a preliminary to the later three volumes on *Rinrigaku*[b] (Ethics). For the Iwanami series on philosophy Watsuji published in 1931 a short introduction to *Ethics,* and in 1934 came out *Ningen no gaku toshite no rinrigaku* (Ethics as Anthropology). The first volume of the later major work in three volumes was but an enlargement and clarification of *Ethics*

a. めずらしさ   b. 倫理学

11) Watsuji Tetsurō, *Fūdo ningengakuteki kōsatsu* 風土人間学的考察 (Climate, an Anthropological Consideration), Iwanami Shoten, 1939; 2 ed. 1951, pp. (first ed.) 2-33; 353-93; 16-27; 230-57; on the Japanese *"mezurashisa"* (novelty-wonder) see pp. 260-82. While preparing this book for publication there came out Watsuji Tetsuro, *A Climate,* transl. by Geoffrey Bownas, Tokyo, 1961. Also in course of publication are *Watsuji's complete works* 和辻哲郎全集 by Iwanami Shoten. Recently was published *Watsuji's Autobiography* 自叙伝の試み, Chūōkōronsha, 1961.

as Anthropology. This consisted of two sections, the first stating Watsuji's basis ethical concepts and the second specifying his methodological procedure of establishing the principles of ethical behavior. For Watsuji ethics was the science of man as such, the only anthropology. Speculative psychology and anthropology in the German sense of the term studied man in the abstract only, dealing too much with problems like soul and body, mind and matter.

Key terms to Watsuji were ethics (*rinri*)[a], man (*ningen*)[b], and being (*sonzai*).[c] Using philological inferences, German social ethics, Indian philosophy and the five Confucianist ethical relations, Watsuji stressed the socio-communitarian nature of his ethics. The first Sino-Japanese character of ethics, that is, *rin*[d], meant for Watsuji *nakama*[e] or the associate and communitarian relationship toward others. The second character or *ri*[f] corresponded to *kotowari* or "reason", that is, the rational order of man to man relationship. Man, too, signified "to be in the world" (*ningen: yo no naka*),[g] while "being" (*sonzai*) implied preservation in time (*son*)[h] and the relation to space or localized subject (*zai*)[i]

The conclusion was that ethics consisted essentially in the *aidagara* or the relationship aspect of contacts between man and man, man and his family, man and society. Taken in its entirety, man is not only an individual or a mere social entity but a being essentially related to the social world to which he belongs. Heidegger's concepts, already evidenced in *Fūdo*, were even more prominent in the first volume of *Rinrigaku* where man, in his

a. 倫理   b. 人間   c. 存在   d. 倫   e. 仲間   f. 理
g. 人間　世の中   h. 存   i. 在

basic elements of ordinary, individual and social aspects, was considered. Absolute and negative elements too, as well as temporal and spatial structures, were discussed and analyzed in detail.

Ethics as Anthropology contained a study of the ethical systems of Aristotle, Kant, Cohen, Hegel, Feuerbach and Marx. This was done for the sake of clarifying the progress made by different thinkers, who, nonetheless, lacked the *aidagara* concept and, therefore, did not perceive the ethical relationship intrinsically connecting man to man. The concept of *aidagara* was for Watsuji similar to the concepts of nothingness and place in Nishida. We can see here Watsuji's tendency toward an Oriental formulation of ethics, while also borrowing from Heidegger.[12]

This Oriental tendency is even more evident in the first volume of *Rinrigaku* where a new stress is laid upon the negative aspects of morality. Moral laws are originated through the absolute negation (*zettaiteki hiteisei*)[a] of the subject. The individual only through the negation of the self can join the whole of the nation. This absolute negation ends in the *kū*[b] (the emptiness of the self), in order to reach the "absolute totality", not dissimilar in purpose to Nishida's nothingness.

This theme was dealt with again in a special chapter where, under the guidance of Simmel, Durkheim and other sociologists, the individual is clearly absorbed into the social reality. Man must dissolve himself in the quest for the absolute emptiness, not

---

a. 絶対的否定性   b. 空

12) Watsuji Tetsurō, *Ningen no gaku toshite no rinrigaku* 人間の学としての 倫理学 (Ethics as Anthropology), Iwanami Shoten, 1934, pp. 2-4; 29-32; 45-46; 187-97

because of reason found in concepts like the "external constriction" of Durkheim (a reason for the limitation of the individual), but rather because of the fundamental void intrinsic to man and society. Society, formed as it is of individuals, is but a dialectical development of self-denying units toward the great void which is social totality.[13]

Obviously Nishida's influence and Buddhist thinking can be easily traced in these considerations. An Oriental background is manifested also in the emphasis upon confidence (*shinrai*)[a] and veracity (*shinjitsu*)[b] as well as the unselfish love of the "heavenly true hearth" (*tenshin na magokoro*).[c] Evil depends on the voluntary betrayal of confidence.

The second volume of Watsuji's *Rinrigaku* dealt mostly with ethical problems of the family, with geographical and cultural communities and their ethico-economic ethos. Nations, too, are studied in detail. The third volume considered the historical dimension of man, and *fūdo* or climate ideas were taken up again.

The political implications of what we could call Watsuji's "social relationism" was especially prominent in the second volume during the discussion of the idea of the state. This consideration, amounting to a totalitarian state-ethics, was corrected in the revised edition of post-war times.[14]

---

a. 信頼   b. 真実   c. 天真な真心

13) Watsuji Tetsurō, *Rinrigaku* 倫理学 (Ethics), *jō* (vol. I). Iwanami Shoten 1937, pp. 1-35, where the basic concepts are considered, and the methodology, on pp. 35-67; for the "absolute negation" see, especially, pp. 193-95

14) Watsuji Tetsurō, *Rinrigaku* 倫理学 (Ethics), *chū* (vol. II). Iwanami Shoten, 1942, pp. 475 ff. which must be compared with post war edition (1949), same pages, to see his changed view of the state.

Adequate studies on Watsuji's philosophy have not yet been published. However, a special issue of the magazine *Risō* contains several articles by his former pupils and friends. The leading paper is by Kaneko Takezō who considers in detail the different influences of Western philosophers upon Watsuji; for example, Windelband's theory of values and Dilthey's *Auslegung* or the interpretative method of studying cultural phenomena. But Watsuji's main ideas were inspired by Husserl and Heidegger. The concept of *Umwelt-Mitwelt* is essential for the comprehension of Watsuji's *aidagara* as well as for *fūdo*. Furukawa Tetsushi in a short survey of recent Japanese ethical trends emphasizes the importance of Watsuji's system, which can be said to represent a progress if compared with the ethical theories of Inoue Tetsujirō and Nakajima Rikizō. Indeed Watsuji's thought cannot be confused with the ultra-nationalist ethical movement very flourishing during his long career.[15]

Nonetheless, he over-stressed the concept of nation, and the post-war changes made in his books are still open to question. Furthermore, Watsuji's "social relationism" and ethics were based too heavily on the influence of *fūdo* on man's existence. This notion lacked interiority and a scheme of values which could transcend the social aspects of society. Changing social relationship cannot be a solid base for valid ethical principles, which Watsuji tried to establish. He seems to justify the primitive custom of giving the wife to the guest as being a sign of com-

---

15) Kaneko Takezō 金子武蔵 in *Risō*, 1961, 6, pp. 1-19; for Watsuji's world views see his *Rinrigaku* 倫理学 (Ethics), *ge* (III vol.), Iwanami Shoten, 1949, pp. 485-91. Furukawa Tetsushi hen (ed.)古川哲史編 *Rinrigaku* 倫理学 (Ethics), Kadokawa, 1953, 1959, pp. 207-230

munitarian spirit. Watsuji, who wrote an interesting essay on *Mask and Persona* and another on *Personality*, never fully recognized the primacy of individual rights and duties.

Granting these limits, Watsuji's merits should not be minimized, and the systematic nature of his thought entitles him to a prominent place among recent Japanese philosophers.[16]

Tanabe Hajime's Logic of the Species (1885-1962)

Tanabe Hajime[a] was born in Tokyo in 1885. At the University of Tokyo he enrolled in the department of science, and therein may be found the explanation for his early and lasting interest in the philosophy of science and mathematics. Before his graduation in 1908, however, Tanabe switched to the department of philosophy. In 1913, he became lecturer at the Tōhoku University in Sendai, teaching philosophy in the science department. His first work, *Saikin no shizenkagaku*[b] (Recent Natural Science) was published in 1915. *Kagaku gairon*[c] (Outline of Science) appeared in 1918, preceded (in 1916) by his translation of Poincaré's *La valeur de la science*.

In 1918, Tanabe was invited to Kyoto University where he became Nishida Kitarō's most famous successor, and eventually formed the so-called *Kyōto-ha* or Kyoto school of philosophy. From 1922 until 1924, he studied abroad at the universities of Berlin, Leipzig and Freiburg (where Husserl was teaching at the time). After his return to Kyoto he published *Kanto no moku-*

---

a. 田辺元   b. 最近の自然科学   c. 科学概論
16) Watsuji Tetsurō, *Jinkaku to jinruisei* 人格と人類性 (Personality and Humanity), Iwanami Shoten, 1938, pp. 181-87 where there is a brief and clear statement of the meaning of "ethical relationship". The main part of this book is a study of personality and humanity in Kant.

tekiron[a] (Kant's Teleology) to commemorate the two-hundredth anniversary of Kant's birth. In 1925 *Sūri tetsugaku kenkyū*[b] (A Study of the Philosophy of Mathematics) was published. Although he wrote on the subject of philosophy of science and mathematics as late as 1951, the year of 1925 may be considered as the culminating point for Tanabe's interest in that field. His influence in this area of study is still in evidence today.

In passing, it might be well to mention here Ishihara Jun (1881-1947), who, as a physicist, dealt with problems of the philosophy of science at the same university where Tanabe started his teaching career. Although Ishihara soon left his teaching position because of a love affair, his research on relativity, quantum theory and philosophical problems of science made him a pioneer in this field. Funayama Shin'ichi classifies Ishihara with the "idealist" philosophers of Japan. No doubt he was an idealist in the one sense that he saw in nature the mysterious work of the Almighty. As a critic of culture, Ishihara closely followed the tenets of Windelband and Rickert.[17]

Tanabe developed his philosophy of mathematics guided by the principles found in Cohen and the Marburg school of neo-Kantianism. This was clearly stated in the preface of his bulky work *A Study of the Philosophy of Mathematics*. This book,

---

a. カントの目的論   b. 数理哲学研究

17) Ishihara Jun's 石原純 main works are: *Gendai no shizenkagaku* 現代の自然科学 (Contemporary Natural Science), Iwanami Shoten, 1924; *Kagaku to shakai bunka* 科学と社会文化 (Science and Social Culture), Iwanami Shoten, 1941; *Shizenkagakuteki sekaizō* 自然科学的世界像 (Scientific World View), Hyōronsha, 1949. Concerning Ishihara see: Funayama S., *Nihon . . .*, o.c., pp 275-83; Tsuchida K., *Contemporary Thought . . .*, o.c., p. 174

as well as his earlier one on the philosophy of science, also served as a testimony of his dependence on Nishida. As Tsuchida emphasized, the understanding of Western philosophy which Tanabe possessed when he wrote *Recent Natural Science* and *Outline of Science* was derived from the teaching of Nishida. It was apparently the intention of the young pupil to develop the philosophy of science which was only touched upon by the master. Like Nishida, Tanabe at this stage of his philosophical evolution attempted to build up a new metaphysics; that is, to create with the aid of Husserl's phenomenology a new foundation for the realization of values. Tsuchida saw in the conclusive remarks of the *Outline of Science* an "abridgement" of Nishida's *Intuition and Reflection in Self-Consciousness.* Tanabe's "intuitionism" gave a realistic foundation to Kant's epistemology. In the *Recent Natural Science,* the tendency was the same; that is, values must have a realistic ground gained through intuition. However, Husserl's phenomenology was more widely applied. The transcendental values were considered, which, in their essence, are eternal and unchangeable. Moral and religious values, too, are not historically determinable, the intermediate link being "intelligible beauty."

A Study of the Philosophy of Mathematics, Tanabe's most important work in the field of the philosophy of science, gained him his doctoral degree. The *Study* was divided into two sections, the first discussing the philosophical basis of numbers, and the second dealing with problems of geometry. Tanabe discussed various mathematicians and philosophers, especially Kant, revealing as he did so, his deep and extensive knowledge of the subject. He then analyzed the logical formation of natural numbers. Assuming as a starting point that numbers can be logically intuited, Tanabe demanded that, for the basis of the logico-mathematical conception of numbers there be an *ein etwas*, an intuitive something, a concrete thing to which is applied the fundamental intuition. Logic being abstract and its unity potential, it is only when applied to concrete things that we have mathematics. Yet, when passing from logic to mathematics, we have but an explicitation of what lay latent in the primitive intuition. The mediative element between logic and mathematics is the intuitive grasp of the unity which is the basis of the multiplicity of concrete things.[18]

In 1927, Tanabe began a transition from Husserl's phenomenology and Heidegger's existentialism to Hegel's dialectic. In 1932, Tanabe published a study on the latter's dialectic; and in 1933, Tanabe's formulations on absolute dialectic first appeared in *Tetsugaku tsūron*[a] (The Elements of Philosophy), a work that has seen repeated publication. Notwithstanding the title, *The Elements of Philosophy* is not merely a popular explanation of the fundamental problems of philosophy, but a fairly original introduction to philosophical thinking. Tanabe's own dialectic is developed in the last chapters of the book, wherein Hegel's assimilation of being and idea is criticized, as well as the Marxist dialectic. Marx comes under fire because his "inversion", like

a. 哲学通論

18) Tanabe Hajime's 田辺元 works on philosophy and methodology of science and mathematics are: *Saikin no shizenkagaku* 最近の自然科学 (Recent Natural Science) Iwanami Shoten, 1915; *Kagaku gairon* 科学概論 (Outline of Science), Iwanami Shoten, 1918 *Sūri tetsugaku kenkyū* 数理哲学研究 (A Study of Philosophy of Mathematics), Iwanami Shoten, 1925; on Tanabe's thought see: Tsuchida K., *Contemporary Thought* . . ., pp. 93-96; *Tanabe tetsugaku* 田辺哲学 (Tanabe's philosophy), Kōbundō Henshūbu, 1951, pp. 107-23

Hegel's, destroys the immanent contradiction existing between the material and the ideal.[19]

Tanabe's reputation as an original thinker was established by his "logic of species" (*shu no ronri*),[a] a concept which he had evolved in opposition to Nishida's "logic of place". As early as 1930, Tanabe indicated the lines along which his thought differed from that of his master. His conception of species was elaborated in two articles, *"Shakai sonzai no ronri"*[b] (The Logic of Social Being) in 1934, and later in specific articles on the "Logic of Species", published in *Tetsugaku kenkyū*, a philosophical journal published by Kyoto University.

Tanabe's opposition to Nishida was in general due to the excessively "contemplative" nature of Nishida's thought. To state it more concretely, though negatively, Tanabe was of the opinion that Nishida's thought was not social-minded enough. Philosophically speaking, according to Tanabe, Nishida failed to realize the importance of the logical category of species. Therefore in his conception of history, Nishida necessarily lacked an essential element. As in logic we have the genus, the species and the individual, so too in the philosophy of history there is mankind (a sort of universal similar to the genus), the species of which is determined by the nation, and the individual historical being. Nishida stressed the interaction between the individual and the genus, but neglected the mediative role of species, which is paramount in logic as well as in history. What qualifies the uni-

a. 種の論理   b.社会存在の論理

19)   Tanabe Hajime, *Hegeru tetsugaku to benshōhō* ヘーゲル哲学と弁証法 (Hegel's Philosophy and Dialectic), Iwanami Shoten, 1932, pp. 1-13.
       —, *Tetsugaku tsūron* 哲学通論 (Elements of Philosophy), Iwanami Shoten, 1933, pp. 8-15; 42-48; 170-236

versal and the individual is the specific aspect of a thing. Nishida, as well as those who follow formal logic, seems to neglect the role of the species, which is almost lost in the universal, or is reduced to the individual. The state, in the Tanabe system of logic, focuses both terms and gives them the proper perspective.

The political implication contained in Tanabe's early formulation of the "logic of species" has received its share of criticism by left-wingers and liberal thinkers in post-war times. Tanabe himself in the preface to *Shu no ronri no benshōhō*[a] (The Dialectic of the Logic of Species), published in 1947, conceded that his concept was not clear and was susceptible to misunderstanding. He therefore proposed "the absolute dialectic" (*zettai benshōhō*)[b] as a corrective element. He strove, as in his early period, to give a concrete foundation to the concept of national society, which he saw distorted by the two extreme positions of liberalism and totalitarianism. Therefore, to overcome absolutism, the concept of "absolute nothingness" or "absolute dialectic" should be established as a starting point.

In self-criticism, Tanabe said that his former logic was excessively based upon the principle of identity. As with Hegel, who did not entirely discard this principle, the nation became the absolute, depriving the individual of his freedom. A nation as a species is a necessary concept even now, yet it must be considered as opposed to the individual and to mankind in general because of its particularistic ends. The species has therefore a twofold opposition to the individual and to mankind which must be dialectically overcome by the inclusion of

a. 種の論理の弁証法　　b. 絶対弁証法

absolute nothingness, which in turn stems from the individual
but effects the species too. A long analysis of Hegel, Plotinus,
Nishida, and Aristotle's dialectic thinking was included in the
content of *The Dialectic of the Logic of Species*. Tanabe came
close to a Plotinian type of dialectic which, though pervaded
by the absolute nothingness as well as by Christian love, gave
him a keen interest in Christian existentialism.   Similarly
striking was the use, or perhaps abuse, of dialectic to identify
the individual with the whole (*zentai soku kotai*)[a] through the
"principle of mediative union" (*baikai ketsugō no genri*)[b].[20]

To understand Tanabe's post-war conception of the logic
of species, we must go back to *Zangedō toshite no tetsugaku*[c]
(Philosophy as Metanoesis), a book published in 1946, but prepared in the last year of the war, or more exactly in the summer
of 1944, when Tanabe's philosophical evolution took place. The
humiliating national defeat was not foreseen at that time by
most Japanese. Tanabe, though, made a profession of repentance,
as it were, in the name of Japanese intellectuals, who in pre-war
times gave in to the nationalistic trend. *Philosophy as Metanoesis*, or philosophy as repentance, depicted the mood of a de-
feated ideology forced to make a clean sweep of former positions,
yet trying to save what was necessary for future generations.
It is no wonder that Tanabe advocated a "philosophy without
philosophy". By this he meant that old positions were to be
discarded in favor of one based on repentance and having

a. 全体即個体   b. 媒介結合の原理   c. 懺悔道としての哲学
20)   Tanabe Hajime, *Shu no ronri no benshōhō* 種の論理の弁証法 (The Dia-
      lectic of the Logic of Species), Akita-en, 1946, pp. 2-5; 143-58. For a
      Marxist critique of Tanabe see: Hayashi N., *Nishida tetsugaku . . . .*,
      o.c., pp 229-77; Takeuchi Y., ed., *Shōwa . . .*, o.c., pp. 140-82

a transcendental perspective. Former philosophies must die in order to give successful rise to a new way of life. About his own logic of species, he stated that the *zangedō* or repentance element was to be introduced. To state it more simply, Tanabe did not see in his former logic of species the possibility of evil in the Hegelian conception of the state. However, even so moral a substance as the state is for Hegel must pass through absolute negation; if it does not, absolutism will spring up.

Tanabe's absolute negation meant also "absolute criticism"; criticism of self first, but criticism also of philosophers like Kant, Hegel, Nietzsche. The book had predominant religious overtones, especially in those portions where Eckhart and Shinran,[a] the founder of the Shinshū[b] sect of Buddhism, are given special consideration, as well as those portions where the motives of the Jōdo[c] sect of Buddhism are treated.

Repentance, absolute criticism, nothingness, total dependence upon an absolute outside of man were the cornerstone of Tanabe's philosophy. He further claimed that Japanese society, as well as the entire world, should reassert its positions from these terms. Tanabe's religious views were the basis of a new social philosophy.[21]

The long autobiographical preface of *Kirisutokyō no benshō-hō*[d] (The Dialectic of Christianity, 1948) explained Tanabe's early interest in Christianity, beginning when he was a high school student at the Daiichi Kōtōgakkō. At the university he was influenced considerably by Koeber, who advised him to

---

a. 親鸞　　b. 真宗　　c. 浄土宗　　d. キリスト教の弁証法

21) Tanabe Hajime, *Zangedō toshite no tetsugaku*懺悔道としての哲学(Philosophy as Metanoesis), Iwanami Shoten, 1946, see especially the preface and chapters I and VIII

read St. Francis's *Fioretti*. Hatano Seiichi's *Origins of Christianity* likewise made a deep impression upon the young Tanabe.
However, as a student of science, his early relativistic and positivistic tendencies and his later intellectualism did not bring him
any nearer to the Christian religion. Nevertheless, further
studies convinced him that in order to understand Western philosophy, a study of Christianity was necessary. Furthermore,
after the war he came to realize the social implications of this
religion. Although he carefully considered Buddhism, he took
relevant parts of the doctrine on social reconstruction from the
teaching of Christianity and even from Marxism. As an appendix to his volume, he added an article "Christianity, Marxism
and Japanese Buddhism", in which his conciliatory spirit tries
to make Christianity more Buddhistic, and Marxism more Christian. This effort is evident throughout his book, in which he
treats the Protestant theological opposition between Christ as
Savior and Christ as Master as one of the main themes. By his
own dialectic he wished to overcome the opposition inherent in
these two ideas and, transcending St. Paul's theology, to go back
to the Christ of the Gospel. Many interesting views are presented, Barth's theology being predominant. Strange examples of
dialectic, too, were included, such as the Resurrection of Christ.
The gist of the bulky work is summarized in the preface, in
which Tanabe states that, although he cannot say, "I believe,
Lord, help my faith," he nonetheless recognizes the tremendous
task undertaken by the Christian teaching. Both Protestantism
and Catholicism (the latter impressed him by its world-wide
allegiance) figured in his theory for the social redemption of
mankind. It must be recognized that a change must be not
only of a purely social nature but one of a religious nature

as well. Yet there are certain conditions which are pre-requisites to the fulfilment of such a task. Thus Christianity must dispose of all the mythological elements which hamper its development. Tanabe declared that it is necessary for Christianity to pass from the personalistic conception of God, through the "absolute mediative self-negation" (*zettai baikaiteki jiko-hitei*)[a] to the nothingness which is love, operative love, and love that is faith, and which in turn can be adapted to Buddhism.[22]

Tanabe's conceptions of this period were expressed also in *Jitsuzon to ai to jissen*[b] (Existentialism, Love and Praxis, 1947). This work deals with the religious problems mentioned in *The Dialectic of Christianity*, with special emphasis laid on Christian existentialism. Marxism and existentialism being the great themes of discussion in the early post-war years, Tanabe sided with religious existentialism of the Kierkegaard type. His absolute dialectic and total mediation offered a guiding path through the most difficult synthesis, always ending with a socio-religious reform emphasizing religious love with a mixture of Christian charity and Buddhist nothingness.

Tanabe's socio-political tendencies are best expressed in *Sei-ji tetsugaku no kyūmu*[c] (The Urgent Need of a Political Philosophy, 1946). Originally published as a series of articles in various journals, they were slightly augmented and revised when published in book-form in 1947. His political philosophy favored

---

a. 絶対媒介的自己否定   b. 実存と愛と実践   c. 政治哲学の急務

22)   Tanabe Hajime, *Kirisutokyō no benshōhō* キリスト教の弁証法 (The Dialectic of Christianity), Chikuma Shobō, 1948, pp. 1-24; 14-16

a social democracy. Tanabe's social thought is so permeated by such categories as "absolute nothingness" and "absolute dialectic" that it is not difficult for Marxists and socialists alike to recognize a great deal of utopian idealism in Tanabe's interest in social reconstruction.[23]

Typical of Tanabe's philosophy, yet more systematic, are a series of volumes under the general title *Tetsugaku nyūmon*[a] (An Introduction to Philosophy), which came out during the years 1949-1952. *An Introduction to Philosophy* is based upon a series of conferences with a group of teachers. According to the sub-title of the first volume, it deals with some fundamental problems of philosophy, of which the first is to establish the concept of philosophy itself. A formal definition did not satisfy Tanabe. Citing Windelband's *Introduction to Philosophy* as a reliable standard work, Tanabe took up various philosophical problems in the framework of their historical evolution. He believed that this procedure was best suited for pinpointing the essential problems of philosophy. While stressing the necessity of analytical method, for didactical purposes, he wrote that only a total vision of the problem through the dialectical approach could distinguish the inner connection and the opposing aspects of every question. The principle of contradiction cannot be denied in formal logic; yet real philosophy, requiring the commitment of the thinking ego, must use a superior logic or total dialectic.

a. 哲学入門
23)   Tanabe Hajime, *Jitsuzon to ai to jissen* 実存と愛と実践 (Existentialism, Love and Praxis), Chikuma Shobō, 1947, pp. 1-9; *Seiji tetsugaku no kyūmu* 政治哲学の急務 (The Urgent Need of a Political Philosophy), Chikuma Shobō, 1946, 1947, pp. 58-73

For Tanabe this approach necessitated primarily the insertion of *mu* (nothingness), interpreted here as the negation of negation. This concept was needed for the process of dialectical thinking, which progresses through contradiction. Secondly, nothingness and the negative process were required, because of *de aru*[a] and *ga aru*[b]—the duality of essence and existence involved in every reality. Other important themes of Tanabe's thought appeared in his discussion on the dialectic of history and the self-consciousness of nothingness in the philosophy of science. The latter required the negative element of dialectic for the conception of the dual nature of motion, while history needed nothingness to project time into the future. Obviously Marxism cannot be discussed without a thorough understanding of the negative aspects of capitalism, as well as that of every social system, a social system being conceived of as always progressing to new stages and forms and never as an ultimate condition arrived at. The philosophy of history is treated in the second volume of the series of *The Introduction to Philosophy*, where such topics as the thought of Hegel and Ranke and historical materialism are considered. Political philosophy is also studied, while the other volumes deal with the philosophy of science and epistemology and the philosophy of religion and ethics. However no really new ideas are proposed here.[24]

a. である   b. がある

24) Tanabe Hajime, *Tetsugaku nyūmon tetsugaku no kompon. mondai* 哲学入門 哲学の根本問題 (Introduction to Philosophy—The Fundamental Problems of Philosophy), Chikuma Shobō, 1949. pp. 53-61; 115-52 Other volumes are: *Rekishi tetsugaku- Seiji tetsugaku* 歴史哲学一政治哲学 (Philosophy of History—Philosophy of Politics); *Kagaku tetsugaku ninshikiron* 科学哲学認識論 (Philosophy of Science and Epistemology); *Shūkyō tetsugaku Rinrigaku* 宗教哲学倫理学 (Philosophy of Religion— Ethics)

It is difficult to present a thorough evaluation of Tanabe Hajime's thought. In a sense, he seems quite consistent in his logic of species; on the other hand, the content of his logic changed considerably during various stages of development. In a pre-war analysis of Tanabe's position, T. Taketi pointed out that Tanabe differed with Nishida on three points: Tanabe's rejection of a too metaphysical and mystical tendency, his clarification of the distinctive role of philosophy and religion, and the necessity of inserting the nation as mediative element of the logic of space. However, in his post-war phase, Tanabe's philosophy of repentance and his interpretation of nothingness did not greatly differ from Nishida's efforts. On socio-political grounds, Tanabe is known for his stronger commitment, but this is precisely what has been most criticized by the younger generation. Tanabe, more than Nishida, plunged into religious philosophy as well as mysticism. He is, no doubt, the most brilliant thinker after Nishida. Along with Nishida he is the second philosopher who has been honored with the highest cultural prize of Japan.

Until more of Tanabe's works are translated, the Western reader may receive some idea of his religious bent by considering the essay *Memento Mori*, which has been made available in a good English translation through the effort of V.H. Viglielmo. This essay is more than a dialectical theology, of which Tanabe's post-war writings are filled; it is rather a *Zen kōan*[a] (a Zen Buddhist text for meditation), which stresses the necessity of a philosophy of death in the age of the atomic bomb—an age in which the total destruction of mankind has become a macabre

a. 禅公案

possibility. Tanabe stressed the concept of life-death, *shōji ichin-yo*[a] meaning a death-resurrection attitude. This Buddhist conception of life-in-death, carrying also Christian overtones of resurrection, was paramount. Also expressions like "absolute-nothingness-qua-love" were repeatedly formulated. In other words, the Christian conception of God was too strongly based on the existence of God, and Christianity was too much a philosophy of life. Zen Buddhism, to which existentialism approaches, emphasises a philosophy of death. Even better, the central concept of Mahāyāna Buddhism, that is, absolute nothingness, if permeated by love, can be a way of salvation in this "age of death." How Buddhist absolute negation can be combined with Christian love or how such a philosophy of death can be invoked to restore international peace, is difficult to say. At any rate, Tanabe invited the reader to think about these problems, which, for the congenially minded, have a certain appeal.[25]

a. 生死一如

25) Taketi T., Japanische Philosophie der Gegenwart, in: *Blätter für Deutsche Philosophie*, 1940, Heft 3, pp. 277-299; *Tanabe tetsugaku* . . ., o.c., pp. 69-78; 163-200; Kōsaka K., *Nishida tetsugaku* . . ., o.c., pp. 77-89. The essay translated by V. H. Viglielmo "Memento Mori" is in the *Philosophical Studies of Japan*, compiled by the Japanese National Commission for Unesco, vol. 1, 1959, pp. 1-12

Chapter VI

CULTURALISM AND HEGELIANISM; MARXISM
AND WORLD PHILOSOPHY 1926—1945

Culturalism and Hegelianism

The period now to be considered shows, on the one hand, the establishment of an academic philosophy, the fruit of seeds of thought of the early Taishō period. On the other hand, the years beginning with the Shōwa era (1926) up to the end of the war are the least academic in Japanese thought, because of the involvement of thinkers in the problems through which Japan was passing at that time. The Taishō democracy, as it is usually called, which lasted roughly from the first World War till 1926, was a liberal period for Japan, when democratic ideas were freely propagated and discussed. It was also the time when cultural criticism and cultural philosophy fully matured. Especially during the 1920's the so-called Bunkashugi[a] or "Culturalism" became prominent.

Tsuchida Kyōson (1891-1934) is cne of the outstanding exponents of this trend. His interest in the field of philosophical criticism of civilization is evidenced in his work, already quoted, on Japanese thought, in which three chapters are devoted to this subject. I have already mentioned in Chapter 3 thinkers such as Takayama Rinjirō, Tanaka Odō, Abe Jirō and others who dealt with problems of culture and society from a broad or even journalistic point of view. This trend is sometimes called

a. 文化主義

zaiya or "non-official" philosophy in order to distinguish it from
the academic type of thinking which I have been stressing in this
survey. The reason adduced by Tsuchida in favor of this non-
official philosophy and social criticism must be briefly treated
here, however, because of its importance not only in the cultural
history of Japan, but also in understanding the commitment of
some academic thinkers.

Tsuchida vividly expresses the discontent of many critics
with academic philosophers who, according to him, became too
formal and did not attempt to solve the problems which society
was then facing. Tsuchida, as the good philosopher he was,
wanted such criticsm to be based on strict epistemolcgy; yet the
philosopher must still be "engaged", to put it in recent terms,
and discuss actual questions. The works of Tsuchida, such as
his *Bunkashugi genron*[a] (Principles of Culturalism, 1921) or
his philosophy of Japanese literature and social philosophy can
be quoted as good examples of intellectual criticism. Tsuchida
received a good philosophical training at the University of Kyoto.
According to Mutai Risaku, who knew him well, he was a very
gifted thinker. Although he died at the early age of forty-two,
his collected works fill fifteen volumes. He wrote much for
magazines, being the editor of *Bunka*[b] (Culture), yet his books
were quite systematic, not merely collections of loosely connected
essays. Today Tsuchida is mostly remembered for his controversy with Kawakami Hajime[c], with whom we shall deal shortly.
His views on "Culturalism" are stated briefly in his book *Contemporary Thought of Japan and China*. If his ideas are striking
for the noble purposes they manifest, they are so muddled in a

a. 文化主義原論   b. 文化   c. 河上肇

dialectic of "personal anarchy", as he calls his ethical idealism, that one must wonder at his pretenses of sound epistemological premises. At any rate, Tsuchida is for a culture and a society which exists as an ideal to be continously pursued and realized; he is not, therefore, an utopian like Marx, because he does not assign any finite or limited construction of society. P. Lüth compares Tsuchida's cultural stand-point with that of Rudolf M. Holzapfel's "Panideal".[1]

Tsuchida mentions among social and cultural critics Hasegawa Manjirō (1875-1892) who is well known under his penname Nyozekan as a journalist and writer, although he had a short teaching career. Here he must be mentioned only on account of his association with the Society for the Study of Materialism, and for his criticism of socio-political institutions, he being a liberal of the British school. Murobuse Kōshin (Takanobu, 1892-　), is also much more known as a journalist and writer than anything else, and therefore no discussion of his ideas is needed in these pages.[2]

---

1) Tsuchida Kyōson 土田杏村, Bunkashugi genron 文化主義原論 (Principles of Culturalism), Naigai Shuppan, Kyoto. 1921; Shakai tetsugaku genron 社会哲学原論 (Principles of Social Philosophy), Naigai Shuppan, Kyoto, 1925. His complete works Tsuchida Kyōson zenshū 土田杏村全集, Daiichi Shobō, 1935-36, 15 vols. The fourth volume has the original Japanese of Contemporary Thought of Japan and China, often quoted, where at pp. 183-89 his cultural views are related. See also Lüth P., Die japanische . . ., o.c., pp. 91-92

2) Hasegawa Manjirō (Nyozekan) 長谷川万次郎 (如是閑) and Murobuse Kōshin (Takanobu) 室伏高信 see Tsuchida K.. Contemporary Thought . . ., o.c., pp. 166-72. For bibliographical indications: Bonneau Georges, Bibliographie de la Littérature Japonaise Contemporaine, Tokyo, 1938

A philosopher by training, but a scholar who specialized mostly in aesthetics and therefore developed the philosophical basis of literary criticism is Tanikawa Tetsuzō (1895-   ). He belongs to the Kyoto school of philosophy in a very broad sense, because he graduated from that University in 1922 and developed as a philosopher the German type of *Lebensphilosophie*. After he became a professor at Hōsei University[a] in Tokyo he began to cultivate Goethe's thought, but as many of his books are meant for a wide circle of readers, he is generally regarded as a journalistic thinker. His more philosophical works are listed in the following note[3]. As regards his journalistic writings, they were surely of a decidedly higher calibre. His cultural competence in fine arts won for him the post of Vice-Director of the National Museum in 1948.

More important as good philosophers and as well-known cultural personalities in Japan are Abe Yoshishige (1893-   ) and Amano Teiyū (1894-   ). Both could be considered to rank alongside Abe Jirō for the influence they exerted upon several generations of Japanese students, both through their writings and as educators. There are also great differences, however. Abe Y. and Amano became known to the world of students much

---

a. 法政大学

3)   Tanikawa Tetsuzō's 谷川徹三 more philosophical works are: *Kanshō to hansei* 感傷と反省 (Sentimentality and Reflection) Iwanami Shoten, 1925: *Naibu to gaibu* 内部と外部 (The Interior and the Exterior) Koyama Shoten, 193?: *Shisō enkin* 思想遠近 (Far and Near Thoughts), Koyama Shoten, 1933; *Seikatsu, tetsugaku, geijutsu* 生活 哲学 芸術 (Life, Philosophy, Art), Iwanami Shoten, 1930. On Tanikawa's thought see: Tama Giichi 田間義一, *Gendai tetsugakusha-ron* 現代哲学者論 (On Contemporary Philosophers), Ikuei Shoin, 1943, pp. 120-131

later than Abe Jirō. Their first works were studies on Kant, although they devoted much time to popular works also. Abe Yoshishige is a graduate of Tokyo University, while Amano is from Kyoto, although not belonging at all to the Kyoto school of thought. Both have in common many scholarly studies on Kant (Abe also on Spinoza), both are good writers, and both occupied the post of Minister of Education in post-war Cabinets: Abe, soon after the war in the Shidehara Cabinet; Amano, about 1950 with the Yoshida Cabinet. This is a detail which must be mentioned because it implies that neither was committed to nationalist trends in pre-war times. Amano, it is true, gave up his position in the Cabinet, because in the moral chaos of post-war Japan he proposed a morality which left-wingers called too Kantian and therefore not fitting with their own social morality. Still it is to his credit to have had the courage to advance some- thing which would surely lead to criticism from the "progressive thinkers." Amano was one of the few in post-war Japan who was not afraid to incur the disfavor of the left-wing press which was predominant.

Neither Abe nor Amano have any special philosophical system of their own. Amano, however, must be singled out for the clear stand he took against the tide of irrational thinking, which was fostered by the militarists, in his books, *Dōri no kankaku*[a] (The Sense of Reason, 1937) and its continuation *Dōri e no ishi*[b] (The Will to Reason, 1939). These books were sharply criticized by nationalists and militarists, although they look pretty innocuous to a reader today. They are not at all systematic books, being composed of articles written for various

a. 道理の感覚　　b. 道理への意志

newspapers and journals at different times. They touch upon such a variety of subjects as his memories of Heidelberg, praise of Uchimura Kanzō, the subject of poverty, the meaning of life, etc. It is difficult to see any clear connecting idea. Still the ethical meaning of life is the key-note of these two books. Amano was talking to students, telling them that morality must be based on "Reason", which is not particularly either Oriental or Western, and that the sense of duty and responsibility must be based not on nature, but on philosophical, nay, metaphysical principles. In the chapter in which he explicitly deals with *Dōri* or "Reason", he follows M. Scheler in classifying different values; but the gist of his whole lecture is this, namely, that man as an individual must realize for himself this world of values. In the second book where, among other things, Oriental and Western scholarship are considered, Amano, while granting all the existing differences, is for a more unified and universal philosophy.

Since both of them as philosophers were disciples of Kant, they are not at all typical of this period, in which phenomenology or Hegelianism was prevalent. This also indicates their non-conformity to the philosophical trends of the times.[4]   A third

---

4) Abe Yoshishige's 安部能成 main works are: *Kant no jissen tetsugaku* カントの実践哲学 (The Philosophy of Praxis of Kant), Iwanami Shoten, 1924; *Emmanuel Kant dōtoku tetsugaku genron* インマヌエルカント道徳哲学原論 (Principles of E. Kant's Moral Philosophy), Iwanami Shoten, 1926; *Shūkyō tetsugaku* 宗教哲学 (Philosophy of Religion of Kant.) Iwanami Shoten, 1932; *Spinoza rinrigaku* スピノザ倫理学 (Spinoza's Ethics), 10 vol. of the Collection *Dai shisō bunko*, Iwanami Shoten, 1935-36; *Jissen risei hihan kaisetsu* 実践理性批判解説 (Exposition of the Critique of Practical Reason), in *Kant kenkyū* カント研究 (Studies on Kant), Genrinsha, 1936; *Shisō to bunka* 思想と文化 (Thought and Culture), Kōsesha, 1924; *Gendai to bunka* 現代と文化 (Present and Culture), Iwanami Shoten, 1941, in which, pp. 109-258, there is a survey of Meiji

independent thinker could be added here, Itō Kichinosuke (1885-1961), who was the successor of Kuwaki at Tokyo Imperial University, and who became the editor of the standard *Tetsugaku jiten* (Philosophical Dictionary). Itō was no doubt under Kantian influence, but his critical spirit never allowed him to go beyond *mitdenken* (thinking with) Kant, nor did he ever finish his doctoral dissertation.[5]

An original philosopher, as well as an exponent of phenomenology and Hegelian dialectic is Takahashi Satomi (1886-1962), who has been already mentioned as a critic of Nishida's views. He too, like Abe and Amano, never compromised his academic standard with current nationalism or philosophical factions which have been an obstacle to independent thinking. Takahashi was a graduate of Tokyo University, 1919, and for many years was professor at Tōhoku University, Sendai, becoming its President in 1949. In an autobiographical article he writes that the reason why he became a philosopher originated in the need he felt to look for a rational foundation for moral uprightness. He

thought.

Amano Teiyū 天野貞祐, *Dōri no kankaku* 道理の感覚 (The Sense of Reason), Iwanami Shoten, 1937, pp. 264-88; *Dōri e no ishi* 道理への意志 (The Will toward Reason), Iwanami Shoten, 1939, pp. 37-47. Other works by Amano: *Jinkaku to jiyū* 人格と自由 (Personality and Freedom), in *Iwanami Kōza*, 1931-33; *Kant junsui risei hihan* カント純粋理性批判 (Kant's Critique of Pure Reason), vol. 17 of the collection *Dai shisō bunko*, Iwanami Shoten, 1935; *Konnichi ni ikiru rinri* 今日に生きる倫理 (Living Ethics Today), Kaname Shobō, 1950; *Hibi no rinri watashi no jinsei annai* 日日の倫理わたしの人生案内 (Daily Ethics—My Guide to Life), Kantō-sha, 1954. Concerning Abe and Amano see: Tama G., *Gendai . . .*, o.c., pp. 67-87

5) For Itō Kichinosuke 伊藤吉之助 see Yamazaki Masakazu 山崎正一 in *Risō*, 1961, 2, pp. 39-43

himself is always a strong moralist, although his philosophical books are on Husserl's phenomenology, Hegel's dialectic and his own personal type of dialectic. He also took care of translating Bergson's *Matière et Mémoire*.

His moral uprightness, more than his ethical theory, about which he has written little, is described by one of his pupils, Watanabe Yoshio,[a] who remembers Takahashi's critical attitude toward Nishida and Tanabe. During the last ten years before the war everything was supposed to be made *Nihonteki*[b] or Japanese, philosophy included. Takahashi, so Watanabe recalls, did not go for this type of speculation, and was not afraid to tell his students that they had better walk out of the classroom if they did not want to hear the truth and the whole truth. In a book published in 1947, *Tetsugaku no honshitsu*[c] (The Essence of Philosophy), Takahashi states his position, which never changed, namely that philosophy is a quest for pure theory, not in the sense of abstract intellectualism, but of sound rationalism based upon eternal principles. His phenomenology can been seen in his later works, and is best expressed in his *Zentai no tachiba*[d] (The Point of View of the Whole), published in 1932. More linked to Hegel than Husserl is his *Taiken to sonzai*[e] (Experience and Being, 1936), while his rational bent can be seen in the translation made in 1917 of the work of the Italian philosopher Aliotta, *The Idealistic Reaction Against Science*, where the anti-intellectualism in epistemological problems of science is criticized.

The most important work of Takahashi is *Hōbenshōhō*[f] (Pan-Inclusive Dialectic, 1942), where he tries to overcome Hegel's and Nishida's dialectic with an all-embracing method,

---

a. 渡辺義雄　　b. 日本的　　c. 哲学の本質　　d. 全体の立場
e. 体験と存在　　f. 包弁証法

which can be called dialectical only in a very broad sense of the term. In a sense this book can be considered in relation to his previous *Zentai no tachiba*, because he tried to build up a theory which would give the basis for a "Total Vision" which could be truly said to be *Zentai no tachiba*. His Pan-Inclusive dialectic is, as a matter of fact, a critique of several forms of dialectical thinking in favor of a universal logic stemming from a universal love, which is at the basis of Takahashi's epistemological quest for reality. [6]

Another original philosopher who, like Takahashi, cultivated phenomenology as well as dialectic, is Mutai Risaku, about whom we shall have more to say in the following chapter on account of his role in post-war years. Mutai's books belonging to this phase are *Hyōgen to ronri*[a] (Expression and Logic, 1940) and *Genshōgaku kenkyū*[b] (A Study of Phenomenology, 1940). One of the earlier purveyors of phenomenology in Japan is the former professor of Kyoto University, Yamauchi Tokuryū[c]

a. 表現と論理   b. 現象学研究   c. 山内得立

6)   Takahashi Satomi 髙橋里美 *Tetsugaku no honshitsu* 哲学の本質 (The Essence of Philosophy), Fukumura Shoten, 1947, pp. 147-57. Other books are: *Zentai no tachiba* 全体の立場 (The Point of View of the Whole), Iwanami Shoten, 1932; *Taiken to sonzai* 体験と存在 (Experience and Being), Iwanami Shoten, 1936. *Gendai no tetsugaku* 現代の哲学 (Contemporary Philosophy), Iwanami Shoten, 1917. This book is, but for two chapters, the translation of A. Aliotta, *The Idealistic Reaction against Science*, *Ninshikiron* 認識論 (Epistemology), Iwanami Shoten, 1938; *Rekishi to benshōhō* 歴史と弁証法 (History and Dialectic), Iwanami Shoten, 1939; *Hō-benshōhō* 包弁証法 (Pan-Inclusive Dialectic), Risōsha, 1942; *Takahashi tetsugaku* 髙橋哲学 (Takahashi S.'s Philosophy), ed. by Nobechi Tōyō 野辺地東洋. Fukumura Shoten, 1955. This book is a systematic presentation of Takahashi's main concepts. In English see: S. Takahashi, Historical Actuality, in *Philosophical Studies of Japan*, vol. II (1960), pp. 1-20. See also Watanabe Yoshio 渡辺義雄 in *Risō* 理想, 1961, 2, pp. 49-54

(1890-   ), who published two works reflecting this trend in 1929 and 1930 respectively. In *Genshōgaku josetsu*[a] (Introduction to Phenomenology) and *Sonzai no genshō keitai*[b] (The Phenomenological Form of Being) phenomenology is interpreted according to Heidegger's *Seinsfrage*. Yamauchi's dependence upon Heidegger is acknowledged in the preface of the latter book. Mystical elements taken from the West (Nicholas of Cusa), as well as Oriental intuitionism, are also incorporated by Yamauchi.

Kierkegaard's and Heidegger's existentialism have been known in Japan since 1926, and I have already mentioned Watsuji's having been influenced by them. An existentialist philosopher who felt the influence of Heidegger is Kuki Shūzō[c] (1888-1941). He graduated from Tokyo University in 1912, and eventually became a professor at Kyoto University in 1935. His interest in existentialism is manifested in his *Jitsuzon no tetsugaku*[d] (The Philosophy of Existentialism), written for the Iwanami series on philosophy, and *Ningen to jitsuzon*[e] (Man and Existentialism). His artistic spirit (he too was under the influence of Koeber) is stated in *Bungeiron*[f] (A Theory of Literary Arts), and especially in the well-read book, continuously reprinted even now, *Iki no kōzō*[g] (The Structure of "*Iki*",[h] 1930). By *iki* is meant the æsthetic taste as a way of living, peculiar to the Japanese. After having stated that *iki* is something typically Japanese, he looks for the comprehension and extension of this concept in a very logical way, so that anyone studying the Japanese spirit and culture should take this into account.

---

a. 現象学序説   b. 存在の現象形態   c. 九鬼周造   d. 実存の哲学   e. 人間と実存   f. 文芸論   g. いきの構造   h. 粋

This way of life based on *shumi*[a] (taste, elegance) has, no doubt, philosophical premises, but they are latent and therefore hard to discuss. Kuki invites us to live them, but only in Japan the real feeling of this Weltanschauung can be guessed at.[7]

More than phenomenology and existentialism, it is Hegel's dialectic which became predominant in the last ten years before the war. What has been said about Nishida and Tanabe, and what we are going to see about the Marxist interpretation of Hegel or World Philosophy, and the existence of fanatic nationalists like Kihira Masami, are all evident proof of the interest that Japanese philosophers took in Hegel. The centenary of the death of Hegel in 1931 brought about an increase and new developments of Hegelian studies in Japan. Not only were Hegel's complete works translated, but studies like those of R. Haym, K. Rosenkrantz, H. Glockner were rendered into Japanese. That Hegel's dialectical reasoning presents similarities with Oriental ways of thinking is quite a commonplace. It is stated not only by Kihira, who wanted already in 1929 to find a relationship betwen the Wang Yang-min[b] school and Hegel's philosophy, but by almost all the above-mentioned thinkers. The reasons for the fascination of Hegel were no doubt, political, both on the right and the left, as was

a. 趣味   b. 王陽明

7) Kuki Shūzō 九鬼周造, *Iki no kōzō* いきの構造 (The Structure of *"iki"*); Iwanami Shoten, 1960 (9th ed.), pp. 1-17; 130-50; *Jitsuzon no tetsugaku* 実存の哲学 (Philosophy of Existence), *Iwanami kōza Tetsugaku* 岩波講座 哲学 (Iwanami's Lectures: Philosophy); *Bungeiron* 文芸論 (Literary Theory), Iwanami Shoten, 1941; *Ningen to jitsuzon* 人間と実存 (Man and Existence), Iwanami Shoten, 1939; *Seiyō kinsei tetsugaku-shi* 西洋近 世哲学史 (History of Recent Western Philosophy), Iwanami Shoten, 1944; 1949, 2 vols.; *Gendai Furansu tetsugaku kōgi* 現代フランス哲学講義 (Lectures on Contemporary French Philosophy), Iwanami Shoten, 1957.

the case in the West. Deeper or more philosophical reasons are to be found in what has been said about Tanabe's "absolute dialectic", and will be discussed also at the end of this volume; here it is enough merely to state the fact.[8]

Kawakami's Historical Materialism

A link between early socialism and later Marxism of the extreme form of the Kōtoku type, described in the second chapter, is Ōsugi Sakae[a] (1885-1923). He was the only one still to advocate direct action, in the sense of Sorel's syndicalism, even after the tragic death of the Kōtoku group, which put an end to most active members of social action in Japan. Ōsugi, too, met a tragic end, being strangled to death by a police-captain during the disorder following the great earthquake of 1923. Ōsugi was a theoretician of a sort, his inspiration coming from Bergson and Nietzsche. At the time of his death Ōsugi was a communist, and the Communist Party was to be a main factor in the spreading of Marxist philosophy in Japan. In July 1922, under the leadership of Sakai Toshihiko[b], Yamakawa Hitoshi[c] and Arahata Kanson[d], the new party began under great difficulty, and was troubled with factional divisions from the very beginning. Nevertheless, the real spread of Marxism in Japan is due, not so much to the communist leaders, as to Kawakami Hajime (1879-1946). Kawakami's position as professor of economics at Kyoto University, and his frequent writings for leading newspapers and his scientific publications drew Marxism to the attention of all Japanese thinkers.

a. 大杉栄   b. 堺利彦   c. 山川均   d. 荒畑寒村
8) Lüth P., *Die japanische* . . ., o.c., pp. 78-79; Saigusa H., *Nihon ni okeru* . . ., o.c. pp. 183-224.

Kawakami was born in Yamaguchi Prefecture, graduated from Tokyo University in 1902, and joined the staff of the Yomiuri Newspaper[a], as a writer on political and social problems. As a student at Tokyo University he was moved, not so much by the dry lectures of his professors of political science and economics, as by the conferences of Uchimura Kanzō. The Bible was his favorite book. The New Testament and Tolstoi's *My Religion* enflamed him. Later on, his dedication to the movement of "Absolute Unselfish Love" brought him to the verge of death, so many were the privations he underwent for the sake of this social-service organization.

The second period of his life starts with his appointment in 1908 as instructor at the University of Kyoto, and his study of economics which he pursued during his trip abroad from 1913 to 1915. Once back, he became full professor of economics, initiating the translation of Marx's *Das Kapital*. He disclosed his true intentions at this time in his autobiography in the following terms: "Using my position as university professor, I shall make propaganda for socialism". At this time he was not yet a full-fledged Marxist, his position being not very dissimilar to that of E.R.A. Seligman's *The Economic Interpretation of History*, which he translated in 1905. Even less was he a materialist. According to Saigusa, it was only around 1924 that he realized the implications of Marx's materialism in its philosophical aspects. At any rate, his increasing interest in practical social problems is manifested in his *Bimbō monogatari*[b] (Talks on Poverty, 1917), and *Shakai mondai kanken*[c] (A Personal Point of View of the Social Question, 1918). In 1919 he

a. 読売新聞　　b. 貧乏物語　　c. 社会問題管見

started a one-man magazine, *Shakai mondai kenkyū*[a] (Studies on Social Problems) in which he exposed his more Marxist "Studies on Historical Materialism". His *Talks on Poverty*, printed serially in the Ōsaka Asahi[b] reached the wide circle of readers of this influential newspaper just at the moment of economic chaos which Japan was beginning to feel during the Taishō period, when the big *Zaibatsu*[c], or family trusts, were building up their monopolistic capitalism, and poverty and unemployment was spreading.

Kawakami's Marxism and materialism must be related to the criticism of his views by communist theoreticians like Fukumoto Kazuo, who in 1926 pointed out his undue stressing of the economic factor, forgetting the real dialectic of *Das Kapital*. Kawakami was always trying to change men's hearts rather than the economic system. He was even suggesting Malthusianism in order to alleviate misery—a mortal sin to any Marxist. His weakness can be seen especially in his article on "Historical Materialism and Causality." It must be admitted that Kawakami was not an "orthodox" Marxist. Still, Fukumoto's criticism must not be taken at face value, because of the too many political overtones of his criticism. Besides, Kawakami had the merit to have pointed out clearly where the essence of historical materialism was in Marx, i.e., in the "Introduction" to *Zur Kritik der Politischen Oekonomie*. He was also accused of "Yamakawa-ism", a term taken from the position of another communist, Yamakawa Hitoshi, who was for a more liberal policy in the party. At any rate, the criticism of Fukumoto, who also was to be condemned as a deviationist

a. 社会問題研究   b. 大阪朝日   c. 財閥

from the true communist path, was humbly accepted by Kawakami. He resigned from his position at the university in 1928 to run as a candidate for the new Labor-Farmer Party, a communist supported political organization.

Kawakami's stricter Marxism can be seen in his books and articles from 1928 on, as for example, his *Shihonron nyū-mon*[a] (Introduction to Capitalism, 1928). He became a member of the Communist Party, for which he had to pay by going to prison in 1933. As party member his main merit lay in his translation from the German of the so-called "1932 Thesis", which was smuggled into Japan and appeared in translation in the communist paper *Red Flag* in July, 1932. This thesis, a revival of the one of 1931, described by Stalin as "Trotskyist", urged Japanese communists to fight Japanese imperialism, which was taking over Manchuria and going beyond the Russian controlled Chinese Eastern Railway. Another hopeless task imposed upon Japanese communists by this thesis was to attack the emperor institution. Naturally this thesis was the cause of new arrests and further disruption of the party, which had always a very precarious existence. Kawakami also was arrested. But all these trials did not shake his faith in the party—and of faith we have reason to speak, because his Marxism was always tinged with an adhesion similar to that he gave in his early days to the "Absolute Unselfish Movement." Kawakami, we must not forget, was also a poet and an excellent prose writer, as can be seen in the book *Sources of Japanese Tradition*, where are given excerpts of his *Jijoden*[b] (Autobiography, five volumes in the original) and his *Gokuchū zeigo*[c]

a. 資本論入門   b. 自叙伝   c. 獄中贅語

(Prison Ramblings).   The reader can see, for instance, how
he tried to combine scientific materialism and Buddhistic religious experience which, although not fully approved of by him,
as a materialist, still had a special field of human value not to be
totally despised.   No doubt, orthodox Marxists were puzzled at
his idea. [9]

The communist party members, no doubt, were set on pro-
moting Marxism in Japan, but among the early theoretical
leaders a great deal of factionalism sprang up.   "Yamakawa-
ism" is not really much of an ideological problem, if we do not
consider the tactical problems in which Yamakawa Hitoshi
(1880-1958) was involved.   Yamakawa, who never had any
special schooling, but was involved in political activity from his
early years, and familiar therefore with the interior of various
prisons, wrote for the then Socialist magazine *Zen-ei*[a] (Van-
guard) in 1922 a programmatic article on the need of "A
Change of Direction in the Proletarian Movement" (*Musan-kai-
kyū hōkō tenkan*)[b].   This article was an appeal to the ultra-
intellectuals to rally under the banners of communism and go to
the masses who were losing all contact with their leaders. [10]

a. 前衛   b. 無産階級方向転換

9) For a full bibliography of Kawakami Hajime 河上肇 see:
    Amano Keitaro ed. 天野敬太郎, *Kawakami Hajime hakase bunken-shi*
    河上肇博士文献志 (Bibliographical Record of Dr. Kawakami Hajime),
    Iwanami Shoten, 1956 Kawakami Hajime, *Jijoden* 自叙伝 (Autobiogra-
    phy), 5 vols., Iwanami Shoten, 1951. *Sources of Japanese Tradition*, o.c.,
    pp. 820-27; 872-80. See also: Sakisaka I., ed., *Kindai Nihon . . .*, o.c., pp.
    148-60; Saigusa H., *Nihon . . .*, o.c., pp. 265-318; Ōi T., *Nihon . . .*,
    pp. 181-93. Furuta Hikaru 古田光, *Kawakami Hajime*, Tōkyō Daigaku
    Shuppan-kai. 1959, a biographical study with bibliography, pp. 256-60.

10) Yamakawa Hitoshi 山川均, *Aru bonjin no kiroku* ある凡人の記録 (A
    Commoner Record), Asahi Shimbunsha, 1951.   In this autobiography,
    the socialist movement is described up to the so-called "Red Flag Inci-
    dent". June 1908.

The mixed blessings of many intellectuals in a small party, like the Communist Party, can easily be imagined. The special police, or "thought police" as they were usually called, especially after the Kōtoku hanging, left the communists very little to do except to discuss theoretical problems. Besides, as is true today, Japanese university campuses have always been the best ground for left-wing movements (and right-wing movements, too, to be fair); and so it was that by November, 1922, twenty intellectual circles had been organized in different campuses, with the Tokyo Imperial University and Waseda University having the leadership. In these student circles, communist leaders like Shiga Yoshio[a] and Sano Manabu (Gaku)[b] who was directing the students at Waseda University, had their first experiences. Yamakawa's appeal was more than needed, but he was never for a strict party leadership as Lenin had forged in Russia, and therefore he was attacked on several grounds. His point of view was later condemned as disruptive and pernicious by Bukharin, who at the same time, in 1927, also reproached the main antagonist of Kawakami and Yamakawa, Fukumoto Kazuo (1894-).

Fukumoto, a graduate of the department of political science of Tokyo Imperial University, had but a short teaching career, then went abroad for a while, and by 1920 had become a member of the Central Committee of the Communist Party. His leading position as a theorist is due to his criticism of Kawakami and Yamakawa, the latter having also the fault of calling, just after his release from prison, a temporary disbandment of the party. This was not such an unwise measure if we

a. 志賀義雄   b. 佐野学

think of the continuous arrests of the party members, but it was altogether against Moscow's directives, which through the Shanghai thesis, January 1925, expressed dissatisfaction at there not being a well-organized party in Japan. Fukumoto, although he had little social background, went up fast in communist circles, owing in part to the fact that other communist leaders, more known to the police, were always serving prison sentences. He has to his credit the development of the dialectical aspects of historical materialism, as well as practical aspects in the line of Lenin's *What is to be done?* His polemical zest, as well as his knowledge of Marxist theory, won for him the title "a second Lenin". Still, according to his critics, his dialectical materialism and his concept of class consciousness were too much influenced by Lukács, and in epistemological problems he divided the unity of theory and praxis. The term he coined, *Bunriketsugō*[a] (literally, Separation-Unity), by which he tried to join together all the different factions of left-wing leaders, especially Yamakawa's *Rōnō-ha*[b] (Labor-Farmer group), was later labelled as a trend toward fostering factionalism or *Sekutoshugi*, to use the Japanese communist term. His view that Japanese capitalism had already reached the advanced stage of Western capitalism could not square with the view of the Comintern. At any rate, as Swearingen and Langer point out, the anti-Fukumoto trend was backed by the Russian representative of the Comintern in Tokyo, Jacob D. Yanson, and owing to his report seven Japanese communist leaders were invited to go to Moscow in order to straighten up their questions. This resulted in the Bukharin thesis, mentioned above, in which Fukumoto recanted, and "Yamakawa-

a. 分離結合   b. 労農派

ism" as well as "Fukumoto-ism" were rejected. The activity of the Communist Party under Tanaka Giichi's government and his successors had to face new and stricter police surveillance. During the so-called "March 15th Incident" (1928), 500 Communists were arrested. Arrests followed arrests, and in prison some of the communist leaders recanted. Among them were Sano Manabu and Nabeyama Sadachika[a], who wrote an "apology" to the authorities. Fukumoto Kazuo, although undergoing fourteen years of prison life without recanting, rejoined the party only in 1950. Fukumoto is also known in Japan as an expert on *ukiyoe*[b], a realistic type of painting which came in vogue during the seventeenth century, and has in Hokusai one of its best representatives. Fukumoto devoted a volume to Hokusai[c].[11]

Miki's Anthropological Marxism

If Kawakami gave respectability to Marxism in academic circles in general, developing mostly the economic theory of Marx, Miki Kiyoshi (1897-1945) introduced Marxist thought among philosophers as well as a wide circle of students and the general public which avidly read his essays, written in a fairly clear and easy style. Besides, Miki developed the humanistic aspect of Marx, or his "anthropology", as he called it, and thus stressed an aspect of Marxism which could not but arouse the interest of many. Miki's collected works, in sixteen volumes, start with a study on Pascal and end with a consideration of

a. 鍋山貞親   b. 浮世絵   c. 北斎
11) R. Swearingen-P Langer, *Red Flag in Japan*, Cambridge Massachusetts. 1952, pp. 15-26. About Fukumoto Kazuo 福本和夫 see: Oi T., *Nihon . . .*, o.c., pp. 181-90; *Kindai Nihon shisō-shi . . .*, o.c., vol. 3, pp. 584-94.

the meaning of life, covering a wide range of subjects which cannot but impress students of philosophy, critics, and the common reader as well. [12]

Miki was born in Hyōgo Prefecture, and already in high school (Daiichi Kōtō of Tokyo) founded a philosophical study club. Nishida's thought attracted him to Kyoto University which he entered in 1917. More than Nishida, to whom he later acknowledged dependence (see *Tetsugaku nyūmon*, Introduction to Philosophy), the personality and teaching of Hatano Seiichi seems to have made an early impact upon Miki. His interests were very wide, ranging from Sōda Kiichirō's *Problems of Philosophy of Economics*, to French literature and thought. During his college and post-graduate studies, philosophy of history was his main field of research, reading philosophers like Windelband, Rickert, Simmel, Troeltsch, and historians like Lamprecht, Burckhardt and Ranke. This early interest in the philosophy of history was to mature in his later major works, but was already manifested in the essays collected in the second volume of his works entitled "Problems on the Idealistic Conception of History". Going to Germany in 1922, he pursued this type of study under Rickert, publishing two essays in German. In Marburg he had Heidegger as a teacher, and here also came in contact with K. Löwith. Socialist influence was very strong in academic circles in Germany at the time, and Miki was influenced also by M. Weber and Mannheim. During his studies abroad, he was also for a while in Paris, coming back to Japan in 1925. In April 1927 he was appointed

---

12) *Miki Kiyoshi Chosaku-shū* 三木清著作集 (Miki Kiyoshi's Collected Works) Iwanami Shoten, 1946-51, 16 vols.

professor at Hōsei University, where he remained until 1930 when, on account of some help he gave to a friend he was held for a while by the police as a communist sympathizer. He had to resign his teaching position, and from this time on his literary output increased because he now had to make a living by writing. Most of his later publications were articles for magazines, and hence the level was of a journalistic type of philosophy or criticism. Still a work like *Kōsōryoku no ronri*[a] (The Logic of the Power of Imagination), published in 1939, attests his philosophical vigor at its best, this book being one of his most systematic works. During this period he also produced many translations: Marx-Engel's *German Ideology* and some works of Aristotle.

His journalistic activity really began in 1928 when, with the Marxist historian Hani Gorō,[b] he jointly published a magazine. This activity, together with his publications on Marxism, not only made him a suspect in the eyes of the police, but also provoked a storm of criticism from communist circles which, then as now, have the exclusive right to interpret Marx. No doubt this narrow-minded criticism was a reason why he moved more and more away from Marxist ideas. This is why Miki is studied in a collection of "Japanese Idealists", as is done by Funayama Shin'ichi. Although this label is misleading and sounds too much of the sharp ideological division in vogue with Marxist thinkers, Miki's later developments are surely not materialistically oriented. Miki, who was basically an existential humanist tinged with social-liberal ideas, was again taken into custody by the police towards the end of the war on March 28, 1945, after some military service in the Philippines. A left-wing

a. 構想力の論理　　b. 羽仁五郎

friend of his, Takakura Teru, escaped from the police, and went to see Miki to get some food and clothes. Miki died on September 26, 1945, nobody knows how, at the early age of 48. The war was over by then, but he could not benefit by the Occupation Forces' directives which released all the political prisoners only in the following October. [13]

A detail of "petite histoire" may be allowed here. Miki and other left-wingers or communists like Tosaka Jun[a] and Kozai took part in the translation work for a Catholic Encyclopedia which started in 1939. Their dire economic situation in the midst of the military nationalism in Japan moved to compassion the director of the Encyclopedia, Fr. Kraus of Sophia University, who, out of charity, did not hesitate to use them as translators. Miki's *Pascaru ni okeru ningen no kenkyū* (A Study of Man in Pascal), begun already in France and published in 1926, shows decisively his existential humanism which was to continue even in his interpretation of Marxism. "The Problem of Individuality" (*Kosei no mondai*) already attracted him as a student. His contact with Heidegger and existentialism made him find in Pascal's anthropology the elements of the uncertain existence of man who cannot be made the absolute,

---

a. 戸坂潤

13) For Miki's life and thought see:

Miyagawa Tōru 宮川透, *Miki Kiyoshi* 三木清, Tōkyō Daigaku Shuppankai, 1958; Karaki Junzō, 唐木順三, *Miki Kiyoshi*, Chikuma Shobō, 1950; Takakuwa Sumio 高桑純夫, *Miki tetsugaku* 三木哲学 (The Philosophy of Miki), Natsume Shoten, 1946. This book deals mostly with Miki's *Tetsugaku nyūmon* 哲学入門 (Introduction to Philosophy), which is the first part of vol. 7 of Miki's Works; Funayama S., *Nihon* . . ., o.c., pp. 287-304; Takeuchi Y. ed., *Shōwa* . . ., o.c., pp. 269-309; Tama G., *Gendai* . . ., o.c., pp. 88-109.

facing as he does death and nothingness. [14]

His essays on historical materialism date from the years 1927-30 while he was at Hōsei University, and were preceded and followed by other studies on the philosophy of history which are not Marxist at all. Communist thinkers can easily point out his unorthodox interpretation of Marx, given the categories of Heidegger, the influence of G. Lukács, and his overemphasis of what he calls "fundamental experience" (*kiso keiken*)[a], which is the unity of the social relations of being, ultimately the experience of the proletarian class. To me it seems a very intelligent, if free, interpretation of Marxism, which I have seldom read even in the best non-orthodox foreign Marxists. That is why also in Japan he is considered the best advocate of philosophical Marxism which, while provided in the climate of post-war freedom with many faithful interpreters, had but little original thought or even skilful presentation. His anthropological Marxism is not at all a psychological explanation of class consciousness, but an effort to give "the genealogy of theories" (*riron no keifugaku*)[b], in the sense that Mannheim tried to build up a *Wissenssoziologie* (Sociology of Knowledge), quite a vital point in a Marxist system. I do not pretend that Miki fared much better than Mannheim, but at least he was squarely facing the problem, and his stress on anthropology no doubt brings him nearer to Marx than Mannheim himself, who did not have any relevant influence upon Miki.

a. 基礎経験   b. 理論の系譜学

14) *Miki Kiyoshi Chosaku-shū* . . ., o.c., vol. 1 (*Pascaru no kenkyū* パスカルの 研究: A Study of Pascal), pp. 112-14; 127-29; 143. *Kosei no mondai* 個性の問題 (The Problem of Individuality), vol. I., pp. 95-107.

His *Genealogie der Theorien* consists of four aspects, which being all dialectically interwoven cannot easily be distinguished. His starting point is the "fundamental experience", which is not Bergson's pure experience (Miki was opposed to Sorel's Bergsonism), but the Marxist proletarian social experience. From this first stage we must pass through the "logos", or a kind of epistemological experience, to the phases of an ideology which is not thought of as a conscious intellectual framework, but rather as a product of what Miki calls the "Model of Being" (*sonzai no moderu*)[a], or the pattern of social being. Finally anthropology is the historical result of the three former aspects, which indicated the historical aspects of man already patterned in the social framework of the former vital experiences. The basic experience goes through a necessary process of self-abstraction into the pattern of being, which is a natural and unconscious ideological background, out of which conscious and historical anthropology springs forth. This fourfold process is the real Marxism for Miki, or at least, what had value in the essays published under the programmatic title *Yuibutsu shikan to gendai ishiki*[b] (Historical Materialism and Modern Consciousness). Miki in this book, which forms the first four essays of the third volume of his works, tries to free Marxism from all of the "metaphysical aspects" of materialism. Problems like the nature of matter, of consciousness, how the latter comes from the former, etc. are no problems for Miki or for Marx. His emphasis is on the social matter or social consciousness, a position, indeed, true for Marx, but not so for Engels or Soviet Marxists, or for Japanese "orthodox" Marxists, who therefore

a. 存在のモデル   b. 唯物史観と現代意識

criticized Miki for his neglect of the philosophical (metaphysical for Miki) aspects of Marxism. It must be added though, at this stage, that Miki tried to justify more than to explain Marx, which can also be seen in the chapter on the relation between pragmatism and Marxism (he was being accused of pragmatism among other things). But with creative thinkers orthodoxy cannot come to terms, and never will be satisfied. [15]

Miki's *Rekishi tetsugaku*[a] (Philosophy of History, 1932) was written after his release from detention and therefore some spoke of a "change" due perhaps to external pressure. The theoretical change is due to Heidegger's existentialism (*Sein und Zeit* came out four years earlier than Miki's work), as it was Heidegger who revived the concept of Kant's *Einbildungskrafte*, a subject dealt with by Miki in his *Kōsōryoku no ronri* (The Logic of the Power of Imagination) published in 1939. In this work Miki tries to find a new logic, different from the classical one, as well as from the neo-Kantian or Nishida's logic of place. Miki's philosophy of history is based on the analysis of three

---

a. 歴史哲学

15) *Miki Kiyoshi Chosaku-shū* . . ., o.c., vol. 3 has as title *Yuibutsushikan kenkyū* 唯物史観研究 (Studies on Historical Materialism), of which the first four chapters were earlier published under the title *Yuibutsushikan to gendai ishiki* 唯物史観と現代意識 (Historical Materialism and Contemporary Consciousness). See the "introduction" (*jo* 序) at the end of this volume where the *Genealogie der Theorien*, p. 365, is explained. For *"Kiso keiken"* 基礎経験 (Fundamental Experience), Logos, etc. see *passim*, and especially pp. 2-9; 41-43. *"Sonzai no moderu"* 存在のモデル (Model of Being) see pp. 119-20. Miki's anti-metaphysical Marxism is stated at pp. 45-46; 68-69 and *passim*. Chapters 5-8 (not numbered in this edition) were formerly published under the title *Shakai kagaku no yobi gainen* 社会科学の予備概念 (Introductive Concept of Social Science).

main categories, the fourth, i.e. the sources or historical documents, being of no great relevance for the philosopher. The three main categories are: being, or history as the happened-events, the *res gestae;* logos, or the description of the events; and, finally, history as *jijitsu*[a] or reality. This last concept is the true starting point for Miki's philosophy of history, because it is this "reality", or rather, actuality, which gives us an understanding of history. This actual reality, which is the presentness of history, is related also to Nishida's similar idea in his *The Self-Conscious Determination of Nothingness.* Nevertheless, unlike Nishida, Miki presents a special type of existential activism, which makes him contrast Fichte's *Tathandlung* with the *Tatsache.* It is not our thinking activity which gives an understanding of history, but what Miki calls *jittaiteki mono kanseiteki mono,*[b] that is, the existential and sensible experience of life. This experience of the subject or individual experience (*shutaisei,*[c] litt. selfhood) overcomes relativism and a subjective interpretation of history, because it is actual history to which meaning is given by our lived history. History as "logos" can be a subjective description of the past which impinges upon history as being, where strict causal relations exist. History as actuality is man-made reality, where through the *kisoteki keiken*[d], or the fundamental experience, we recreate the past in the present. This fundamental experience which was considered also in Miki's conception of historical materialism, is now the historical consciousness of the subject which gives a meaning to the present. To achieve the future not as a possibility but as an actual present, Miki in-

a. 事実   b. 実体的もの　感性的もの   c. 主体性   d. 基礎的経験

vokes the decision of the subject, supported by the idea of history as "pathos."

This last theme is connected with Miki's *The Logic of the Power of Imagination*, because for him only this kind of logic of the imaginative pathos transcends sensibility and also the *Verstand* or intellectual knowledge, and goes therefore into the intimate reality of things. It is not the intentionality of Husserl, but something similar to it. For Heidegger, the "Power of Imagination" grasps the concrete existence of man. Miki'goes further; he wants to unify or transcend logos and pathos with this power which is creative of a "form", which has its own logic (*katachi no ronri*)[a]. The direct field of this logic, which is not intellectual at all but the operative behaviour of man, manifested especially in the creation of myths, institutions and finally of techniques, has relevance for history, because the latter is essentially technique. Namely, man is the creator of culture, or of the different aspects of socio-cultural and technical "forms". Man's history is but the history of mutations of "forms". Miki thinks that this logic of "form" has its own objectivity, which, if we presuppose the identity between theory and praxis, could be admitted with little consolation for a more critical view of historical knowledge. At any rate, Miki thinks that, by adding the environment, as a more concrete basis, greater objectivity is reached. For Miki, at this stage, social environment is not quite the same as Marx's determining factor, but rather the field where the subjective man continuously operates in creating new forms. This is a kind of subjective-objective reality, which he aimed

a. 形の論理

at also in his *Philosophy of History*. The stress must be laid upon the creative factor inherent in the "Power of Imagination", which in its more intelectual aspect is the *kōiteki chokkan*[a] or the "acting intuition", and its more operative element is the production of "form". [16]

A third aspect of Miki's thought is expressed as humanism on account of several essays he wrote on the subject. In his later activity as a critic, he sponsored many liberal causes, and made efforts to free intellectuals from the chauvinism and political servility of much of the academic thought of the times. I refer especially to the essays on "Society" in the 14th volume of his works. His ideas on Chinese and Japanese culture vividly express the contemporary abuse of history for political purposes. He remained a liberal humanist to the end, but, for the police, an unloyal citizen. To his intellectual personality Nishida Kitarō, and even Tanabe Hajime, although on the other side of the fence, could not but pay the highest praise. [17]

Materialists and Communist Philosophers

For more orthodox views on materialism and Marxist philosophy, rather than Miki, we must now consider the *Yuibutsuron Kenkyūkai*,[b] or Society for the Study of Materialism, and think-

---

a. 行為的真観   b. 唯物論研究会

16) *Miki Kiyoshi Chosaku-shū* . . ., o.c., vol. 6: *Rekishi tetsugaku* 歴史哲学 (Philosophy of History), pp. 32-34; 39-40; 164-67. vol. 8: *Kōsōryoku no ronri* 構想力の論理 (The Logic of the Power of Imagination), pp. 6-11; 311-66.

17) *Miki Kiyoshi Chosaku-shū* . . ., o.c., vol. 12, pp. 171-79; vol. 10, pp. 385-99 for Miki's humanism; vol. 14, pp. 16-23 on Japanese and Chinese thought; vol. 14, p. 441 on Nishida and Tanabe. See also: Satō Nobu? 佐藤信衛, *Nishida Kitarō to Miki Kiyoshi* 西田幾多郎と三木清 (Nishid⌐ K. and Miki K.), Chūō Kōronsha, 1947.

ers like Nagata Hiroshi[a] and Tosaka Jun. The Society for the Study of Materialism, which began in October, 1932, was composed of about forty members led by Hasegawa Nyozekan, Hattori Shisō[b], Hani Gorō, Honda Kenzō[c], Saigusa Hiroto, Tosaka, and others. The program was to propagate knowledge of materialism in the various fields of natural and social sciences, as well as in philosophy. A magazine was published called *Yuibutsuron kenkyū*[d] (Studies on Materialism), and a series of books on Materialism, *Yuibutsuron zensho*[e], also appeared. The Society was dissolved in 1938, but in the meanwhile it brought to the knowledge of the general public all the facets of Soviet disputes about Mitin versus Deborin, who was translated into Japanese, as well as Stalin's criticism, first of Bukharin, who was widely read in Japan, and afterwards of the idealistic tendency of the dialectic of Deborin. Stalin favored the position of the young Mitin, who later became the spokesman of the Stalinist position. Already in the early thirties in Japan, therefore, even more so than in the West, there was a deep knowledge of Soviet philosophy, which was in the stage of a double-front fight of Stalin against his adversaries, that is, a fight against practical and theoretical deviations on the left (Trotsky) and on the right (Bukharin).

The writer, who has written extensively on Soviet philosophy, can testify that, while the West made much more thorough studies of Marxism, Japan, already in pre-war times, had a much more complete grasp of the subtleties of Soviet philosophical disputes. There is no country, apart from Soviet

a. 永田広志　　b. 服部之総　　c. 本多謙三　　d. 唯物論研究
e. 唯物論全書

Russia itself, where Soviet thought has been so thoroughly studied as in Japan. This was partly due to the *Yuibutsuron Kenkyūkai* as well as to the amount of translation from the Russian of all the outstanding Soviet thinkers, such as Deborin, who have never been translated into any other foreign language except Japanese. It is true that not much original thought is to be found, most of it being merely the work of translation and introduction. Still scholarly work was done. Naturally materialistic trends in early Japanese thought too were considered, as we shall see in the works of Nagata Hiroshi or Saigusa, both more historians than systematic philosophers. For a systematic study of the different fields of Marxist philosophy, such as epistemology, dialectic, the identity of theory and practice, the so-called *partiinost* in Russian and *tōhasei*[a] in Japanese, which can be rendered in English by "partisanship" and means the class-conditioning of ideology, I can but refer to specialized studies like those by Ōi Tadashi. [18]

Nagata Hiroshi (1904-1946), owing to his excellent knowledge of the Russian language, was a good interpreter of Soviet philosophy. Nagata had no special philosophical training, but

---

a. 党派性

18) *Yuibutsuron kenkyū-kai* 唯物論研究会 see: Oi T., *Nihon* . . ., o.c., pp. 203-45; *Kindai Nihon shisō-shi* . . ., o.c., vol. 3, pp. 595-606; Miyagawa Tōru 宮川透 *Kindai Nihon no tetsugaku* 近代日本の哲学 (Recent Japanese Philosophy), Keisō Shobō, 1961, pp. 228-29.

Yuibutsuron zensho 唯物論全書 (Series on Materialism) was planned in 50 voll., followed by similar *Mikasa zensho* 三笠全書 in 16 voll. Mikasa Shobō was the publishing House of both series. The first series comprehends all aspects of philosophical and social problems, starting with *Kagakuron* 科学論 (A Theory of Science) by Tosaka Jun 戸坂潤 covering the history of science, past and present materialism, logic (by Saigusa H.), aesthetics, political problems, theory of war, fascism etc.

graduated from the Tokyo University of Foreign Languages in 1924, having majored in Russian. He was a prolific writer, and his writings are contained only in part in the volumes of his collected works published in 1946. His work as a translator began with the works of Akselrod and Deborin, and ended with Stalin's *Dialectical and Historical Materialism*, which established his authority among Japanese communists and materialists. His best essays, still praised by Marxists today, are those which show his most strict fidelity to the changing ideological trends of Soviet philosophy, i.e., that about the criticism of Deborin by Mitin written in 1932, and others concerning the then much-disputed identity of formal logic, dialectical logic and epistemology. His lack of knowledge of Hegel's philosophy, however, was surely an impediment to a full understanding of the richness of the dialectical method. Other major works on dialectical and distorical materialism have, no doubt, good points, although they reveal too much the character of manuals rather than of specialized studies. He must be termed a popularizer, in the good sense of the term, rather than a specialist. As a historian and author of Japanese Philosophy and Thought (*Nihon tetsugaku shisō-shi*,[a] 1938), and History of Japanese Materialism (*Nihon yuibutsuron-shi*)[b] Nagata displays a good knowledge of Japanese sources. The interpretation, though, is strictly Marxist; and if these books are a good counterbalance to idealist historians, still his point of view is far removed from standard works on Japanese thought. [19]

a. 日本哲学思想史   b. 日本唯物論史
19) *Nagata Hiroshi Senshū* 永田広志選集 (Collected Works of Nagata Hiroshi), Hakuyōsha, 1946-49, 9 vols. Concerning Nagata see: Takeuchi Y. ed. *Shōwa* . . ., o.c., pp. 302-34.

A more brilliant philosopher than Nagata is another communist thinker, Tosaka Jun (1900-1945). He graduated from Kyoto University in 1924, in which year his translation of the work of Windelband also appeared. His philosophical training was along the line of neo-Kantianism and phenomenology. His graduation work was on the problem of space in Kant. After lecturing at various schools, he became professor at Otani University in 1929. Around this time he came under the influence of Miki Kiyoshi and so turned to materialism and later on to communism. He was one of the main figures of the *Yuibutsuron Kenkyūkai* and wrote for the collection published by this society *Kagaku hōhōron*[a] (Methodology of Science), where his philosophy of science grows into materialism. He is more known, though, for his *Ideorogii no ronrigaku*[b] (The Logic of Ideology) and, in 1935, *Nihon no ideorogiiron*[c] (On Japanese Ideology), in which the influence of Marx-Engels' *Deutsche Ideologie* can be felt. He spoke, at this time, against the militaristic fascism which was already gaining control of Japan. He had to pay for his courage with prison, where he died at the early age of 45. He came from Kyoto to Tokyo, becoming a lecturer at Hōsei University in 1931, but the police were always after him, so he too had to give up his teaching and make a living by writing for magazines and doing translation work. [20]

As a conclusion to pre-war Marxist thought in Japan, we must mention here the *Collection on the History of the Growth*

---

a. 科学方法論   b. イデオロギーの論理学   c. 日本のイデオロギー論

20) On Tosaka Jun's 戸坂潤 thought see: Saigusa H., *Nihon* . . . o.c., pp. 319-49; Ōi T., *Nihon* . . ., o.c., pp. 228-38; Takeuchi Y. ed., *Shōwa* . . ., o.c., pp. 336-74; Hirabayashi Yasuyuki 平林康之, *Tosaka Jun*, Tōkyō Daigaku Shuppankai, 1960.

of Capitalism in Japan, in which the main writers were Hani Gorō, Hattori Shisō, Hirano Yoshitarō[a]. These Marxist historians went against the government interpretation of the Meiji Restoration, linking the growth of capitalism with state-intervention and absolutism. The official view of the Meiji Restoration was that of a political restoration of power in favor of the emperor, while economic historians like Honjō Eijirō[b] stressed the natural development of economic life in pre-Meiji Japan, without any political commitment. Marxist historians insisted, instead, that the Restoration was a movement toward absolutism, and against the *Rōnō-ha* (Farm-Labor group), that it was not a bourgeois revolution, but rather a form of modern Japanese capitalism, semi-feudal and autocratic by nature. Naturally this interpretation fits in better with the term "Asiatic Despotism" and "Asiatic Mode of Production" of Marx. The influence of the *Kōza-ha*[c] (the Marxist group responsible for the Collection) became prevalent in pre-war Japan and was a great factor in influencing historiography in Japan and even today it remains very strong.

World Philosophy and Nationalism

The post-war histories of Japanese thought, all written by young Marxists if not communists, have long chapters on the "Imperialist Philosophy" of the followers of the *Kyōto-ha* or the philosophical school which has Nishida for originator and Tanabe as the best disciple. Nishida himself is not much criticized, although, as we shall see, he too is not spared. Tanabe's *Dialectical Logic of Species*, 1934, is especially pointed out, as

a. 平野義太郎   b. 本庄栄次郎   c. 講座派

is his article on *Kokka sonzai no ronri*[a] (The Theory of the Being of the Nation) for criticism. In many other passages also Tanabe can easily be indicted for his irrationalism, which was divinizing the state and the emperor. Watsuji's *Fū.o*, too, can be easily turned into a *Lebensraum* conception, not too different from the Nazi one. Watsuji naturally does not belong to the Kyoto school of philosophy. As nationalist philosophers of this trend are especially singled out Kōsaka Masaaki (1900-   ), Kōyama Iwao[b] (1905-   ) and Nishitani Keiji[c] (1900-   ), as well as the less important Suzuki Naritaka.[d] The first three are mentioned also because of their philosophical importance, being even now among the leading professors of philosophy in Japan. All three graduated from Kyoto University, and all for a while belonged to the staff of their alma mater, but had to retire for a while during the purges of post-war times. All, except Kōyama, returned to Kyoto University, and their recent publications, which will be dealt with in the following chapter, prove their intellectual ability.

Their early publications show a similarity of interests, which make them an easy mark for sweeping generalizations so common to Marxist interpreters of thought. Kōsaka already in 1932 published a work on the philosophy of history which was to be the common field of research of these pupils of Nishida. In 1937 he published his *Rekishiteki sekai*[e] (Historical world), and 1942 *Minzoku no tetsugaku*[f] (Philosophy of the Nation), while also working on three studies concerning neo-Kantianism and Kant himself. Kōyama, better known for his two volumes

a. 国家存在の論理   b. 高山巌   c. 西谷啓治   d. 鈴木成高
e. 歴史的世界   f. 民族の哲学

on Nishida's philosophy, also has works on *Bunka ruikeigaku*[a] (Typology of Culture, 1939), and *Sekaishi no tetsugaku*[b] (Philosophy of World History, 1942). Nishitani, the least productive of the three, but not the least capable, besides being an expert on the philosophy of Aristotle, wrote *Kongenteki shutaisei no tetsugaku*[c] (The Philosophy of Fundamental Selfhood, 1940) and *Sekaikan to kokkakan*[d] (World View and State View, 1941). For magazines like the *Chūōkōron*[e], the three together with other intellectuals were forced to discuss during the war problems of world history and Japan, and even such philosophical problems as *"Sōryokusen no tetsugaku"*,[f] i.e., the "philosophy of total war".

I will not quote here passages which taken out of context can be read in the books quoted in the note, and which prove abundantly the thesis of their modern critics. If it is obvious that to write on such subjects, especially during the war years, was practically impossible without giving in, more or less, to nationalistic tendencies, it is also clear that not much choice was left to them. At the same time, though, it must also be stated clearly that books like Kōsaka's *Historical World* try to establish a concept of *Universalgeschichte*, which is not limited only to European history, but which includes the Oriental world as well. It is enough to read the chapter on racial interpretation of history to see how far from racist or Nazi ideas Kōsaka is. Kōyama's studies on *Typology of Culture* are an attempt to place the culture of Japan in a special category, and in the edition which came out during the war

a. 文化類型学　　b. 世界史の哲学　　c. 根元的主体性の哲学
d. 世界観と国家観　　e. 中央公論　　f. 総力戦の哲学

it was criticized by some because he did not consider Japanese culture unique and superior to all others. His *Philosophy of World History* is but an application of Ranke's view of the state and the individual, and Meinecke's *Staatsraeson*. Naturally stress was laid upon the supposition that world history was shifting from the West to Asia. More questionable is Kōyama's *Nihon no kadai to sekaishi*[a] (The Task of Japan and World History, 1943), where the emphasis on nationalism is overstressed. Kōsaka, too, relies heavily upon Ranke, and he is very critical, especially of Troeltsch, because, all in all, history was but a European consciousness, and Asia was totally neglected. [21] For Oriental thinkers this was, no doubt, a sore point which, under the stimulus of nationalism, they tried to overcome. That they overdid it is beside the point. Their masters though were at times no less nationalistic.

A nationalistic view of history was also given by Hiraizumi Kiyoshi[b], who in his *Waga rekishikan*[c] (My Interpetation of History, 1934) and *Dentō*[d] (Tradition, 1940) extolled the Imperial House and the superiority of Japanese culture. A center of nationalist trends was the Cultural (Spiritual) Research Institute (Seishin bunka kenkyū)[e] in which Minoda Kyōki[f] of Keiō University played a leading role. Minoda committed suicide at the end of the war. Other fanatical nationalists were

---

a. 日本の課題と世界史   b. 平泉清   c. わが歴史観   d. 伝統
e. 精神文化研究   f. 蓑田胸喜
21) Kōsaka Masaaki 高坂正顕, *Sekai-shi no tetsugaku* 世界史の哲学 (Philosophy of World History), Iwanami Shoten, 1942, pp. 1-7; 183-217; 447-86. For a sharp criticism of this trend see: Takeuchi Y. ed., *Shōwa . . .*. o.c., pp. 359-421; 1-83; *Kindai Nihon shisō-shi . . .*, o.c., vol. 3, pp. 715-33.

Satō Tsūji[a], Kanokogi Kazunobu[b]; but as a philosopher of value and an ardent nationalist, we must here single out Kihira Masami (1874-1949).

Kihira, who graduated from Tokyo University in 1900, was active in the philosophical world already in the last decade of Meiji times, and took part in compiling many philosophical collections and dictionaries, already mentioned in the third chapter. He became a full professor of the Gakushūin (Peers's College) already in 1919, but was associated also with many other educational institutions which were centers of studies on Japanese culture, like the Kokugakuin University[c], working along the same line as Inoue Tetsujirō. His early work on *Ninshikiron*[d] (Epistemology, 1915) is a very critical study of this field of philosophy and does not show any bias. Later on, though, in his *Gyō no tetsugaku*[e] (The Philosophy of *Gyō*[f],1923) and *Nihon no seishin*[g] (The Spirit of Japan, 1930), his nationalism, based on Hegel, was to become prominent. Kihira was not only a translator, but had also a good knowledge of Hegel's dialectic. His Philosophy of *Gyō* (a term which defies translation; "Action" does not convey its meaning) is compared by Tsuchida to Fichte's *Tathandlung* or Nishida's "self-consciousness", and is practically man's action as seen from the angle of the national ethical spirit. For Kihira history is made by the folk-spirit, which resembles Hegel's *Geist* in which we have to take consciousness of our power and active role in creating the march of history. It is through the whole, the "great *Gyō*" which is the real process. The pattern of the "Absolute

a. 佐藤通次   b. 鹿子木員信   c. 国学院大学   d. 認識論
e. 行の哲学   f. 行   g. 日本の精神

Spirit" of Hegel can be clearly seen in the threefold evolving of the spirit in the realm of art, religion and logic. In this work Kihira is critical of the Buddhist $Gō^a$ or *Karma*, because of its fatalism, while his appreciation of Oriental values is more evident in "The Spirit of Japan". Still, it is the dialectic of Hegel, so often used for the purpose of fighting nationalism by materialist thinkers, that Kihira exploits. In his *Naru hodo no tetsugaku* (The Philosophy of Becoming) Hegel's way of thinking is used to explain the coming into being of Japanese mythology, heaven and earth stemming from the Japanese gods, while the center of such eternal and evolving movement is the Imperial line. [22]

An early Hegelian and an ever-increasing nationalist Confucian ethician was Nishi Shin'ichirō[b] (1873-1943), who has to his credit also important historical studies. Tsuchida who reviews his earlier works, *The Fundamental Problems of Ethics* (1923), and *Education* and *Morality* (1923), compares him to Nishida because of Nishi's stress upon "pure consciousness", the only reality, in which moral consciousness plays the leading part. It is only in the realm of freedom, i.e., of moral-

---

a. 業   b. 西晋一郎

[22] Kihira Masami 紀平正美. *Nihon no seishin* 日本の精神 (The Japanese Spirit), Iwanami Shoten, 3rd ed. 1931. This book deals with the Japanese spirit based upon Confucianist filial piety, patriotic loyalty. *Chi to gyō* 知と行 (Knowledge and Action), Kōbundō. 4th ed. 1941. This book deals with Confucianist-Japanese morality. *Naru hodo no tetsugaku* なるほどの哲学 (The Philosophy of Becoming). 1942. Hegel's dialectics adapted to the Japanese spirit.

On Kihira's thought see: Funayama S., *Nihon kannenronsha* . . ., o.c., pp. 212-17; Ōi T., *Nihon* . . ., o.c., pp. 78-80; Tsuchida K., *Contemporary Thought* . . ., o.c., pp. 105-13.

ity, he contends, where man realizes his self-consciousness, the opposition from others, and all the social relations which constitute the whole of morality. Kant, too, and Mencius, and the samurai spirit, or *Bushidō*, are invoked in order to rationalize and moralize the irrational nature. Nishi speaks of a rational feeling, which must accomplish this task. His criticism of Western ethics and his partiality for Confucianist morality is obvious in his learned commentary published during the war, on the famous Imperial Rescript on Education, about which we spoke in the second chapter of this survey. Nishi is quite an eclectic ethician, trying to combine Western and Oriental morality. Naturally *Chūkōron*[a], which is the title of a book of his (On Loyalty and Filial Piety), the Japanese-Chinese blend of Confucianism, is always paramount, and Western principles must be adapted to Oriental standards. [23]

Chapter VII

POST-WAR PHILOSOPHICAL TRENDS

1945—1962

The Existentialism of the Kyoto School

The end of the war found Japanese philosophical circles deprived of such leading philosophers as Nishida Kitarō, Miki Kiyoshi, while post-war screening of politically compromised

a. 忠孝論

23) Nawada Jirō 縄田二郎. *Nishi Shin'ichirō sensei no shōgai to tetsugaku* 西晋一郎先生の生涯と哲学 (Life and Philosophy of Nishi Shin'ichirō sensei), Risōsha, 1953. Tsuchida K., *Contemporary Thought* . . ., o.c., pp. 97-105.

professors did little to bring new hope to the shattered academic world.

The courageous attitude of self criticism taken by Tanabe Hajime in the post-war years (which we have already review-ed to some extent) was no doubt a stimulus to his followers not to stand idly by and leave the philosophical field and the solu-tion of social problems entirely open to the Marxist thinkers. The Marxists, enjoying the newly established freedom of a capitalist democratic regime, were making a big headway in these two areas. Writing during the early post-war period in *Tembō*[a] (Vista), a short-lived magazine of the time, Tanabe readily conceded that the pillar upon which they had leaned so heavily had suddenly collapsed and that nihilism might natural-ly be expected to fill the void. He then tried to indicate a new path to the re-examination of philosophical and social problems. Whether Tanabe's philosophy of repentance and his socio-political ideas were consistent with his earlier position is open to question. Still his attitude of renewed hope and faith in the future had a tonic effect in some circles. In view of the cala-mitous defeat, existentialist philosophy with its pessimistic mood could not but be taken up by the followers of the *Kyōto-ha*, or the disciples of Nishida and Tanabe. Kōsaka Masaaki, in the September, 1947, issue of *Tetsugaku Hyōron*[b] (Philosophical Review), saw in existentialism a proof of the emptiness of modern civilization.

Before examining the development of philosophers of the Kyoto school of philosophy, which manifested more than a mere passing interest in existentialism, it should be pointed out that

a. 展望   b. 哲学評論

German existentialism and religious existentialism were the main concern of the disciples of Nishida. Sartre's existentialism was very much in vogue among journalist philosophers, as well as among other members of various literary circles. His Marxist leaning had quite a following among intellectuals; and, if as much can be assumed by the recent translation of his complete works, the number of his followers is still considerable. This popularity, though, can hardly be attributed to the Kyoto school of philosophers who rather commented on and explained the thought of Kierkegaard, Heidegger, and Jaspers. More recently, Gabriel Marcel's popularity has been enhanced by a series of nation-wide lectures that he delivered under the auspices of the International Association of Philosophy. This group, numbering among its leading members Kojima Takehiko[a] of the Kyoto school, hardly ranks with the stronger and more influential *Nihon Tetsugaku-kai*[b] (The Philosophical Society of Japan). Until a few years ago, this Society stood in direct opposition to the philosophers of Kyoto, dominated as the former was by more progressive, not to say Marxist, members.

The denomination of the Kyoto group of philosophers as a special "school" of thinkers can be said to have a theoretical basis if we recall what has been said in the previous chapter about the "philosophy of world history". Furthermore, a certain identity as a group was acquired when in the immediate post-war years the disciples of Nishida lost no time in editing the complete works of their master, as well as publishing studies on both Nishida and Tanabe. Still there is also an ideological build-up conveniently exploited by Marxists who want to split

a. 小島威彦　　b. 日本哲学会

the Japanese philosophical world into the "two camps" of idealists and Marxist-progressive thinkers. The natural rivalry existing between Tokyo and Kyoto universities also contributed to this superficial characterization.

Schematization is one of the necessary evils in writing a summary-survey of philosophical thought, and so the reader should not be deceived by the apparent simplicity of what is in reality a complex of diverse systems of thought. The reduction of vast material into some recognizable general trends is an unavoidable necessity. The analysis of the thinking of Kōsaka, Kōyama Iwao, and Nishitani Keiji, for example, reveals as many differences as similarities. Still, in the light of their writings on existentialism, ethical problems, and the philosophy of religion, a marked similarity can be noted, and, as such, these three thinkers can be termed exponents of a certain trend. These marked similarities can be recognized among other schools of philosophy as well (to be considered later), but among the Kyoto philosophers, who had in Nishida and Tanabe two creative thinkers as models, the trend of similarity is more in evidence.[1]

Kōsaka expressed his views about *Politics, Freedom and Destiny* in a work published in 1947 under the title *Seiji jiyū*

---

1) For a general survey of the first years after the war see: *Tetsugaku nenkan* 哲学年鑑 1945-1947, (Yearbook of Philosophy), ed. by Tetsugaku Nenkan Kankō-kai 哲学年鑑刊行会, Sōgensha, Osaka, 1949. The survey of pp. 1-33 is by Mutai Risaku 務台理作. For a Marxist survey see: *Bunka nenkan* 文化年鑑 (Cultural Yearbook), ed. by Minshushugi Bunka Renmei, 1949, pp. 27-32. Among the various *Nenkan* (Yearbooks) the most useful are the *Mainichi nenkan* 毎日年鑑 ed. by the Mainichi Publishing House.

oyobi ummei ni kansuru kōsatsu. Here he clearly admits that the conditioning of man is due to his socio-political environmental nature. No *metanoesis* is invoked by Kōsaka. Instead, while not escaping from a relativistic historicism, he still expresses hope in the "Logic of Research" (*Tankyū no ronri*)[a], or, the quest for serious knowledge of a reality which is a phenomenological manifestation of universal nothingness (*muteki fuhen*)[b]. While it is difficult to determine whether Kōsaka himself subscribed to existentialism, his exposition of the subject can be found in two works. The first is *Jitsuzon tetsugaku*[c] (Philosophy of Existentialism), and the second is in a treatment of Heidegger in which he debates the question as to whether or not Heidegger is a nihilist. *Japanese Thought in the Meiji Era* was edited in the post-war years, and greatly attests to Kōsaka's ability as a historian of ideas. This work was freely consulted by the author in preparing the first chapters of this survey[2].

Kōyama Iwao in 1948 published *Risei seishin jitsuzon*[d] (Reason, Spirit and Existence) a work, which marks a bold attempt to trace the deep linkage between Kant's critic of reason, Hegel's *Geist*, and the existentialism of Kierkegaard, Heidegger and Jaspers. In this book, Kōyama holds that philosophy must be a philosophy of reason which progresses into the philosophy

---

a. 探究の論理   b. 無的普遍   c. 実存哲学   d. 理性精神実存

2) Kōsaka Masaaki 高坂正顕, *Seiji jiyū oyobi ummei ni kansuru kōsatsu* 政治自由及び運命に関する考察 (Reflection on Politics, Freedom, and Destiny), Kōbundō Shoten, 1947, pp. 2-7; 207-23; 225-38.

——, *Heidegga-wa nihirisuto ka* ハイデッガーはニヒリストか (Is Heidegger a Nihilist?), Sōbunsha, 1953, pp. 196-98.

of spirit with its necessary pantheism. But freedom of man, which can take a leap either into mysticism or to existentialism as a revolt against pantheism, should instead take the direction of existence. This new direction does not necessarily mean an existentialist philosophy. The deep interest of Kōyama in the religious problems of modern civilization appears in *Gendai no fuan to shūkyō* (Present Anxiety and Religion, 1955). The present secularized civilization, which was brought about also by the religiously-inclined people as well by the intellectuals, must find a way of coexistence and harmonious development if it is to overcome the chaotic situation of modern man. This attempt at a solution to the condition of modern man's peculiar difficulty recalls in a more systematic, if less original form, the religious works of Tanabe's post-war phase. In dealing with such problems as the existence of God, Kōyama states that we cannot speak of God in terms of existence or non-existence, as when we deal with things of the physical world. Rather, he prefers the Buddhist terminology which presupposes a *satori* or illumination rather than formal logic. The importance of religion is due to the fact that it can create a civilization based on love of mankind along with moral values which, in turn, can only be based on the absolute goodness of God.

Moral problems are dealt with in another of Kōyama's works, *Dōtoku no kiki to shinrinri*[a] (The Crisis of Morality and the New Ethics, 1954). As he states in the preface, he is is not satisfied at all with the new ethics of the post-war period, which after all had been a nineteenth century form of liberalism, or the undemocratic ethics of communism. The slogan of

a. 道徳の危機と新倫理

novelty might also be applied to the recent fascist ethics (in so far as it is newer than Marxism), and as has been proved in this instance by a disastrous war; novelty for its own sake (as far as a code of morality is concerned) is no guarantee of its basic soundness. All the forms of ethics proposed in post-war Japan were quite old. The new ethics must be made by the Japanese themselves who have the advantage of a long tradition of ethics. After a critical survey of those "old" views, Kōyama proposes as the most sensible solution of the moral problems an ethic that takes into consideration both the unchanging aspects of ethics and the changing historical elements of ethics unified in the internal ethical personality, i.e., the religious man. He further advocates the adaptation of the terminology of Rousseau's *Volonté générale,* the "universal character of moral will" (*dōtoku ishi no fuhensei*)[a], as a fundamental principle of ethical effort, always keeping in mind the limits of theoretical formulation of ethical theories. For Kōyama morality must come from the eternal, of which it is as an apparition in the world, or the "third creation", as he calls it.[3]

Nishitani Keiji, who contributed articles on the social problems of modern man (*Gendai no shakai no shomondai to shakai*)[b], and a learned essay on the problem of evil (these articles were very much in demand by scholarly journals after the war) also published an important book on *Nihirizumu* (Nihilism, 1949). The book originated with a series of lectures

---

a. 道徳意志の普遍性   b. 現代の社会の諸問題と社会

3) Kōyama Iwao 高山岩男, *Gendai no fuan to shūkyō* 現代の不安と宗教 (Present Anxiety and Religion), Sōbunsha, 1955, pp. 2-5; 189-90; 196-202.
——, *Dōtoku no kiki to shinrinri* 道徳の危機と新倫理 (The Crisis of Morality and the New Ethics), Sōbunsha, 1954, pp. 1-4; 31-50; 164-65; 200-02.

on nihilism presented according to Dostoevski and Nietzsche; the latter having made the mistake of comparing Buddhism's "emptiness" (*kū*) with European nihilism. Nishitani instead sees in "creative nihilism and finitude" a fundamental unity which can span East and West. He further tries to discover a new dimension of man in this type of philosophy of crisis. The concept of "creative nothingness" is taken from Stirner, but in its twofold negation of the phenomenal world as well as of the world of eternal essences (through Nietzsche and Heidegger), there is a fundamental oneness with European nihilism. European civilization, though, has a metaphysics founded on being, and an old logical tradition which is lacking in the Orient. Nishitani nevertheless sees many positive values in Buddhism and therefore does not dispair of the future of Oriental civilization.[4]

The impact of existentialism in post-war time is not limited to the Kyoto school of philosophy only. Ethicians like Kaneko Takezō, (*The Philosophy of Rational Existence*, 1954), and Ōshima Yasumasa,[a] who has to his credit one of the most scholarly works on existentialist "situational ethics", showed how wide the influence of existentialism was and still is. Both of these philosophers, one of Tokyo University and the other of Tokyo University of Education, will be considered more in de-

---

a. 大島康正

4) Nishitani Keiji 西谷啓治, Aku no mondai 悪の問題 (The Problem of Evil), in *Shinrinri kōza* 新倫理講座 (New Ethics-Symposium), ed. by Abe, Amano, Mutai, Watsuji, etc., vol. II, Sōbunsha, 1952, pp. 1-27.
—, *Nihirizumu* ニヒリズム (Nihilism), Kōbundō, 1949, pp. 224-29.
—, *Shūkyō to wa nani ka* 宗教とは何か (What is Religion?), Sōbunsha, 1961. See, for the English translation of the first essay of this book, *Philosophical Studies of Japan*, vol. II (1960), pp. 21-64.

tail in the following pages.

As a further sign of the existentialist trend, reference here can be made to Watsuji Tetsurō already mentioned and his *Sören Kierkegaard* published in 1947. This book is a new edition of a much earlier work.

An entirely new work on existentialism was put out by the phenomenologist, Yamauchi Tokuryū. His book is entitled *Jitsuzon to shoyū*[a] (Existence and Having), and is reminiscent, in title at least, of a similar work by G. Marcel, *Etre et Avoir*. It might be noted here that Yamauchi also completed his first two volumes on *Greek Philosophy* in 1947. These volumes are a study of the foundations of Western civilization in general. This series as of 1960 has reached its fifth volume, therefore forming the most thorough study of Greek thought there has been to date.[5]

Tanaka Michitarō[b] (1902-   ) might be said to be a member of the Kyoto school by association. He graduated from that institution in 1926, and returned there to teach in 1954. Never professing a great interest in the finer distinctions of existentialism, Tanaka is known rather as one of the outstanding Platonic thinkers. He is the author of a fine introduction to philosophy, and of many learned essays. On the subject of Plato, his interests center on evolving his own brand of Platonism or idealism rather than acting as a mere commentator or philologist. His major work is *Rogosu to idea* (Logos and Idea, 1947), and the more recent *Zen to hitsuzen to no aida ni*

---

a. 実存と所有   b. 田中美知太郎

5) *Yamauchi Tokuryū's* 山内得立 works on Greek philosophy in five volumes are edited by Kōbundō, 1961. The first volume covers the Pre-Socratic philosophers, two volumes respectively deal with Plato and Aristotle.

(Between Good and Necessity, 1952). Both works were formerly published in philosophical journals as separate essays. The
linking thread of identity between the two works is to be found
not only in Tanaka's grounding in Platonic philosophy, but also
in his systematic presentation. The first, *Rogosu to idea*, presents the logos-idea metaphysical view of reality; the second,
Zen to hitsuzen to no aida ni is a sort of anthropological study
wherein the presuppositions of human freedom are discussed.
Although Tanaka devoted three essays to Plato's concept of time
in the first book, his object was not an analysis of this idea.
Rather, he strove to gain a better knowledge of reality. For
Plato, as well as for Tanaka, the second main problem is to see
the relation between reality and good, which is also the main
theme of the second book where his ethical anthropology is discussed. His knowledge of the Greek language (Tanaka is also
the author of a Greek grammar) also enhances his reputation
as the best Plato scholar in Japan today. In the two philosophical works mentioned above, Tanaka displays a marked advance beyond the level of being a mere commentator. His
achievements show a truly independent philosophical development inspired as it was by the Greek thinker.[6]

6) Tanaka Michitarō 田中美知太郎, *Rogosu to idea* ロゴスとイデア (Logos
and Idea), Iwanami Shoten, 1947, pp. 335-44.
— *Zen to hitsuzen to no aida ni* 善と必然との間に (Between Good and
Necessity), Iwanami Shoten, 1952, pp. 325-35. Other works by Tanaka
on Greek thought are: *Girisha kenkyū to humanizumu* ギリシャ研究とヒ
ューマニズム (Studies on Greece and Humanism), Kaname Shobō, 1955;
Koten no chie 古典の智慧 (The Wisdom of Classical Antiquity), Kawade
Shobō, 1955.

Post-War Marxism and Materialism

The most popular philosophical trend in Japan in the post-war years has been by far Marxist. The first years after the war brought to left-wing thinkers the freedom that only a capitalist and democratic society can make possible, and the communist and Marxist thinkers have made the most of this freedom. The great output of communist or Marxist inspired philosophical publications, the belligerent attitude maintained by communists and their fellow-travellers at philosophical congresses, the theoretical hair-splitting stress applied to communist squabbles which result in the emergence of diametrically opposed political party lines, all point to the degree to which Marxist ideas have pervaded Japanese philosophical thinking. Borrowing terminology from the Marxists themselves, this widespread adoption of Marxist ideas might be seen in its dialectical counterpart as sort of an antithesis to the frenzy of pre-war nationalism. Although the book-stores are generally crammed with publications of all sorts on communist and Marxist philosophy, original works by Japanese authors are few. The translation and commentaries offered cover the field from the classics of Marx and Lenin (and more recently, of Mao Tse-tung) to such authors as Rosental, Konstantinov and Aleksandrov. Non-Russian communist writers also have found their place on the shelves of the ubiquitous book-stalls; these writers too receive their share of laudatory reviews. The most popular among these latter are Britain's Cornforth, France's Garaudy and Lefebvre (presently in disgrace), East Germany's Oelsener and Bloch (the latter also not holding the "party line"), and Italy's Gramsci. The recently published Russian *Istoriya Filosofii* has been widely acclaimed among the Japanese philosophers. However, not many countries outside the Soviet satellites can count among its current translation of foreign periodicals a year-book on Soviet philosophy (*Gendai Sovieto tetsugaku*) which brings together the best articles published in the *Voprosy Filosofii*, the Soviet Journal of Philosophy.

This preoccupation with Marxist-communist thought has had regrettable results in the field of scholarly research. Any number of histories of Japanese thought dealing with the period from the time of Meiji until the present have fallen under this communist wave and consequently have lost much of their historical and philosophical accuracy. For lack of anything better this author was forced to make at least partial use of these materials.

The fascination, as it were, with Marxist philosophy has spread not only among those who openly proclaim themselves to be communist, but also among those who can make a distinction between social reforms and Marxist thought. In the past ten years, the Marxist philosophers have cleverly exploited the ranks of the liberal professors in Japanese universities and have gained at least their partial support. The Philosophical Society of Japan (*Nihon Tetsugaku-kai*) until recently had also been under the domination of communist philosophers. At philosophical conventions and congresses sponsored by this organization, it was not uncommon to hear heated discussion on such topics as the peace movement, condemnation of the atomic bomb, etc.[7]

The reasons why communism and Marxism have been so widely endorsed in post-war Japan are not easy to explain. One of the reasons might be found within the Japanese publishing world. Beginning in the late pre-war years and continuing during the war, many left-wingers lost their academic positions in the universities and turned to the publishing firms for employment. In this field their talents most often as not were utilized in translation work and in other non-influential capacities. After the war, as many of these former professors stayed on with the publishing firms they soon found themselves advanced to more influential posts. As a result, many publishing firms in Japan today are known for their "left-wing fringe". Typical is the case of Iwanami—one of the biggest and most respected publishing firms in Japan—which took a sharp turn to the left after the war. Awata Kenzō[a], an avowed Marxist, takes care of publications on philosophy for Iwanami, which explains also why the widely read journal *Shisō* (Thought), published by Iwanami, at times appears to be more Marxist than the communist philosophical journal *Riron*[b] (Theory).

Still another cause for Marxism's grip on Japanese think-

---

a. 粟田賢三   b. 理論

7) *Gendai Sovieto tetsugaku* 現代ソヴエト哲学 (Contemporary Soviet Philosophy), ed. by Terazawa Tsunenobu 寺沢恒信 Hayashi Reiji 林礼二, vol 1, 1955, vol. 2, 1956. From volume 3 (1958) on, the publisher is the Gōdō Shuppansha. It is imposs'ble to enumerate all the translations of Soviet books on philosophy. The most recent enterprize is the several volume edition, both in hard cover and in paperback, of the *Istoriya Filosofii* (History of Philosophy), Moscow, 5 vol. 1957-1960 rendered into Japanese as *Sekai tetsugaku-shi* 世界哲学史 (History of World Philosophy). Shōkō Shuppansha, 1958-1961, 7 vols.

ers may be alluded to as originating in the frenzy of war-time. Police surveillance in the literary field was so complete that any reference to communism by writers called for immediate and permanent confiscation of the material. As an example of the nervous attention paid to this matter by the police, it can be noted that the German Jesuit Cathrein's book criticising socialism was confiscated on the pretext that even objective criticism afforded this unwanted philosophy an underserved publicity. War-time library cards on works by Kawakami, Tosaka, and others all bear the inscription "Confiscated by Police". One is led to believe that today incidents such as these have not been easily forgetten by the Japanese, and that furthermore, they are convinced that the complete freedom they now enjoy in this matter of study and propagating Marxism is not going to be perpetually endorsed by the government.

More immediate, and perhaps still more cogent reasons for the widespread endorsement of Marxism by Japanese thinkers are to be found in the impact of Soviet world-power, and more recently that of Red China. Added to this is the quasi-guilt complex found in evidence among certain thinkers who blame themselves for the government's disastrous pre-war course by not having taken a more firm stand in resisting the government's policies. Finally, the magic of Hegelian dialectic as well as many social reasons are not to be overlooked. However, the roles of these influences have been both superficial and complex at the same time; of necessity, the analysis of their causes must be left to more extensive studies.

The most debated questions among post-war Marxists have been "Freedom under Socialism" (read Communism), handled at length in the progressive philosophical magazine *Shisō*, and

that of the role and value of formal and dialectic logic. In Soviet Russia, formal logic was again introduced into the curri-
culum of studies on the order of Stalin himself, in 1947.
Consequently, the problem arose of how to conciliate the previously much despised formal logic with the dialectical method—
the only one emphasized by Engels. In Russia this question has
been debated continuously in the post-war years, and even now
a clear solution has not been arrived at. But the fact remains,
that since Stalin's death, formal logic has been considered an
integral part of philosophical teaching. Communists abroad, and
especially in East Germany and Japan also took up this issue
and some of the thinkers in Japan have turned out to be more
orthodox than their Soviet counter-parts. Others who were
not communists but who had become interested in the debate
delivered stinging criticism against those who thought a fusion
possible. On this question of dialectic logic, the name of Matsumura Kazuto (1905-   ) must be singled out. A materialist of
long standing and a student of Hegelian philosophy, he is the
author of *Hegeru ronrigaku kenkyū* (A Study of the Logic of
Hegel, 1946). More recently, in connection also with the above-
mentioned debate, he published a book on the dialectic of Mao
Tse-tung who wrote an essay entitled *On Contradiction.*[8]

In addition to Matsumura, other prominent communist and
materialist philosophers are discussed in the following pages.

8) Ohc Seizo, *Ph:losophy in Japan,* in *Philosophy in the Mid-Century, A Survey,* ed. by R. Klibansky, Firenze, 1959, pp. 273-75.
Matsumura Kazuto 松村一人, *Hegeru ronrigaku kenkyū* ヘーゲル論理学研究
(A Study on the Logic of Hegel, Hokuryōkan, 1946.
, *Benshōhō no hatten -Mao Takuto mujunron o chūshin toshite* 弁証法
の発展毛沢東の矛盾論を中心として (The Development of Dialectic:
on Mao Tse-tung's Theory of Contradiction), Iwanami Shoten, 1953.

However, it should be noted that the listing is not complete because the younger generation has been omitted due to their great number.

One of the conquests made by the communists which caused quite a stir in Japanese university circles was that of a well-known professor of Tokyo University. Ide Takashi, born in Okayama in 1882, graduated from the Imperial University in Tokyo where he became a full professor in 1935 when he took over the chair vacated by his old master, Kuwaki Gen'yoku. Given the complete change in religious-philosophical thinking of this man, one hesitates to analyze the metamorphosis in so short a survey. The following is but an attempt to indicate the general trend of the change of views by briefly investigating his published works, viewed within the framework of his biography.

According to a statement made by Ide himself, and as quoted in a book published by Swearingen and Langen, Ide's gradual change from Christianity to communism developed largely from his own practical experiences rather than by any penetrating and profound analysis of the intellectual merits of the latter philosophy. Born of a poor samurai family, he developed a great dislike for the rich merchant class with which he came into contact during his school days. Although Kōtoku's *Essence of Socialism* made a deep impression on him, it was an idealistic and Christian form of socialism that he dreamed of as a young student. As Christianity was the only religion free of the many superstitions he saw practised about him, and being what he called, "the most ethical religion", he began attending church services. In time as he progressed up the

academic ladder from student to assistant professor to full professor, coupled with a trip through England, France, and Germany, his youthful ideas on socialism gradually vanished. In
their stead, Greek philosophy became his chief, and almost sole,
interest. Today, Ide has to his credit the best Japanese rendering of Aristotle's *Metaphysics*.

The war which soon followed with the sufferings it brought
effected a great change on Ide; and discouraged by the chaos
he witnessed about him, Ide began to see academic philosophy,
and even Greek philosophy and Christianity as tools for the
exploitation of the working class. This disillusionment with the
academic world was so complete that for a long while after the
war, Ide thought of resigning his position at the university.
Nineteen-hundred and forty-eight was also the year when the
communist party in Japan applied the "soft sell" policy in
order to gain popular support in the national elections. Ide upon
the suggestion of a neighbor, abruptly joined the communist
party. The reason which he gave at the time for this move
was that he wished to get rid of "half-baked, opportunistic ideas"
about social reforms, and the Marx-Lenin philosophy of praxis
afforded the best means to greater efficiency in resolving social
ills.

Those who have come to know Ide Takashi cannot but pay
a deep respect to his gentle personality, wrapped as it is in
shyness and modesty, though broken as it is occasionally by
some witticism and at times by sarcastic remarks. The nature
of these modest outbreaks lead one to believe that Ide at times
resents his "lapse" into Christianity and his early explorations

in the field of Christian socialism. This resentment toward his "Christian period" can be detected in his later edition of *Kami no omoi* (Thoughts on God) which might be labeled a collection of "sermons", or religious-philosophical talks based on the Gospel. To what extent Koeber influenced Ide is difficult to determine; in the above mentioned work, Ide pays him honor with a tribute of high respect. Kuwaki's influence of critical analysis is more easily discerned in the short study *Kaigiron-shi* (History of Scepticism) a work dealing with the Greek and Roman sceptics published in 1932, and re-issued at a later date.

Ide's religious inclination can be detected in his translation of Plotinus's *Enneads*. His most widely read book is *Tetsugaku izen* (Before Philosophy, 1932) which is an introduction to philosophical thinking; a work of some originality.

Ide's contribution to Marxist thought, or to philosophical thought in general since becoming an active member of the Communist Party, are marked by neither progress nor originality. *Tetsugaku kyōtei* (Manual of Philosophy, 1950) is but a routine party line introduction to Marxist-Stalinist philosophy. In one portion of this work, Ide follows Stalin's essay *Dialectical Materialism and Historical Materialism* which at one time had been incorporated into the *Short Course History of the Communist Party of the Soviet Union* but which recently has been eliminated. At present, most of Ide's activity is devoted to work as co-editor in charge of a group which is translating Marxist or Soviet philosophy. The previously mentioned translation of Aristotle's Metaphysics (the second part), a work to which he devoted many years of painstaking labor, has recently found its way to the book-stalls.[9]

Yanagida Kenjūrō (1883-   ), a former member of the Kyoto school, is another well-known professor who as a long-time promoter of Marxist philosophy recently (1960) became an official member of the Communist Party. Unlike Ide, Yanagida is outspoken and somewhat of an extrovert. He is a prolific writer, and a good speaker who has attracted a popular following especially among the younger readers. In his *Waga shisō no henreki* (The Wandering of My Thought, 1951), a kind of philosophical odyssey recently translated into Russian, Yanagida describes how he passed from an idealist position to materialism and militant atheism. His life presents the uncommon feature of a father of three children who quits his job in order to enter Kyoto University, where he specialized in ethics, graduating in 1925. Although he heard lectures by Nishida and Tomonaga Sanjūrō, it was the criticism of Marxism delivered by his professor of ethics Fujii Kenjirō that Yanagida claims to remember the best. At the time, the popular trend was toward neo-Kantianism, and Kroner's *Von Kant bis Hegel* (From Kant to Hegel) seems to have made the deepest impression on him. Around 1929, he became interested in Fichte. This study of Fichte, Yanagida claims, helped him to understand Nishida in retrospect. In 1935, Yanagida began to write on the philosophical thinking of his former master.

9) Ide Takashi 出隆, *Kami no omoi* 神の思い (Thoughts on God), Kadokawa Shoten, 1948, pp. 6; 245-56.
—, *Tetsugaku kyōtei* 哲学教程 (Manual of Philosophy), Komeji Shoten, 1950 (Aoki Shoten, 1951), pp. 93-130; 93-130; 138-15.
—, *Kaigiron* 懐疑論 (Scepticism), Kadokawa Shoten, 948.
—, *Tetsugaku izen* 哲学以前 (Before Philosophy), Iwanami Shoten, 1930.
R. Swearingen-P. Langer, *Red Flag in Japan*, o.c., pp. 194-95.

In 1941, Yanagida resigned his position at Taihoku University in Taiwan and returned to the city of Kyoto where he began teaching at various colleges. His previously published works *Benshōhōteki sekai no rinri*[a] (The Ethics of the Dialectical World, 1939) and *Nihon no seishin to sekai no seishin*[b] (Japanese Spirit and World Spirit, 1939), his study on Nishida and other books, afforded him an easy access to Kyoto academic circles. The end of the war accelerated the transition from a rejection of nationalist ideals and interest in ethical problems to materialism and finally to communism.

Yanagida, although a talented writer who has covered almost all fields of philosophical research with his post-war published books, is not what might be called profound. With the apparent intention of propagandizing and directing his writing to a popular reading public, Yanagida's contribution to scholarly research does not bear the hallmarks of deep analysis or profound insights. Notwithstanding his campaigns for pro-Soviet causes, his visit to the Soviet Union, and his more recent adhesion to communism, Yanagida still cannot be called a "hard core" communist philosopher. Only the future will show whether another *henreki*, or change of mind, will take place in this flexible thinker, who might be termed a passionate romantic.[10]

---

a. 弁証法的世界の倫理   b. 日本の精神と世界の精神

10)   Yanagida Kenjūrō 柳田謙十郎, *Waga shisō no henreki* わが思想の遍歴 (The Wandering of My Thought), Sōbunsha, 1951, pp. 72-77; 109; 124; 158; 171-75.
Among his many works the most important are: *Kannenron to yuibutsuron* 観念論と唯物論 (Idealism and Materialism), Sōbunsha, 951; *Rinrigaku* 倫理学 (Ethics), Sōbunsha, 1951; *Rekishi tetsugaku* 歴史哲学 (Philosophy of History), Sōbunsha, 1957.

Another idealist-turned-materialist of pre-war vintage though, is Funayama Shin'ichi. Funayama, born in 1907, is at present a professor in Ritsumeikan University[a] in Kyoto. Grounded in idealism at Kyoto University (1930), he soon produced *Kannenron kara yuibutsuron e*[b] (From Idealism to Materialism), and in 1932, *Ninshikiron toshite no benshōhō*[c] (Dialectic as Epistemology). The latter work is highly prized by Ōi Tadashi, who, although under the strong influence of Soviet philosophy is still considered the best historian of Marxist thought in Japan at present. Consequently, Ōi's appraisal of Funayama's work is full of criticism, directed mainly toward the latter's concept of praxis. This notion of Funayama's, Ōi claims, is influenced too strongly by Nishida, and is even tinged with the fascist interpretation of political praxis. This is but one of the criticisms levelled by Ōi against Funayama, who admittedly manifests a good grasp of Lenin's philosophy. Funayama obviously has never been regarded as an orthodox thinker, nor has he ever claimed to be such. It should be added, however, than in addition to a translation of Hegel and Feuerbach, Funayama is also the author of a history of Meiji philosophy which represents the work of a scholarly mind.[11]

A materialist of long-standing is the previously mentioned Saigusa Hiroto. Saigusa should be remembered for his role in the *Yuibutsuron Kenkyū-kai* (Society for the Study of Mate-

---

a. 立命館大学　　b. 観念論から唯物論へ　　c. 認識論としての弁証法

11) Funayama Shin'ichi's 船山信一 works on the history of recent Japanese thought have been already indicated in the footnotes and see also the Selected Bibliography. About Funayama see: Ōi T., *Nihon* . . ., o.c., pp. 206-08; 220-28; Tama G., *Gendai* . . ., pp. 209-21. pp. 209-21.

rialism) as well as for his numerous volumes on Japanese materialist thinkers. He is also the editor of important collections on Japanese thought. Saigusa's speciality is the philosophy of technology, out of which he has formulated his own theory of materialism. Saigusa is convinced that materialism is the result of an inter-action between the progressive social or technological development of society inspired by the basic material needs of a people, and the "conservative" elements within a society, which out of lack of social consciousness, are opposed to this progress.[12]

A communist philosopher strictly speaking is Kozai Yoshishige[a], known for his work as co-editor of many works including the recent *Small Dictionary of Philosophy*. This latter work bearing as it does the trademark of the Iwanami Publishing Company should in time become one of the most popular of philosophical dictionaries.

Many other professors and scholars could be mentioned here but the list would be too long. It would suffice to recall the names of Ōi Tadashi and of Yamazaki Masakazu[b], assistant professor at Tokyo University who is often associated with Marxist writers of the history of Japanese thought.

Analytical Philosophy and Other Trends

Development of philosophical thought in post-war Japan

---

a. 古在由重   b. 山崎正一

12) Saigusa Hiroto's 三枝博音 works on the history of Japanese thought have already been indicated in the footnotes. See also the Selected Bibliography. Other books by him are: *Gijutsu-shi* 技術史 (History of Technics), Tōyō Keizai Shuppansha, 1940; *Gijutsu no tetsugaku* 技術の哲学 (Philosophy of Technics), Iwanami Shoten, 1952. Concerning Saigusa see: Tama G., *Gendai* . . ., o.c., pp. 102-13.

was by no means limited to the battle between the followers of the Kyoto School and the belligerent Marxists. The attempt by certain Japanese philosophers to introduce analytical philosophy into Japan constitutes another major trend in the over-all picture of the growth of Western thought in Japan. The attempt made in this respect has been marked by an auspicious beginning and manifests signs of future development. Since 1954, a series of yearbooks has been published which contains important studies on logical positivism, the philosophy of language, symbolic logic, and the philosophy of science—all geared to the analytical method. The yearbooks are the official organ of the Association for the Study of American Philosophy, an organization which came into existence after the war with the help of an American foundation. Although the yearbooks are published in Japanese, as often as not they contain articles in English by eminent foreign philosophers. In the past, articles have appeared by Sidney Hook, Everett W. Hall, Willard Van Quine, and others. Consequently, by "Study of American Philosophy" can be taken to mean philosophical research along pragmatic, and more recently, analytical lines.

Ueda Seiji (1902-   ) a scholar of long-standing on Anglo-American thought is well-suited as editor of these yearbooks. Furthermore, as professor of philosophy at Waseda University in Tokyo he is situated in a university long known as the center of pragmatism in Japan, a fact alluded to in a previous chapter. Ueda has to his credit several studies on present English-American philosophy. Among his books, Ueda's *Keikenteki sekai*[a] (The Experimental World, 1942), and *Kōdōteki sekai*

a. 経験的世界

(The Behavioral World, 1946) must be singled out. These two
works constitute an attempt to present a psychological study
of American and English culture and spirit. They are in reality
a history of ideas.[13]

Among the English philosophers most widely read in Japan
today, (if not the most carefully studied) is Bertrand Russell,
whose complete works have been recently translated into Japanese. The *Wiener Kreis*, or Vienna Circle had its representative in Nakamura Katsumi[a] (d. 1952), Hirano Tomoharu[b],
Shinohara Takeshi[c], and Itō Makoto[d] who are now associated
with the analytical movement.

To an extent distinct from this analytical movement is a
current of thought centering around the Association for Philosophy of Science, which was rejuvenated after the war. Its official publication, the *Journal of the Japan Association for Philosophy of Science*, has been coming out since 1955. Forerunners
in the fields of philosophy of science were Ishihara Jun and
Tanabe Hajime. The latter, according to Ohe Seizō,[e] is still in

---

a. 中村克己   b. 平野智治   c. 篠原雄   d. 伊藤誠
e. 大江精三

13)   Ueda Seiji 植田清次, *Kōdōteki sekai* 行動的世界(The Behavioral World)
Risōsha, 1946, pp. 1-3.
Uyeda Seizi (a different Romanization of Ueda) is the editor of the series
Bunseki tetsugaku kenkyū rombunshū 分析哲学研究論文集 (Essays in
the Philosophical Analysis) published by the Waseda Shuppambu (Waseda University Press): I. *Ronri jisshōshugi* 論理実証主義 (Logical Positivism), 1954; II. *Gengo Imi Kachi* 言語意味価値 (Language, Meaning, Value), 1956; III. *Bunseki tetsugaku no shomondai* 分析哲学の諸
問題 (Problems of Analytical Philosophy), 1957; IV. *Kagaku tetsugaku e
no michi* 科学哲学への道 (A Way to the Philosophy of Science), 1958;
V. *Gendai tetsugaku no kiso* 現代哲学の基礎 (The Basis of Contemporary Philosophy), 1960.

the forefront chiefly as a critic of Suetsuna Joichi[a] (1898-), a leading philosopher of mathematics. Suetsuna, who makes use of Nishida's concept of "acting intuition", in the sense of unity of spacial intuition and temporal action, does not hold for abstract, formal mathematics. He attempts rather to build up classical mathematics "as well as a closed system with concrete intuitive meaning on the basis of the concrete totality of natural numbers and linear continuum." Ohe, a professor at Nihon University (Tokyo), claims that he himself takes a position similar to Suetsuna's on account of his own epistemological view of "the multiple structure of our external knowledge."

Ohe makes reference also to the development of the philosophy of physics by Tanabe, and of the Nobel prize winning physicist Yukawa Hideki[b]. Others who have contributed important historical works on the development of the philosophy and history of science in Japan are Shimomura Toratarō[c] and Nagai Hiroshi.[14]

Still another well-known name in the field of philosophy of science is that of Miyake Gōichi[d] (1895-), a professor of Tōhoku University. Miyake is also known for his study of Heidegger's thought, while in the field of philosophy of mathematics the influence of B. Russell is to be noted.

There are in addition to the societies devoted to studies of Anglo-American philosophy and the philosophy of science, a large number of learned societies covering almost every branch of ancient and modern philosophy. Included in this number

a. 末綱恕一   b. 湯川秀樹   c. 下村寅太郎   d. 三宅剛一

14) Ohe Seizo, Philosophy in Japan, in *Philosophy in Mid-Century* . . ., o.c., pp. 275-76.

are societies devoted specifically to the study of such individual philosophers of the past and present as Spinoza and
Jaspers. The Association for Medieval Studies with its branch
for philosophy and its annual publication deserves also a mention. The study of Patristic and Medieval philosophy in Japan
dates back to the time of Professor Koeber who to a great extent
influenced Iwashita Sōichi (1889-1940) in this line of research.
Iwashita, a well-known figure in the philosophical world in pre-
war times, was a graduate of Tokyo University. While abroad
doing post-graduate work, Iwashita decided to become a Catholic
priest and in time his writing came to the attention of philosophers and religious thinkers alike. Among his best works is
Shinkō no isan (The Legacy of Faith, 1942), where many religious philosophical problems are studied.

Yoshimitsu Yoshihiko (1904-1945), perhaps more productive than Iwashita, is largely responsible for the introduction
of the thought of Maritain and Gilson into Japan, while Matsumoto Masao, professor at Keio University, is at present known
as the exponent of Thomism. In his doctoral dissertation, *Sonzai
no ronrigaku kenkyū* (A Study of the Logic of Being, 1944),
Matsumoto attempts to ontologize the various types of logic
including the dialectical on the basis of the Aristotelian table
of categories.[15]

15)   Iwashita Sōichi 岩下壮一, *Shinkō no isan* 信仰の遺産 (The Heritage of
       Faith), Iwanami Shoten, 1942.
       Yoshimitsu Yoshihiko choshaku-shū 吉満義彦著作集 (Yoshimitsu Yoshihiko's
       Selected Works), 4 vols., Misuzu Shobō, 1948-1952.
       Matsumoto Masao 松本正夫, *Sonzai no ronrigaku kenkyū* 存在の論理学研究
       (A Study of the Logic of Being), Iwanami Shoten, 1944.

While the centers for Medieval studies in Japan are to be found in Catholic institutions such as Sophia University in Tokyo, and in Kyoto where the Dominican Fathers are collaborating on a translation of S. Thomas's *Summa Theologica*, many other scholars are actively engaged in Medieval studies. Most active in this field are those engaged in the philosophy of religion among whom Ishihara Ken (1882-   ) deserves chief mention. Ishihara, for many years engaged in teaching at Tōhoku University, later became president of the Tokyo Women's College (Joshi Daigaku)[a]. Ishihara is a well known expert on St. Augustine, who, like Pascal, is widely read in Japan. Another Protestant and a specialist in the theology of Karl Barth is Takizawa Katsumi (1909-) presently at the University of Kyūshū (Fukuoka). Takizawa is also noted for his research on the philosophy of Nishida. Nieda Rokusaburō (1907-) of Waseda University deserves attention for his *Shinkō no ronri* (The Logic of Faith) a comparative study of Shinran (founder of the Shinshū branch of Buddhism) and Pascal.[16]

Turning to individuals who independently of any specialized philosophical trend have made notable contributions to the development of philosophical thought in Japan, the following are

a. 東京女子大学

16) Ishihara Ken 石原謙. *Shūkyō tetsugaku* 宗教哲学 (Philosophy of Religion), Iwanami Shoten, 1922.
Takizawa Katsumi 滝沢克己, *Kāru Baruto kenkyū* カールバルト研究 (A Study on K. Barth), Tōkō Shoin, 1941.
——, *Gendai tetsugaku no kadai* 現代哲学の課題 (**The Task of** Contemporary Philosophy), Yōyōsha, 1953.
Nieda Rokusaburō 二戸田六三郎. *Shinkō no ronri Shinran to Pascaru* 信仰の論理新鸞とパスカル (The Logic of Faith: Shinran and Pascal), Ikeda Shoten, 1954.

among the most outstanding.

Ikegami Kenzō (1900-1956), a professor at Tokyo University in the tradition of Kuwaki and Itō, was by far the most capable of a long list of post-war thinkers. Ikegami's interest had always centered on epistemological problems and more than his predecessors, he displayed an independent creativity in his research. Although Ikegami's first published work of merit was *Ronrigaku*[a] (Logic), his other works are characterized by an epistemological approach which stemmed from phenomenology. His intention was to systematize all the various forms of knowledge in a kind of ontological and basic self-consciousness. In *Bunka tetsugaku kisoron* (The Theoretical Basis of a Philosophy of Culture, 1939) he considered creative knowledge in cultural activities of man. In his main work *Chishiki tetsugaku genri* (Principles of Philosophy of Knowledge, 1946), Ikegami attempts to systematize, or rather, proposes as the general principle and method of self-knowledge as it appears through the different forms of knowledge: artistic, cultural, and scientific. He further holds that philosophy should be the unity of all these types of knowledge. This latter point was also well expressed in the last chapter of *Tetsugaku gairon* (Outline of Philosophy, 1952), in which the highest forms of knowledge are considered. Ikegami whose brilliant career was cut short by cancer was also noted for his research in the field of philosophy of language.[17]

a. 論理学

17)   Ikegami Kenzō 池上謙三, *Bunka tetsugaku kisoron* 文化哲学基礎論 (The Theoretical Basis of Philosophy of Culture), Iwanami Shoten, 1939.

——, *Chishiki tetsugaku genri* 知識哲学原理 (Principles of Philosophy of Knowledge), Iwanami Shoten, 1946. See the preface.

——, *Tetsugaku gairon* 哲学概論 (Outline of Philosophy), Yūhikaku, 1952, pp. 295-346.

Kaneko Takezō (1905-   ), a graduate of Tokyo University, first taught at Hōsei University (Tokyo) but returned to his alma mater in 1938 where he took over the chair of ethics formerly occupied by Watsuji Tetsurō. Kaneko's original position stems from Hegel, concerning whom he had published a work on the latter's idea of the state (*Hegeru no kokkakan,* 1944). The impact of Hegel's' *Phenomenology of the Spirit* can be felt in Kaneko's later works also, though one is led to believe that the popularity of post-war existentialism also left its mark on his thinking. In addition to his contributions to *Rinrgaku jiten*[a] (Dictionary of Ethics) in the capacity of editor, his ethical theory can be found expounded in such works as *Jissen tetsugaku e no michi*[b] (A Way to Philosophy of Praxis, 1948), and *Contemporary Humanism and Ethics,* 1950. His book on the philosophy of praxis was preceded by still another titled *Keijijōgaku e no michi*[c] (A Way to Metaphysics, 1945). Although both works—the one on praxis and the other on metaphysics—were the result of a series of published articles, they display a definite unity, based as they are on definite metaphysical presuppositions. Kaneko's metaphysics is not permeated so much by Aristotle as it is by Hegel's dialectic of the spirit. In this, the influence of Schelling can also be detected. Oriental influences are also at work in Kaneko's thinking and these elements of Oriental thought are evident in his writing. Future historians of Japanese thought will undoubtedly have a great deal

a. 倫理学事典   b. 実践哲学への道   c. 形而上学への道

to say about this deep and complex thinker.[18]

Ōshima Yasumasa (1917-   ), a professor of ethics at Tokyo University of Education, is the editor of *Shinrinri jiten*[a] (Dictionary of New Ethics, 1961) as well as the author of several books on ethical and historical problems of culture. Ōshima's most scholarly contribution to the field of ethics is *Jitsuzon no rinri no rekishiteki kyōi—jinshin to shinjin*, published in 1956. As he states in a long introduction, the title of the book is a translation of the German *Die Geschichtliche Grenzensituation der Existenz-Ethik*, or, "the historical limit-situation of the ethics of existence". This ponderous work of more than eight-hundred pages deals as might be supposed from the translated title with situational ethics, and especially with Jaspers. Heidegger and Kierkegaard are discussed at length also.

With the sub-title *"Jinshin to shinjin"*, or, "God-man and Man-God", Oshima introduces a concept of Dostoevski (in reality of V. Soloviev's) which was widely used by Berdyaev. Ōshima nevertheless uses it as a dialectical concept in order to study the spirit of European culture.

One cannot do justice to the wealth of ideas and insights contained in this work by attempting an analysis in so short a survey. Much simpler to categorize and at the same time

---

a. 新倫理事典

18)   Kaneko Takezō 金子武蔵, *Hegeru no kokkakan* ヘーゲルの国家観 (Hegel's View of the State), Iwanami Shoten, 1944.
——, *Keijijōgaku e no michi* 形而上学への道 (A Way to Metaphysics), Chikuma Shobō, 1945.
——, *Jissen tetsugaku e no michi* 実践哲学への道 (A Way to Philosophy of Praxis), Iwanami Shoten, 1948.
——, *Kindai humanizumu to rinri* 近代ヒューマニズムと倫理 (Contemporary Humanism and Ethics), Keisō Shobō, 1950.

more typical of the point of view held by Oshima on the burning problem of moral education in post-war Japan is his *Kore kara no rinri* (Ethics for Tomorrow, 1953). Ōshima spoke out bluntly in favor of moral education at a time when to do so was to be labelled a reactionary and obscurantist by left wing educators. It was the thesis of this latter group that any sort of moral education advocated for primary and secondary schools was in reality a return to prewar militarist ideology. Oshima's ethics are grounded on *shutaisei* selfhood or individuality which must be fully established within a framework of freedom and democratic thinking and behavior.

Ōshima concludes *Kore kara no rinri* with observations on the pitfalls to be avoided by Japanese in assimilating Western ideas, and also in preserving what is good in the Oriental heritage. The remarks if taken to heart by both right- and left-wingers, would undoubtedly cause a new spirit to prevail in the Japanese culture. Further observations on Ōshima's thought are to be found in the following chapter where some conclusions are drawn.[19]

The Third Humanism of Mutai Risaku

As a conclusion to this chapter where existentialism and Marxism as predominant post-war trends were surveyed, the thought of Mutai Risaku might well serve as a synthesis of the above currents. Born in 1890 in Nagano Prefecture, Mutai

---

19) Ōshima Yasumasa 大島康正. *Jitsuzon rinri no rekishiteki kyōi-Shinjin to Jinshin* 実存倫理の歴史的境位神人と人神 (The Historical Limit-Situation of the Ethics of Existence), Sōbunsha, 1956, pp. 7-65.
——, *Kore kara no rinri* これからの倫理 (Ethics for Tomorrow), Shibundō, 1953, pp. 192-211.

today, after Tanabe Hajime's death, is considered the most important living philosopher of the older generation. A graduate of Kyoto University in 1918, Mutai obtained his degree under the tutelage of such eminent scholars as Tomonaga, Nishida, and Hatano. In Europe in 1926-1928, he broadened his scope under Husserl at the University of Freiburg, which might help to understand his early interest in phenomenology. Upon his return from Europe, Mutai was appointed professor at the newly established University of Taiwan, and from 1939 he taught at the Tokyo Bunrika University[a] (now Tokyo University of Education), of which he became president. Tama Giichi[b], a chronicler of Japanese philosophers, speaks of Mutai as the originator of a school of philosophy at the Bunrika University. Prof. Mutai is highly esteemed by his pupils (among whom this author at one time numbered himself) not only for his personal qualities of dedication and kindness but also for his good grasp of philosophical problems and clarity of exposition.

Professor Mutai, who has always been interested in the living problems of modern man, and who has always tried to sound the deep philosophical basis of human historical experience, felt thoroughly the impact of the war. From this sad experience he developed what he called the theory of "Third Humanism", the wording being taken from an article which first appeared in the February issue of *Shisō* in 1951. The theory which stands somewhat in opposition to Renaissance humanism on the one hand, and to the abstract notions of Kant on the other was later to be developed in book-form. His paci-

a. 東京文理科大学 ·   b. 田間義一

fism, and his stand against Japan's re-arming herself after the war, along with other public issues surprised many who in the light of his earlier association with the Kyoto school considered him of a more conservative bent. Mutai's "Third Humanism" in time became a popularly accepted view. Still, this view, if considered in the light of his published works, is not a mere eclectic combination of existentialism and Marxism as might first appear. As will be explained below, it is rather a further development of both Nishida and Tanabe's positions, tempered by a novel experience, and as such can be said to be rooted in tradition.

Tetsugaku gairon (Outline of Philosophy, 1958) constitutes Mutai's best post-war endeavor by far. Other works as *Shūkyō to bunka* (Culture and Religion, 1947), *Gendai rinri shisō no kenkyū* (Studies on Contemporary Ethical Thought, 1956) are collections of articles of different merit. Much in demand, Mutai wrote with a prolific flare for magazines and newspapers alike. In the course of this great output, an uneven quality developed in his writing, and at times it became confused with political issues of the moment.

Mutai's ideas developed in *Outline of Philosophy* may be found now in an abbreviated form in the essay "Two Conditions of Human Reality", translated by the Japanese Commission for UNESCO. As stated in *Culture and Religion*, it is Mutai's belief that Japanese philosophy in the past has been mostly a philosophy of history. Mutai's present concern is to find a philosophy of *Zentaiteki ningen*[a], or, "total man" in relation to the concept of mankind (*jinrui*)[b]. A concept only recent historical experi-

---

a. 全体的人間　　b. 人類

ence has brought vividly to the attention of philosophers. The idea of mankind in the past has been too abstract, and not realized fully as functioning within the two basic conditions of "human reality", (*ningen genjitsu*)[a], viz., the existential or individual condition and the social aspect of man. The actual man (the German, *menschliches Dasein*) can and must transcend the historical situation in which he lives, for the individual, while the existential and social aspects are dialectically related, the one does not necessitate or explain the other. Marxism in this sense takes a one-sided view of man in overstressing the social conditioning of man. On the other hand, this much must be said that for Mutai, sociality is in a sense a primary source since it spurns existence and the individual. Still both of these elements must be taken into account when the total man is considered, since this totality remains on a higher level of the actual man, conditioned by the two above elements. In other words, totality for Mutai means transcendency, i.e., the potentiality to overcome the existential and social conditioning of man and create new historical perspectives. Existence is really the humanizing and creative factor of the social condition.

Mutai here resorts to a new concept of mankind as the mediative element of total man. To understand the total man, we must have an ideal concept of mankind. This ideal concept of mankind is of a genus type not used either by Nishida or Tanabe. Nishida overstressed the concept of the individual, and the genus mankind was a very abstract and mystical term. Tanabe, on the other hand, rightly pointed out the importance of the species or the nation as a social conditioner for the indi-

a. 人間現実

vidual. Nevertheless, he too advocated an "absolute nothingness" in explaining the species, which then suffered for the lack
of historical conditioning. For Mutai, Tanabe's species has only
a logical value, and he fails to see the historical elements involved. Consequently, in order to correct Tanabe's species-
nation concept, Mutai subtitutes for it his own interpretation.
In the dialectic of Tanabe, which still rejects to a great degree
Hegel's concept of the state, only the mediation of mankind can
obviate the danger of totalitarianism. In this way the self-
egotism of the state is limited by the corrective influence of the
peace and the welfare of mankind, and the freedom of mankind
remains safeguarded. To this logical consideration of mankind
as a mediative concept, Mutai adds the historical consideration
of humanity. Thus for Mutai the purely abstract and logical
concept is brought to conform with the full measure of reality.
Herder and Kant, according to Mutai, considered mankind only
in the light of man's essence as the individual prescinding, as
it were, from man's historical content. Pure reason and rationalism were at the core of this vision of history centered
on such a concept of man.

Even after the works of Dilthey, Windelband, and Rickert
what we have is the merely logical content of history. Nietzsche,
existentialism, and the consequences of two world wars more
and more brought to the foreground the consciousness of a new
world community; a peaceful mankind intent on building up
an international solidarity. It is a new consciousness of mankind which, while not destroying the identity of individual nations, works toward the peace of all mankind.

In his *Ningen no rinri* (Ethics of Man), published in 1960,
Mutai adheres to a form of eudaemonism based on his total con-

cept of man. Man's happiness, according to Mutai, lies in this concept which has as its practical-ethical motivation the fostering of world peace. Furthermore, it is a eudaemonism which strives to gain man's happiness by maintaining a high regard for both humanity and personal liberty, and is to be brought about through the integration of sociality and existentiality.

These lofty ideals of Mutai Risaku cannot but be admired; and, philosophically speaking, the logical structure does not lack originality and consistency. Still, its weakness can be said to lie in going too far in attempting to rectify Nishida and Tanabe's position. In Mutai's theory, the contingent historical applications are overemphasized. The sad experiences of the last war should have been an inspiration for a more realistic type of humanism. One wonders how much utopian thought is still latent in the rosy path which the "Third Humanism" advocates.[20]

---

20) Mutai Risaku's 務台理作 bibliography up to the year 1951 can be found in *Gendai tetsugaku no kiso mondai Mutai Risaku hakase rombunshū* 現代哲学の基礎問題 務台理作博士論文集 (Basic Problems of Philosophy -Dr. Mutai R. Festschrift), Kōbundō, 1951, pp. 317-18.
——, *Bunka to shūkyō* 文化と宗教 (Culture and Religion), Kōbundō Shobō 1947, pp. 77-79.
——, *Gendai rinri shisō no kenkyū* 現代倫理思想の研究 (Studies on Contemporary Ethical Thought), Miraisha, 1956.
——, *Tetsugaku gairon* 哲学概論 (Outline of Philosophy), Iwanami Shoten, 1958, pp. 41-45; 172-75. See also *Shisō* 思想, 1951, n. 2, pp. 89-101; Mutai Risaku, *Daisan humanizumu to heiwa* 第三ヒューマニズムと平和 (The Third Humanism and Peace), Baifūkan, 1951, p. 1-36; Mutai Risaku, *Gendai no humanizumu* 現代のヒューマニズム (Contemporary Humanism, Iwanami shinsho, 1961; Mutai Risaku, *Ningen no rinri* 人間の倫理 (Ethics of Man), Daimeidō, 1960, pp. 183-92; in English: Mutai Risaku, Two Conditions of Human Reality, in *Philosophical Studies of Japan*, vol. I, 1959, pp. 13-31. Tama G., *Gendai* . . ., p. 13.

Chapter VIII

CONCLUSIONS: WESTERN PHILOSOPHY VERSUS ORIENTAL CULTURE

The Birth and Diffusion of Ideas and Philosophies

At the end of this survey the reader may well expect a balance sheet of the hundred years of Japanese philosophy which we have reviewed. Furthermore, he may feel entitled to some judgments on vast problems like the Japanization of Western thought or the possibility of the meeting of Eastern and Western philosophy, given the currency that such ideas have today in the cultural and political world. Not to disappoint the reader, I shall state at once that, though I will offer some tentatively and necessarily superficial generalizations on Japan's modern philosophy, I am of the opinion that problems like those mentioned in the preceding sentence are so complex and frequently have so little to do with the history of ideas, that the better part of wisdom is not to write about them instead of trying to solve them by recurring to the unqualified generalizations of the journalist or dilettante.

Since, however, too many write about these problems, and with a great deal of self-assurance, it will be useful to state in a negative way some of the most common pitfalls that can swallow up the overly ambitious student of comparative cultures. This negative approach, it need hardly be said, will not save me from succumbing to the weakness I have just condemned. In partial atonement for these lapses into "generalization-itis", I encourage the reader to take my generalizations with the classical grain of salt. In other words, in the course of this chapter

I will deny and try to remind the reader occasionally that the few positive judgments which I feel bound to pass are based upon good though inadequate sources. In no sense can the reader in this field of history of ideas expect statements which have a "scientific" validity, even if we interpret science in the broader and more humanistic sense.

As a typical example of hasty generalizations I shall adduce, first of all, the unqualified statement on the lack of originality in Japanese thought in the past and in the present. Orientalists of past generations were almost all experts in Indian and Chinese rather than Japanese thought and tended, as a consequence, to look down on Japanese Buddhism and Confucianism as by-products of small importance. Confronted with such giant brothers, Japan indeed looked like a small pygmy. Early Japanologists, like B. H. Chamberlain, spread the idea that the Japanese people had little speculative power. Later foreign experts, as well as some Japanese who were fond of stressing the peculiarity of the Japanese soul in its emotional and artistic achievements, perpetuated this hasty judgment.

I will not enter into a refutation of such evalutions as they bear on the past except to say that they are not corroborated by detailed studies of the thought of early Japanese thinkers. As far as recent philosophy goes, it must be said that thinkers like Nishida, Tanabe, Takahashi Satomi, Watsuji, Hatano, Miki Kiyoshi and Mutai Risaku deserve a place in world philosophical history. Whether the best of these can be compared with recent great philosophers of the West is obviously an open question, not least because the stature of contemporary Western thinkers is very debatable. At any rate, it is safe to say that in Japan, in the very short span of the past one-hundred years of a Western type of philosophical activity, new terminology, new systems, and even a kind of new logic have been elaborated. Naturally, if global systems like those of India, China and the whole of western Europe are taken as the standard for the evaluation of philosophical creativity, Japan comes out very badly indeed. But if instead of taking the whole of western Europe as a unit, we consider individual countries, then we see that many Japans can be found in the West also. That is to say, in the past and in the present, many other nations have failed to produce great philosophical systems.

Later in this chapter I shall consider this question of philosophical creativity in greater detail, but now I would like to present a second example of the type of hasty generalizations which should die an unlamented death. This one is advanced in different forms as an "explanation" of the claim that only idealistic or conservative ideology has been developed in Japan. In post-war times social, or rather, Marxist-minded critics, irritated at not finding materialistic thought, much less democratic ideas in their Oriental heritage have shown as much imagination in explaining this phenomenon as their fanatic, nationalist colleagues of pre-war days who saw originality and deep thought everywhere in Japanese culture. One of these "progressive" thinkers, a professor of Nihon University, Yamazaki Ken, invites Japanese people to think with "the head", explaining that in the past "the poverty" of philosophy in Japan was due to the fact that thinking, being a monopoly of the bureaucracy and not spread among the masses, was only a function of absolutism.[1]

1) Yamazaki Ken 山崎謙, *Nihon gendai tetsugaku no kihon seikaku* 日本現代哲学の基本性格 (The Basic Feature of Japanese Philosophy) Bunshōsha, 1957, pp. 9-28.

For this reason, very likely, Marxist philosophers write books with the captivating title *Philosophy for the Millions*.

Saigusa Hiroto, the materialist philosopher already mentioned and an expert on the history of Japanese thought, takes a much broader cultural view to illustrate why in the past neither materialism nor philosophy in the Western sense ever developed. Saigusa goes back to Kitabatake Chikafusa's[a] *Jinnō Shōtōki*[b], written in 1339 to relate the history of the true succession of the divine emperors from the era of the gods to his own times. In this work of six centuries ago Saigusa sees already well established what he believes to be the major obstacle to the rise of materialistic thinking, namely, the claim for the divine origin and support of Japan polity. The national spirit of Japan, unified into the harmonic whole of the *Kunshi fushi no kuni*[c] (The Immortal Land of the Princely Man), could not allow the individual to express free and progressive ideas. Buddhism, Confucianism, and the *Geidō*[d], or the "Way of the Arts", so influential in Japanese life, created a culture which became too pliable an instrument in the hands of the ruling upper classes.

Saigusa ventures further into the question why, not only in Japan, but in the Orient in general, there has not been much materialistic philosophy. India, for instance, while developing mathematics, did not make use of it for technical applications, and therefore (Saigusa claims) materialism did not grow, for materialism and progressive ideas are generated from the conflict between man's technical needs and the conservative trends of the time. Saigusa also quotes the materialist thinker of Meiji times, Nakae Chōmin[e], who advanced the view that in the Orient

a. 北畠親房   b. 神皇正統記   c. 君子不死の国   d. 芸道
e. 中江兆民

no clear cut thesis (*shugi no kakuritsu*)[a] has ever been formulated and that no logic has ever taken root in the East. Saigusa, much more conversant with Indian thought than Nakae, drew his most striking explanation for the absence of materialism in Oriental thought from a consideration of the differing attitudes toward nature found in the East and West. The ideographs or characters for nature in Sino-Japanese language form the compound *shizen*[b], which, according to Saigusa, denote a spontaneous process (*onozukara shikaru mono*)[c], where man is absorbed in the becoming of things. In the West on the other hand, men is looked on as the conqueror of nature, which is expressed as an objective reality, in opposition to the subject. Indian thought in the Rig-Veda, expresses the fundamental elements of things in unreal terms based on negation, quite differently from those used in Greek philosophy. Even China, with its very practical social philosophy, has nothing to compare with the Greek *physis* or the Roman *natura*, but finds its philosophical center in the abstract *li*[d] pervading all things.[2]

Saigusa's considerations are not hasty generalizations as in the case of Yamazaki. They are, though, sweeping generalizations in another sense pretending to embrace the whole of Eastern or Western thought. Against this holistic trend, the reader is invited to see in a much more systematized form and with much more wealth of material the same questions treated in the important volume of Nakamura Hajime, *The Ways of Thinking of Eastern Peoples*. From Nakamura's work, as well as from that of another professor of Tokyo University, Kawada Kuma-

a. 主義の確立　　b. 自然　　c. 自ずから叱る物　　d. 理
2) Saigusa Hiroto, *Nihon* . . . . ., o.c., pp. 11-38.

tarō[a], the reader learns first the shallowness of such generalizations as "the Oriental mind" or "Western thought". Experts, both in the West and in the East, know that such terms have no more than a geographical connotation. Nakamura, and with him all the experts in the field, is against a terminology which would incorporate into one way of thinking the thought life of Indians, Chinese, Tibetans and Japanese. Each people has is own characteristic and to speak of the "soulful" or "mysticointuitive" Oriental mind, in contrast to the "materialistic" or "positivistic" Western mind, is to ignore all the different and contrasting tendencies which have flourished both in the East and in the West. No expert today dares to affirm that there are features exclusively shared by all the East Asian peoples as a whole. A detailed analysis of different peoples reveals their different characteristics even within some common religious background, which, it may be remarked in passing, is common mostly because it is not analyzed in detail. [3]

In the West, where socio-anthropological studies of cultural phenomena are fairly advanced, the great majority of scholars is against any form of holism, integralism, or biologico-organicist unity of cultural phenomena. Some writers have even coined new terms to express the complexity of individual cultures. Sorokin speaks of "cultural congeries", Gurvitch of "heterogeneity" of cultural traits, German sociologists following Alfred Weber, of *Konstellation;* and Kroeber, the dean of American anthropologists, has indicated at least five "cultural strata" or

a. 川田熊太郎

3) Nakamura Hajime. *The Ways of Thinking of Eastern Peoples.* Japanese National Commission for Unesco. 1960. pp. 623-44.

layers in Mexican culture. Historians, like Marrou and Bar-raclough (to cite only two recent examples), are even more skeptical about the alleged unity of cultures and civilizations.

From such considerations we may modestly conclude that the greater the geographical and temporal extension of cultures the less meaningful are generalizations concerning them. Hence, judgments about "the East" or "the West" are little more figures of speech than statements with a definable meaning. This is obviously true of the so called super-civilizations or terms like East and West, which comprehend half of the globe and run for thousand of years.

Even the serious work of Nakamura is occasionally marred by overly broad generalizations, for one will find lumped together testimonials and quotations from periods a hundred, even a thcu-sand years apart, as if one common label or one "ideal type" could include so many changing cultural trends. The way of thinking, even in the pretended more static societies of the East, cannot be fossilized into one formula, if the span of time is so long. The terms and expressions of one age may be retained in later ages but they usually assume a different connotation with the passing of centuries, or even shorter periods.

Returning now to the problem of the birth of cultures and philosophical ideas or rather the correlation between one cul-tural phenomenon and philosophy, we can do no better, it seems to me, (because no grounded "imaginative" theory has been proposed about the birth of culture in general), than consider a few remarks taken from the masterly work of A. L. Kroeber, *Configuration of Culture Growth.*

First of all, Kroeber shows clearly the "spottiness" or rarity of philosophical creativity. India, China, the Eastern Mediterranean area (Greeks and Arabs), and Western Europe have been centers of philosophical activity. Many other cultures did not produce any great philosophy. Secondly, this creativity does not last very long; it comes and disappears or dies down after a period of two or three hundred years of activity, for no plausible reason at all. Thirdly, neither geographical, nor racial, nor economic nor technical "causes", not even the general flourishing of other spiritual aspects of a culture can explain the rise of a new philosophy or a new wave of philosophical activity.

No real patterns, let alone laws, can be detected in this intriguing process of the birth and diffusion of ideas. If Western medieval philosophy, as well as Indian thought, are born within religion, the philosophies of Greece and China are conceived outside that womb. While there is some relation in the Arabic-Muslim world between philosophers and natural-scientists no counterpart in the Indian, Chinese and European medieval world can be found. Writing, an important tool for cultural development though it is, seems to have little to do with philosophical thought. In Mesopotamia and Egypt writing was commonplace thousand of years ago, but no philosophical system has come from those lands. Greek philosophy starts some three hundred years after the Greeks learned how to write, Chinese philosophy followed more than six hundred years after the beginning of writing in China, while systematic Indian thought may be even earlier than Indian writing. Historical materialism or what strikes me as its more sophisticated version, economic materialism, has to explain why the Hellenistic Alexandria for all its prosperity did not produce any philosophy comparable to that of the Athens of Plato and Aristotle or why Soviet economic and technical achievements are accompanied by a "poverty of philosophy" which has few equals. But even leaving aside technico-economic explanations, why is it that the culturally flourishing Renaissance did not produce great philosophers? [4]

Concluding this point, we must state frankly that the outburst of philosophical creativity is not only a rare phenomenon, very erratic in its course, and not easily correlated with other aspects of culture, but also that it is a cultural mystery, to which nobody has as yet given a satisfactory explanation. The only positive result of the arduous labors of those who have studied this question is the demolition of many theories of the past which with scanty illustrations have tried to explain this baffling problem. Only the uninitiated will undervalue the importance of this seemingly negligible finding.

Another contribution made by contemporary cultural anthropologists—one which can help us in our understanding of the value of Japanese culture—is the new evaluation given to such a pejorative term as "borrowing". Far from being a sign of cultural inferiority, the willingness to borrow and to assimilate foreign traits and especially cultural systems is interpreted as evidence of vitality. To use the words of an expert on *Acculturation of Culture,* A. Ferguson, people "borrow often that which they are disposed to invent". Assimilation of cultural phenomena is far from being equivalent to passive receptivity; rather, it involves local adaptation, a kind of creativity. Those who disparage Japanese "borrowing" contend, of course, that foreign elements have been superimposed on, rather than har-

4) A. L. Kroeber, *Configuration of Culture Growth,* Berkley and Los Angeles, 1944, pp. 75-94.

moniously assimilated into, the earlier culture. Leaving aside the question of Pre-Meiji borrowing and considering only the importation of a Western type of philosophy, I do not think it can be denied that a new type of philosophical thinking has taken root in Japan and that it has flowered in new themes and formulations which may be called original and creative. I shall return to this point later when I discuss the characteristics of recent Japanese philosophy.

Coming now to the diffusion of ideas, it must be admitted that in the past as well in the recent development of Japan the socio-political situation was not always favorable to the spreading of cultural systems from abroad. Thus, for example, the political power of the Tokugawa checked the spread of Christianity, while it favored a special brand of Confucianism. Nonetheless, before looking for external reasons from the sociopolitical sphere for the spread and diffusion or the distortion and adaptation of a system, we should consider its dynamics and self-asserting logical content. The internal logical dynamism of Western thought prevailed, after all, over the seclusion policy of the Tokugawa. The cultural impact of a system can also prevail upon a too static conception of a mythical "soul" of nation. Lest the term "Japanese mind" be misunderstood, I hasten to add that it is not to be considered as an organic entity, but, rather, a cultural phenomenon which is formed, changed and regenerated from generation to generation. [5]

If we keep these points in mind we can explain more economically, I think, why Western philosophy from the Meiji times on was imported as a new learning, remained as such, and was

5) P. Sorokin, *Social and Cultural Dynamics*, Boston, 1957, pp. 630-46.

not much Japanized in the sense of being reduced to Buddhist and Confucian categories. Eager Japanese going abroad found a new way of thinking, they had no qualms about adopting it as something new and different, no qualms either about becoming adepts of Western philosophy. Adaptation of a fashion did take place, but it followed new paths which had never before been explored by Japanese thinkers. New wine was poured into old vessels, if you will, but the vessels, though made of Japanese clay, began to change their shape as they received the wine.

The points of resemblance between Western and Japanese philosophers during the past one-hundred years are much more numerous than the differences. I emphasize these points partially to call attention to the inadequacies of those attempts to explain why neither materialism nor positivism, but rather German idealism, became prevalent in Japan.

First of all, it is not true that such trends did not develop, both materialism and positivism having had no little success in Japan. Again, German idealism (another holistic and excessively wide concept) did not enjoy the sway which is claimed for it. Finally, the reason given by P. Lüth for the comparative flourishing of various kinds of idealism—the congeniality between the soul of Japan and the German *Geist*—, and the explanation that political reasons were behind the acceptance of idealism are more ingenious than convincing. The facts will not support them. The pioneers of Western philosophy, like Nishi Amane and Tsuda Mamichi, imported the empiricism and positivism they found abroad. Katō Hiroyuki cultivated Darwinian materialism, which was in vogue in the West. In the following years, as Japanese philosophers progressively discovered the wealth of German philosophy in all its forms they imbibed and propagated all types of German thought, from its most idealistic trends to the most materialistic ones. In a sense, there is no other country which can boast of such a variety of philosophical trends as Japan. Developing within the common cultural heritage of the past, the history of the last hundred years of Japanese philosophy shows so many different orientations that it is a real problem to summarize some specific trends. This is another clear indication that cultural phenomena are not so strictly correlated and that changes in one aspect of culture may have little or no influence on other phases of the same culture.

There have been nationalist philcsophers, like Inoue Tetsujirō and Kihira Masami, who were inspired by political ideology in their philosophical ideas. It is undeniable, too, that some of the Kyoto school of phlosophy succumbed to political pressure. These facts, however, do not yet explain why Inoue took up the *Identitaets* theory to overcome materialism and idealism nor why Kihira was fond of a special brand of Hegel's dialectic. We must not forget that German philosophy, so rich in its creativity in the past three centuries, has influenced not only Japan but every nation in the world. If we consider this matter more closely, we might ask why it is that Tokyo University, the most important center of learning of Japan, never went much fcr themes which were characteristic of her rival Kyoto University? A critical spirit based on Kantian studies has prevailed there. Not only did this type of idealism produce such a staunch democrat as Kuwaki Gen'yoku, but also no nationalistic trends were much supported by Tokyo University professors. We might also ask those who write lcosely about "special affinities" and political ideologies as the key to understanding Japan's assimilation of Western philosophy, why in the years after the first world war, many Japanese students brought home not only conservative German thought, but, as did Miki Kiyoshi, much socialism and Marxism from Heidelberg.

As a last remark on the subject of the diffusion of ideas, I would like to state that, with all the consideration due to general cultural reasons, which are advanced as the reasons to explain the choice of a line of thought by a philosopher, they are not of much relevance to the student of the history of philosophy. If we take Nishida as an example and consider his evolving philosophical thought, we can determine that his general inspiration stems from the background of Mahāyāna Buddhism and Zen. Nonetheless, this background does not give even a hint why Nishida in his study of Western thinkers started from James and Bergson, went through Fichte and Hegel, and produced in the end a "logic of place" which, though inspired by many other ideas, is finally Nishida's own formulation. In other words, we cannot explain the flowering of a great philosopher by pointing to the cultural soil in which he is rooted. We must go much further and consider who tilled that soil, what rains fell upon it, and—most important of all—what was the inner quality of the seed, namely the creativity and novel approach of the great thinker.

Some Characteristics of Japanese Philosophy

Being skeptical of generalizations and nevertheless not able to escape the predicament of describing some patterns of recent Japanese philosophy, I shall limit myself to some observations which make no pretense to be exhaustive. Let us recall at the outset of this section that the initial task of Japanese thinkers was to study thoroughly everything which had been produced in the West, from Thales to Sartre, and to explain the "new thought" to their collegues in other fields and, more broadly, to the educated public. That they did a superb job is beyond dispute. Only because of their success can we explain the variety of philosophical trends which in the short span of one-hundred years were imported and diffused and, in varying degrees, domesticated. Many Japanese philosophers were more than purveyors of Western ideas. The most creative thinkers among them set out to supply what was felt to be the most striking lack in the Oriental philosophical heritage, namely, a new logic which would enable them to compete with Western philosophers. In this quest the best minds, like Nishida, Tanabe, Takahashi S., Mutai and others have spent and are spending a great deal of time and energy. The earlier vogue of Kantianism as well as the current popularity of analytical logic in philosophical circles is a sign of the same fundamental desire to work out a new logic.

To highlight as a characteristic feature of recent Japanese philosophy the quest for a new logic is to invite the objection that this is in contrast to what is so often repeated—namely, that the Japanese are almost congenitally disinclined to logical thinking. Nakamura Hajime has a long chapter in his *The Ways of Thinking of Eastern Peoples* on the "Irrational Tendencies" of Japanese people. These tendencies can be summarized in the following points: disregard for logical rules, lack of logical coherence, lack of ability in forming complicated ideas and a fondness for simple symbolic expressions, disregard for the objective order, and a general immaturity of logic connected with the preference for an intuitive and emotional way of thinking. [6]

Whether the remarks of Nakamura are convincing I am not going to dispute. Quite a different picture could be painted, however, if Japanese philosophers and their way of thinking were studied instead of that of the man on the street or that revealed in literary documents and religious formulations. It is true also that the *jōteki bunka* or culture based on feeling described by Nishida as typical of Japan presupposes a logic of emotion and of an intuitive reasoning rather than a logic of concepts and definitions. It must be also admitted that a Western reader will detect many alogical transitions in the way of thinking of Nishida, Inoue Tetsujirō, Kihira and others.

Nonetheless, this aspect of Nishida's thought (to deal with him now) is not his strongest. Furthermore, it is precisely this "alogical" aspect which led Kuwaki and with him many other philosophers to show a more or less open disdain for the founder of the Kyoto school of philosophy, and to oppose to it the more critical Kantian epistemology. The relation between newer types of logic and that of the past poses a question which defies a simple solution.

Funayama Shin'ichi has characterized the logic of Japanese idealists as based upon the Buddhist term of *soku* or *sunawachi*, which expresses the relation of identity between two different terms or between opposing aspects of things. Typical in this sense is Inoue Tetsujirō's *"Genshō sunawachi jitsuzai-ron"* (Phaenomenon as Realism). In this article Inoue superimposed the Buddhist term *soku*[a] (*sunawachi*) on the *Iden-*

---

a. 即

6) Nakamura H., *The Ways* . . ., o.c., pp. 462-527.

titaetsrealismus in order to go beyond materialism and idealism by identifying the phenomenon with reality. I have already mentioned how Tanabe Hajime used *soku* to express the contrasting and nonetheless coexisting aspects of reality in the same subject. Other thinkers too could be mentioned, who while not directly using such a term still were fond of dialectical identification of opposite elements of phenomenological reality. [7]

Funayama's generalization, however, does not stand critical and more detailed examination. Recent Japanese philosophy has too many different forms of idealism to be squeezed into this Procrustean bed of *soku* logic. Ōnishi, Kuwaki, Itō, Abe Yoshishige, Amano, as well as many of the Kyoto school are not so fond of this type of logic. Nishida's logic of place, Takahashi Satomi's "Pan-inclusive dialectic", and even the *soku* logic when used by Inoue or Tanabe are quite different in specific content from a single type of *soku* logic.

Mutai Risaku in his *Basho no ronrigaku*[a] (The Logic of Place, 1944) is more correct when he described the Japanese logic of the past as a "existential way of thinking" rather than a formal logic. In the West, Mutai observed, Aristotle's logic, Kant's transcendental logic, and Hegel's dialectic have been developed but in the East, except for Indian logic, not much has been done. Therefore, following Nishida, Mutai searched for a logic of space to be based on *kokoro*[b] (Pascal's *coeur?*), wherein intuitive understanding of social relationships would be paramount. Out of this a logic of social communication could arise. This emphasis of Mutai is well grounded when we consider the

a. 場所の論理学   b. 心

7) Funayama S., *Nihon* . . ., o.c., pp. 309-10.

importance that the "social nexus" had and still has in Japan.

It is regrettable that Mutai has not evolved this type of logic in post-war years, perhaps because he has realized some of its possible weaknesses.

I will conclude this discussion on the attention paid to logic by Japanese philosophers with the suggestion that a shift in meaning of the term *shisaku*[a] or thinking (the closest equivalent to *tetsugaku* or philosophy) may give a hint as to how logic will develop in Japan. This term in the past connoted that thinking was about abstruse matters. Nishida, who used it in the title of two of his books, gave it the nuance of what it means to the ordinary Japanese—namely, a living and existential approach to philosophical problems. This meaning of *shisaku*, vague though it be, may well be a characteristic of the philosophical approach typical of Japanese thinkers.

Another characteristic feature of recent Japanese thinkers is the use and abuse of the dialectical method. The quest for a new logic has landed them often enough, not in the fog of Hegelian dialectic in the strict sense, but in the mistiness of a wide dialectical approach, which, as Ōnishi has said about Inoue Enryō, tried to combine "oil with water". Some Japanese have themselves been very critical of this method. Yoshimitsu, for instance, remarked that the tendency to apply the panacea of dialectic to problems which could be easily solved by traditional logic was a sign of the spiritual poverty of Japanese philosophy. He added ironically that, "if this method is described as typically

a. 思索

Oriental and Japanese, the effect on weaker minds is magical". [8]
While granting the fondness for "dialectical mannerism" on the part of some thinkers, we must not forget the good points which even such a method has. It is not too surprising, given the fact that Japanese society has passed through critical moments marked by the fast changing tempo of its structure and ideology, that even independent and capable thinkers were attracted by a method which seemed to present a key to the interpretation of strongly contrasting and paradoxically coexisting aspects of culture. This condition of Japanese culture is, I think, a good instance of the way in which the general cultural background produces a common mood. Needless to say, this fact must be balanced by the consideration that specific forms of dialectics must be evaluated in their own logic and formulations.

Another typical feature of Japanese philosophy is its interest in man and even in the individual. Perhaps, because in the past the function of the individual was neglected and personality not much cared for, a wave of personalistic trends in philosophy and cultural studies can be noticed. This interest has taken different forms in Takayama Rinjirō (Chogyū), Abe Jirō and others according to their different philosophical inspirations. So strong was this interest that even when the tide of Hegelianism rose high and the individual was again submerged in the dialectic of the state, this trend persisted, becoming increasingly a dialectical process where, more than the individual as such, the problem of *shutaisei* became prevalent. *Shutaisei*, which can be

---

8)   Yoshimitsu Yoshihiko's 吉満義彦 preface to the translation of J. Maritain, *Elements de philosophie: Keijijōgaku joron* 形而上学序論 Kōchō Shorin, 1942. pp. 27-28.

translated as "selfhood" or better as "individuality", means the personal experience of the individual with society and the state, or, in the case of philosophy of religion, the place of the individual in front of the absolute. It has little connection with subjectivity in the epistemological sense, meaning rather the subject in the ontological or existential sense. It seems, at times, to mean the affirmation of the self against the political and social reality or an establishment of a place of escape in the interior solitude of the ego. This tendency to highlight *shutaisei* can be noticed in Nishida, Tanabe, Watsuji and Miki Kiyoshi. In postwar times it has been a common subject of discussion among Marxist and socialist minded philosophers. Just as in the early year of this century different conceptions of man appeared, such as those of nationalistic personalism, religious and ethical individualism, the Nietzschean cult of man and worship for representative personalities, so later many forms of *shutaisei* emerged. Today at least three views can be discerned: the existentialist, the Marxist, and the socio-pacifist of Mutai Risaku.

This interest in man and the individual did not result in a really new anthropology. Even if we include the attempts of Watsuji Tetsurō, who made a systematic effort to build up a new ethical anthropology, no new school of thought has emerged. Lack of adequate epistemological premises or eclecticism may be adduced for this failure in the early thinkers, while cultural factors may be used to account for deficiencies of later philosophers. Whatever the reasons for this failure, the fact that philosophers are deeply concerned about the individual must be noticed and recognized. This lively interest will no doubt pervade the works of future thinkers also.

Two fields of philosophy which have more relation with the

Japanese cultural background are no doubt ethics and philosophy of religion. Here we can easily point to an Oriental mood and way of thinking which heavily influenced the ethical philosophy of Watsuji Tetsurō, and the philosophy of religion of Nishida, Tanabe, Nishitani Keiji and others of the school of Kyoto.

It is well known that Confucian tradition adapted to the Japanese reality played a paramount role in ethics from the Meiji times up to the end of the last war. The Imperial Rescript on Education and the compulsory textbooks on moral-national training did obviously hamper academic freedom, even in the universities, not even Watsuji escaping from this restriction. Still there were some outstanding exceptions such as Ōnishi Hajime, Amano Teiyū, and Fujii Kenjirō, to mention but the most famous ethicians. As a broad characteristic of Oriental or rather traditionally minded ethicians, we can say that they studied "social morality" rather than ethical principles, that is, the moral behavior of man in society more than the philosophical basis of ethics.

In post-war years when the problem of a new morality became a burning question and the old tenets had to be rejected, different forms of Western ethical ideas have been considered and discussed. Neither outstanding solutions nor new approaches are yet in view. In the educational field nobody, obviously, wants to go back to pre-war Confucian moral training, and Buddhism, too, seems to have very little to offer. Ōshima Yasumasa, the ethician already considered in the preceding chapter, in his *Kore kara no rinri* (Ethics for Tomorrow) invites the Japanese to use a more critical approach to ethical problems, to build up a better *shutaisei* (selfhood), to avoid basing ethical principles, as in the past was done, upon *ninjō*[a] or human feeling. He also criticizes both the propensity of the Japanese people for extreme points of view, be they of the right or the left, and even more so the attitude to take the present and most recent trend as the best and truest. Sound as those views are, they lack a positive philosophical basis. [9]

If we consider philosophy of religion as a special field, it is interesting to note that Christian-oriented philosophers are rather numerous, Hatano Seiichi being the most outstanding example. Religious philosophers, rather than specialists in philosophy of religion, like Nishida, Tanabe, although undeniably influenced by Christian existentialism, are more inclined to a type of Buddhist nothingness as presented in the cultural Japanese heritage. Nishitani Keiji, too, is definitely a purveyor of an Oriental type of philosophy of religion.

Funayama emphasizes that Japanese idealists are neither pantheists, nor, to be sure, theists in the Christian sense of admitting a transcendent God. They are, rather, "spiritualists", or philosophers of the *kokoro* or "mind". As a matter of fact though, the meaning of *kokoro* varies greatly even among "spiritualists". The real philosopher of *kokoro* or mind was Ishida Baigan[b] (1685-1744), the founder of *Shingaku*[c] or of the "Learning of Mind", who tried to combine Confucianism, Buddhism and even Shintoism in his new doctrine. But philosophers, like Nishida, Tanabe, and others are too well trained in Western philosophy to be vulnerable to the charge of confusing their terminology. Nishida, for instance, qualifies his position

a. 人情　　b. 石田梅巌　　c. 心学

9) Ōshima Yasumasa, *Kore kara no rinri* . . .., o.c., pp. 191-211.

as "panentheismus" and thereby does disassociate himself from any traditional type of pantheism. It must be confessed, however, that the more one probes Nishida's mind the more one would like further clarification on this key concept. But Japanese thinkers like Nishida refuse to enter into these ultimate problems and transmit them to religion. And here we enter into a field which is not easily dealt with in Western philosophical categories, which, it must be said in passing, cannot easily cope even with Western religion.

Among many other things which could be mentioned about Japanese religion, we must remember that in Japan the three main forms of religious allegiance—Shintoism, Buddhism and Confucianism—created a culture where a relativistic syncretism came to permeate the way of thinking of the people at large, as well as experts in the specific field of religious philosophy. Classical examples of syncretist thinkers were Inoue Enryō, Nishimura Shigeki. Against syncretism and eclecticism, the above mentioned professor of comparative philosophy, Kawada Kumatarō, spoke in strong terms urging, in addition, that not only Western thought be considered as philosophy, but Buddhism also. To Western readers this last point may come as a surprise accustomed as they are to many books on the philosophy of Buddhism. In Japan though, especially among the professional philosophers, very little has been done to explain the philosophical content of Buddhism and important studies on the relation of Nishida's thought and the religious world of Buddhism are almost non-existent. Kawada in order to emphasize his point remarks that it was unfortunate that the term *tetsu-gaku* (philosophy) was introduced by Nishi Amane, while Miyake Yūjirō and others were in favor of *rigaku*, the science of "*ri*" or "reason", if this Chinese term can be so translated. The semantic problem is a very debatable one because both terms have a Confucianist connotation (less, obviously, *tetsugaku*), while the literal translation of philosophy *aichi*[a] (love of wisdom) and the more indigenous *shisaku* (thinking) have never been widely used. [10]

Kawada is certainly correct, however, in calling attention to the fact that post-Meiji philosophers have cultivated only a Western type of thinking, leaving Buddhism and Confucianism to other specialists, chiefly those connected with religious or politico-cultural institutions as in the case of Confucianism. In this situation, those who would like to study more deeply the connection between past thought and present philosophy and to see the continuity of a traditional way of thinking with the recent philosophical experience face many difficulties. It is to this question and to the larger problem of the tasks awaiting Japanese philosophers that I will devote my final remarks.

The Tasks of Japanese Philosophy and the Oriental Heritage

Among the characteristic features of recent Japanese philosophy I purposely omitted one in the previous section in order to consider it more fully in this conclusion. I refer to the continuing interest of many Japanese philosophers in the philosophy of culture. I have spoken in the sixth chapter about *Bunka-*

---

a. 愛智

10) Kawada Kumatarō 川田熊太郎, *Bukkyō to tetsugaku* 仏教と哲学 (Buddhism and Philosophy), Heirakuji Shoten, Kyoto, 1957, pp. 140-46.
See for Miyake Yūjirō 三宅雄二郎, *Meiji tetsugaku-kai no kaiko fuki* 明治哲学界の回顧附記 (Appendix to Meiji Philosophy in Retrospect) of Inoue Tetsujirō 井上哲次郎, *Iwanami kōza tetsugaku* 岩波講座哲学 Iwanami's Symposium: Philosophy), Iwanami Shoten, 1933, pp. 87-92.

shugi or "Culturalism" as an area of interest cultivated by Tsuchida Kyōson. Many other thinkers could be mentioned along with Tsuchida, especially if we would go into the so-called *zaiya* or non-academic type of philosophy. Even if we limit ourselves to philosophers in the strict sense, it is true to say that philosophy of culture verging upon philosophy of history has been a main theme of the entire Kyoto school, and even philosophers like Kuwaki, Ikegami Kenzō have dealt extensively with this subject. In a sense the *Bummeiron no gairyaku* (Outline of Civilization) or the dialogue between Western civilization and Japanese culture initiated by Fukuzawa Yukichi in the early years of Meiji has never ended and perhaps never will.

The influence of Japan's past culture on the lives of the people is obviously too pervasive to allow philosophers to avoid the problem of continuously re-evaluating past thought. As I mentioned before, Japanese philosophers are usually too technically minded to enter into a field which presupposes the wide historical knowledge of ancient thought which would carry them beyond their specialty. Still, the problem was felt, and also philosophically considered. Nishida and Tanabe tackled the problem of Oriental logic, Kōsaka and others studied the relation of Japan in world history, while Abe Jirō was one of the first to apply skillfully Dilthey's categories to the Japanese cultural situation.

Mutai Risaku in two articles written respectively in 1945 and 1947 on the tasks of Japanese philosophy, noticing that its main interest had been in philosophy of history and culture, stressed the point that the future of philosophy in Japan was to make a better study of the relationship between different cultural phenomena. According to Mutai, in order to avoid past pitfalls in this field, Japanese philosophers should adopt a wider approach or rather a much more thoroughly critical and scientific method. With this as their guide, they should study the limits and tasks of each field of enquiry, seeing them always in the perspective of the general cultural life of Japan. The different branches of philosophy, social sciences and even natural sciences should be considered together. Epistemological research should be vigorously and preferentially furthered to clarify concepts and to open a new path to a better understanding of this complex task. [11]

Mutai hailed as an important achievement in this direction the epistemology of Ikegami Kenzō, which, as we have seen, was based on a broad cultural approach. Mutai's suggestions are, in a sense, being vigorously carried out by the Society of the Science of Thought (*Kagaku no shisō-kai*)[a], which links together many intellectuals and specialists who through their journal *Kagaku no shisō*[b] try to examine critically many cultural problems. The spirit of the Society is prevalently positivist and empirical and to be sure the members show more opposition than amity and understanding toward the past heritage.

Other thinkers, apart from such well known writers as Suzuki T. Daisetsu, are more positive and think that contemporary Japanese are not much different in their way of thinking from their forebears. Really a great variety of interpretations exists, as can be seen in the copious extracts given in the book *Sources of Japanese Tradition.* The compilers of this volume present the social and liberal critic Hasegawa Nyozekan, who

---

a. 科学の思想会　　b. 科学の思想

11) Mutai Risaku, *Bunka to shūkyō* . . ., o.c., pp. 77-95.

advocates a realistic approach to the post-war reforms which are for him a must if Japan is to fulfill her task in the world community of nations. From a very different angle, namely cultural and artistic, quite different conclusions are proposed by the literary critic and writer, Kamei Katsuichirō[a], who emphasizes instead the need for Japan to return to her cultural heritage. [12]

These opposing views are amply manifested in the several *Kōza*[b] (Lectures) or Symposia edited in post-war times on Japanese thought, the great majority of them being definitely "progressive" and even Marxist. If we except *Kōza* dealing with religion or ethical problems, not much respect is paid to the past, nor for that matter to academic philosophy. That, incidentally, is why very little use could be made of them in this survey.[13] Nonetheless, more artistic or religious minded thinkers show a nostalgia for the great cultural past of Japan. Nationalistic feeling on the upsurge nowadays will in all likelihood strengthen this trend.

As a ray of light in this dialogue between Western trends

---

a. 亀井勝一郎   b. 講座

12) *Sources of Japanese Tradition* . . ., o.c., pp. 891-906.

13) Among the various kōza see: *Iwanami Kōza Gendai shisō XI Gendai Nihon shisō* 岩波講座 現代思想 XI 現代日本思想 (Iwanami Symposium, Contemporary Thought, vol. 11: Contemporary Japanese Thought), Iwanami Shoten, 1957. Maruyama Masao in the first lecture says that in Japan there is not a tradition in this type of historical writing; *Kōza Kindai shisō-shi IX Nihon ni okeru Seiyō kindai shisō no juyō* 講座近代思想史 IX 日本における西洋近代思想の受容 (Symposium on the History of Recent Thought, vol. 9: The Reception in Japan of Recent Western Thought), Kōbundō, 1959; *Kindai Nihon shisō-shi kōza 1 Rekishiteki gaikan* 近代日本思想史講座 1 歴史的概観 (History of Recent Japanese Thought -Symposium, vol. 1: Historical Introduction) ed. by Ienaga Saburō 家永三郎, Chikuma Shobō, 1959.

and Japanese themes, the efforts of students of comparative philosophy should be mentioned. Foremost among such is the scholarly Nakamura Hajime, a specialist in Indian thought and Buddhism. Nakamura is strongly opposed to the "bigotry" of some Western intellectuals, who, especially in the past, did not want to see any philosophy in Indian and Chinese thought. For him, all philosophers in different cultural setting have dealt with the same fundamental problems of the universe and of man. Changing times are bound to produce different solutions, and even new problems emerge from the waves of history, but a fundamental oneness can be found in all philosophical endeavor. In an essay on "The Rise of Philosophy" among the Upanishadic thinkers of India and the Ionian philosophers of Greece at approximately the same time, Nakamura sees many common points in both ways of thinking. Writing from the point of view of Indian thought, Nakamura reduces these themes to the following: yearning for the beyond; the protest aganist ritualism and polytheism; water-ether-wind or breath and numbers as fundamental elements; the absolute and the self; the world as being as such; the absolute subject; transmigration, deliverance; and, finally, ethics based upon monism.

In the same spirit Nakamura has also presented "Buddhist Philosophy in the Western Light", in order to show better the philosophical nature of Buddhism which, it must be confessed seems at times to come to the negation of any philosophy, given the refusal of Buddha and most of his followers to discuss strictly philosophical problems. The philosophical re-evaluation of Buddhism pursued by Nakamura, is no doubt an important contribution to comparative philosophy. However, some may wonder at this "secularization" of the religious content of

Buddhism and Indian thought. After all, mystics in the West too scorned the wisdom of this world, given as they were to contemplation of celestial things. Naturally some schools of Buddhism, unfaithful to the silence of Buddha, did enter into speculations which can well be called philosophies. Nakamura though, seems to stress as matter of philosophy what most people usually call religious themes. Obviously, no hair-splitting distinctions can be made between the subject-matter of the two disciplines, but their methods and purposes are so different that there is plenty of room for distinction. Religion, in effect, cannot be so easily confused with philosophy.

Less known abroad than Nakamura is Kawada Kumatarō, professor of comparative philosophy at Tokyo University. Kawada in his *Bukkyō to tetsugaku* (Buddhism and Philosophy) is, as above mentioned, against any form of eclecticism, and is not at all happy in seeing in Japan several different forms of thought coexisting and tending to create a dangerous syncretism of Buddhist thinking, Confucianist ideas and Christian ideals. He proposes a thorough study of the fundamental unity of different philosophical systems in order thus to create the basis for mutual discussion among them. Kawada sees the pervading unity in Greco-Roman thought in the concept of being and the love of wisdom embracing reality as its primary concern. Chinese philosophy is the philosophy of *Tao* or of the "Way" rather than a system in the Western sense. Buddhistic philosophy is centered on the concept of *chiken* or knowledge as illumination. Kawada sees its unity in the wisdom or knowledge (Sanskrit *prajñā;* Japanese *hannya*) of the *dharma* (*hō* in Japanese) or universal norms (law) and principles which affect all men. Kawada's analysis of Buddhist philosophy—he

too like Nakamura is a strong defender of the philosophical content of Buddhism—faces the difficulty of uncovering "the fundamental Buddhism" or the unity which is certainly not too evident
in the different sects and schools of Buddhism. On purpose he
leaves out Zen Buddhism and the Jōdo sect which are too hard
to classify.

According to Kawada, the task of comparative philosophy
is not merely to give an analytic description of the unity of the
great systems of philosophy. The descriptive task is only a
stepping-stone to the choice of our own philosophy. The ideal
would be to discover a truly universal human philosophy. He
seems to incline to a kind of Buddhist naturalism, but offers no
positive answer to this vital question. The danger that the
individual's choice is bound to be another variety in the already
staggering number of philosophical theories, is not considered
by Kawada. [14]

Students of comparative philosophy are facing a dilemma
which in the past has been faced by their colleagues in comparative religion and all other forms of comparative studies.
The fundamental unity of mankind and its way of thinking have
become more and more clear, while at the same time the specific
differences have become even more evident. So much so that
it has been said about comparative religion that "the chief

[14)   Nakamura Hajime's articles in English, The Rise of Philosophy and Bud-
         dhist Philosophy in the Western Light, are respectively in vol. II, pp.
         417-500, and III, 401-75 of the series edited by Ueda Seiji, see Ch. 7.
         note 13.   See also: Nakamura Hajime 中村元 Hikaku shisō-ron 比較思
         想論 (A Theory on Comparative Thought), Iwanami Shoten, 1960.
       Kawada Kumatarō, Bukkyō to tetsugaku . . ., o.c., passim. See about Na-
         kamura and Kawada's comparative philosophy: Perez Ruiz F., Dos Voces
         Japonesas en el Dialogo Oriente-Occidente, in: Pensamiento, vol. 17
         (1961), pp. 199-218.

service (of the comparative method) was to show the necessity of a better method". The wisdom of this comment is confirmed by, among others, the result of post-war philosophical meetings on East-West philosophy sponsored by the University of Hawaii. Harold E. McCarthy who took part in several of these conferences writing on "The Problem of Philosophical Diversity", suggests as a good working rule for those engaged in comparative philosophy: "seek resemblances but distrust them. And distrust them because resemblances normally exist in a context of differences and must always be seen in relationship to these differences." [15]

The problem of conciliating fundamental unity with no less fundamental specific differences has admittedly not been studied very much in the past, and only as contacts between philosophers of widely different background multiplied has it become a real problem. Whether a "philosophia perennis" will be worked out or has been already found is a question which depends so heavily on what fundamental experience is chosen as a point of departure that no definite answer can be given. Critical minded specialists agree mostly on the reality of fundamental differences, and they do not see any way to bridge these differences. More conciliatory thinkers are more hopeful, but it must be said clearly that the theoretical ground has not yet been formulated for what is emphatically only a hope.

At any rate, whatever the future may bring, it is true that in this country where so many different trends are coexisting, comparative philosophy should be thoroughly studied.

15) Harold E. McCarthy, The Problem of Philosophical Diversity, in *Philosophy East and West*, vol. IX, n. 3-4 (1960), pp. 107-28.

Whether this is one of the most important tasks of philosophy in Japan is another matter. Many writers have offered to open new paths for Japanese philosophy, ranging from the Marxists through Tanabe's philosophy of repentance to the technic and democracy of the West. Others are in favor of the contemplative and artistic East. All lines in the philosophical spectrum are represented, and the difficulty for the individual lies only in the choice, something being available to satisfy every taste!

If we ask what will determine the future of Japanese philosophy, I will answer unhesitatingly that it is, when all is said and done, the vitality and creativity of their future thinkers. I believe that philosophers, in Japan as well in other countries, are not so conformist as social or cultural critics would like to make them. Even less are they going to follow prefabricated patterns. In the general framework of philosophical categories, there will still be a great variety of systems, concepts and points of view which will be difficult to tuck neatly away in the cultural sheath which, more national than philosophy itself, only partially encircles the individual thinkers. After all, recent philosophy is not the common way of thinking, but quite a specialized discipline; as such it does not know geographical or even cultural barriers.

This point of view, a very debatable one I fully agree, seems actually to be widely shared by professional philosophers in Japan for they dislike being considered a localized Oriental tribe not able to communicate with Western philosophers. Their intent and hope is not only to be put on the same platform as their colleagues in the West but also to produce ideas and systems which are truly universal. Professional philosophers in general, while not neglecting their Oriental heritage, are very moderate, even to the point of not committing themselves on large questions concerning philosophies of East and West. They realize clearly how much catch penny, journalistic writing and thinking is involved in such questions.

A last remark must be here added. Many speak of the fundamental unity or the fundamental experience as the characteristic note of a system of thought, which may be very well true of cultural phenomena at large. However, for the philosophers is vital the systematization or elaboration of such fundamental experience. He has not merely to choose a Weltanschauung, but to *say* something, which is his own experience and therefore not determined by the cultural background. As I have repeated perhaps too often, a general common denominator cannot explain the variety which we find in recent philosophy.

As a conclusion to this discussion I shall here include the view of one of the professional philosophers in Japan, well versed in the history of Japanese thought. Shimomura Toratarō. Recalling at the end of a survey on recent Japanese philosophy Japan's great accomplishments in this field, Shimomura clearly acknowledges that philosophy has been born in the West and that, though Buddhists and Confucianists have produced in the past hundred years excellent historical studies on the old thought, they have done little more. Japanese philosophers, Shimomura continues, have a universal task to accomplish, just because philosophy is neither Western nor Oriental. Philosophy must be universal with the different cultural backgrounds serving only as starting points for different philosophical experiences. The concrete task of the philosopher in Japan is not to absorb only Western thinking, nor to emphasize the differences between East and West or to make a mixture of both, it is rather to think as a real universal philosopher by thoroughly deepening the philosophical consciousness. Shimomura sees in Nishida Kitarō a good example of a thinker rooted in the tradition of Japan but also capable of transcending it and reaching a truly universal philosophy. [16]

On this note we may well close this survey, which has tried to show something of the vitality and variegated creativity of the many Japanese philosophers who have created for the next hundred years of Japanese philosophy a new heritage of philosophical thinking. In what sense their work will influence future philosophers only the future will tell. For my part, I hope that the coming generations of philosophers will bring to their task the same openness of mind which has characterized their forebears of this past one-hundred years and that, standing on their shoulders, they will try sincerely to offer a real universal contribution to the philosophical heritage of man.

---

16) Shimomura Toratarō in *Tetsugaku kenkyū nyūmon* . . . o.c., pp. 322-23.

SELECTED BIBLIOGRAPHY*

Asō Yoshiteru 麻生義輝, *Kinsei Nihon tetsugaku-shi* 近世日本哲学史 (History of Recent Japanese Philosophy), Kondō Shoten, 1943

Bessatsu tetsugaku hyōron 別冊哲学評論, *Nihon ni okeru seiyō tetsu-gaku no keifu* 日本における西洋哲学の系譜 (The Genealogy of Western Philosophy in Japan), Minyūsha, 1948

Dai jimmei jiten 大人名事典 (Great Biographical Dictionary), ed. by Heibonsha 平凡社編, 1953-1955, 10 vols.

Funayama Shin'ichi 般山信一, *Meiji tetsugaku-shi kenkyū* 明治哲学史研究 (Studies on the History of Meiji Philosophy), Minerva Shoin, 1959

——, *Nihon no kannenronsha* 日本の観念論者 (Japanese Idealists), Eiōsha, 1956

Gendai Nihon jimmei jiten 現代日本人名事典 (Biographical Diction-ary of Contemporary Japan), ed. by Heibonsha 平凡社編, 1955

Gendai Nihon no shisō 現代日本の思想 (Contemporary Japanese Thought) ed. by Kuno Osamu 久野収, Tsurumi Shunsuke 鶴見俊輔, Iwanami Shoten, 1956.

Gendai no tetsugaku kōza V Nihon no gendai shisō 現代の哲学講座 V 日本の現代思想 (Contemporary Philosophy—Symposium, vol. 5 Contemporary Japanese Thought), ed. by Yamazaki Masakazu 山崎正一 and Others, Yūhikaku, 1958

Holzman Donald, with Motoyama Yukihiko and Others, *Japanese Re-ligion and Philosophy: A Guide to Japanese Reference and Research Material*, Ann Arbor: The University of Michigan

---

* Only general works on the history of philosophical thought and reference works are indicated, not studies on individual thinkers, for which see the footnotes. For further bibliographical references among the above listed books see: Funa-yama Shin'ichi, *Meiji tetsugaku-shi kenkyū*, pp. 396-400 and *Kindai shisō-shi*, ed. by Tōyama S. and Others, vol. 4, pp. 35-59

Press, 1959

Ienaga Saburō 家永三郎, *Nihon kindai shisō-shi kenkyū* 日本近代思想史研究 (Studies on the History of Modern Japanese Thought), Tōkyō Daigaku Shuppankai, 1953

Inoue Tetsujirō 井上哲次郎, *Kaikyūroku* 懐旧録 (Reminiscences), Shunjūsha, 1943

——, *Meiji tetsugaku-kai no kaiko* 明治哲学界の回顧 (Meiji Philosophy in Retrospect), Iwanami Kōza, Iwanami Shoten, 1932

Japan Biographical Encyclopedia & Who's Who, 2 ed. 1961, Rengo Press

Kindai Nihon shisō-shi 近代日本思想史 (History of Recent Japanese Thought), ed. by Tōyama Shigeki 遠山茂樹 & Others, Aoki Shoten, 1955, 1960, 4 vols.

Kindai Nihon shisō-shi Kōza I Rekishiteki gaikan 近代日本思想史講座 歴史的概観 (History of Recent Japanese Thought, Symposium, vol. I: Historical Introduction), ed. by Ienaga Saburō 家永三郎 Chikuma Shobō, 1959

Kiyohara Sadao 清原貞雄, *Meiji jidai shisō-shi* 明治時代思想史 (History of Thought in Meiji Era), Daitōkaku, 1921

Kōsaka Masaaki ed., *Japanese Thought in the Meiji Era*, translated and adapted by David Abosch, Pan-Pacific Press, 1958

Koyama Hirotake 小山弘建, *Nihon Marukusushugi-shi* 日本マルクス主義史 (History of Japanese Marxism), Aoki Shoten, 1956

Kuwaki Gen'yoku 桑木厳翼, *Meiji no tetsugaku-kai* 明治の哲学界 (Meiji Philosophical World), Chūōkōronsha, 1943

——, *Tetsugaku yonjūnen* 哲学四十年 (Forty Years Philosophy), Eikensha, 1946

Lüth Paul, *Die japanische Philosophie*, J.C.B. Mohr (Paul Siebeck), Tübingen, 1944

Meiji bunka zenshū XV Shisō-hen 明治文化全集 XV 思想編 (Collected Works on Meiji Culture, vol. 15: Thought), ed. by Yoshino Sakuzō 吉野作造 and Osatake Takeki 尾佐竹猛, Nihon Hyōron-sha, 1929

Miyagawa Tōru 宮川透, *Kindai Nihon no tetsugaku* 近代日本の哲学 (Recent Japanese Philosophy), Keisō Shobō, 1961

Miyake Yūjirō (Setsurei) 三宅雄二郎 (雪嶺), *Meiji shisō shōshi* 明治思想小史 (Short History of Meiji Thought), Hinoeuma Shuppansha, 1913

——, *Daigaku konjaku-tan* 大学今昔譚 (University Reminiscences), Gaikansha, 1946

——, *Meiji tetsugaku-kai no kaiko fuki* 明治哲学界の回顧 附記 (Appendix to Meiji Philosophy in Retrospect of Inoue Tetsujirō), Iwanami Kōza —tetsugaku—, Iwanami Shoten, 1933

Miyanishi Kazumi 宮西一積, *Kindai shisō no nihonteki tenkai* 近代思想の日本的展開 (The Japanese Development of Recent Thought), Fukumura Shoten, 1960

Nagata Hiroshi 永田広志, *Nihon tetsugaku shisō-shi* 日本哲学思想史 (History of Japanese Philosophy and Thought), Mikasa Shobō, 1938, Hakuyōsha, 1948

——, *Nihon yuibutsuron-shi* 日本唯物論史 (History of Japanese Materialism), Mikasa Shobō, 1936, Hakuyōsha, 1949

Nihon no tetsugakusha 日本の哲学者 (Japanese Philosophers), a special issue of *Risō* 理想 (Ideal), 1961, 2, n. 333

Nihon no shisōka 1 日本の思想家 1 (Japanese Thinkers, vol. 1), ed. by Asahi Jānaru 朝日ヂャーナル編, Asahi Shimbunsha, 1962

Nihon shisō 日本思想 (Japanese Thought), a special issue of *Risō* 理想, 1939, n. 102

Nihon tetsugaku shisō zensho 日本哲学思想全書 (Complete Collection of Works on Japanese Philosophy and Thought), ed. by Saigusa Hiroto and Others, Heibonsha, 1955-1957, 20 vols. See especially vol. I *Tetsugaku-hen* 哲学編 (Philosophy); II *Shisaku-hen* 思索編 (Thinking); V *Yuibutsuron-hen* 唯物論編 (Materialism). This collection, and even more so the pre-war one *Nihon tetsugaku zensho* 日本哲学全書, ed. by the Saigusa, Daiichi Shobō, 1936-1937, 12 vol.—, covers mostly pre-Meiji thought.

Ōi Tadashi 大井正, *Nihon no shisō—Fukuzawa Yukichi kara Amano Teiyū made*— 日本の思想 福沢諭吉から天野貞祐まで (Japanese Thought—From Fukuzawa Y. to Amano T.), Aoki Shoten, 1954

——, *Nihon kindai shisō no ronri* 日本近代思想の論理 (The Logic of Modern Japanese Thought), Gōdō Shuppansha, 1958

Saigusa Hiroto 三枝博音, *Nihon ni okeru tetsugakuteki kannenron no hatten-shi* 日本における哲学的観念論の発展史 (History of the Development of Philosophical Idealism in Japan), Bunshōdō, 1932, Sekai Shoin, 1947

——, *Nihon no yuibutsuronsha* 日本の唯物論者 (Japanese Materialists), Eiōsha, 1956

Sakisaka Itsurō, ed., 向坂逸郎編 *Kindai Nihon no shisōka* 近代日本の思想家 (Recent Japanese Thinkers), Wakōsha, 1954

Sengo Nihon no shisō 戦後日本の思想 (Post-War Japanese Thought). ed. by Kuno Osamu 久野収 Tsurumi Shunsuke 鶴見俊輔 Fujita Shōzō 藤田省三, Chūōkōronsha, 1959

Sengo Nihon seishin-shi 戦後日本精神史 (History of Post-War Japanese Spirit) ed. by Nishitani Keiji 西谷啓治 Kōsaka Masaaki 高坂正顕 and Others, Heibonsha, 1961

Shōwa shisō-shi 昭和思想史 (History of Shōwa Thought), ed. by Takeuchi Yoshitomo 竹内良知, Minerva Shoin, 1958

Takayama Rinjirō (Chogyū) 高山林次郎 (樗牛), *Meiji shisō no hensen* 明治思想の変遷 (Changes in the Meiji Thought), in the IV vol. of *Chogyū zenshū* 樗牛全集, pp. 404-449, Hakubunkan, 1905

Tama Giichi 田間義一, *Gendai tetsugakusha-ron* 現代哲学者論 (On

Contemporary Philosophers), Ikuei Shoin, 1943

Takizawa Katsumi 滝沢克己, *Gendai Nihon tetsugaku* 現代日本哲学 (Contemporary Japanese Philosophy), Mikasa Shobō, 1940

Teikoku toshokan wakan tosho bunrui mokuroku—shūkyō tetsugaku kyōiku no bu 帝国図書館和漢図書分類目録—宗教 哲学 教育の部 (Classified Catalogue of Japanese-Chinese books of the Imperial Library),ed. by Teikoku Toshokan, 1904

Tetsugaku jiten 哲学事典, ed. by Heibonsha 平凡社編, 1954

Tetsugaku nenkan 哲学年鑑 (Yearbook of Philosophy), vol. 1, 1942; vol. 2, 1943, ed. by Usui Jishō 臼井二尚 and Others, Seibunsha, Osaka, 1943-1944

Tetsugaku nenkan 1945-1947 哲学年鑑 (Yearbook of Philosophy), ed. by Tetsugaku Nenkan Kankō-kai 哲学年鑑刊行会編 Sōgensha, Ōsaka, 1949

Tetsugaku nempyō 哲学年表 (Chronological Table of Philosophy), ed. by Hayami Keiji 速水敬二編, Iwanami Shoten, 1939-1941

Torii Hiroo 鳥井博郎, *Meiji shisō-shi* 明治思想史 (History of Meiji Thought), Chikuma Shobō, 1935, Kawade Shobō, 1953

Tsuchida Kyōson, *Contemporary Thought of Japan and China*, London, 1927

Tsunoda R., Wm. Th. de Bary, D. Keene, editors, *Sources of Japanese Tradition*, New York, 1958

Yamada Munemutsu 山田宗睦, *Gendai shisō-shi nempyō* 現代思想史年表 (Chronology of Contemporary Thought), San-ichi Shobō, 1961

Yamazaki Masakazu 山崎正一, *Kindai Nihon shisō-shi tsūshi* 近代日本思想史通史 (A Comprehensive History of Recent Japanese Thought), Aoki Shoten, 1957

Appendix 1

THE PHILOSOPHICAL THOUGHT OF JAPAN FROM 1963 TO 1996

Naoshi Yamawaki
Translated by Jeremiah L. Alberg

The philosophical thought of Japan has changed in profound ways in the more than 30 years since this book was originally published. The two dominant streams of thought at that time, namely existentialism (cf. Ch. 7 Sec. 1) and Marxism (cf. Ch. 7 Sec. 2) began to ebb away, and many new philosophers, who do not fit into dogmatic schools of thought, began to appear. I would like to present a brief outline of this activity.

Decline of Marxism and one Exceptional Philosopher

1. The most telling occurrence of this 30-year time period was the decline of Marxism, which had been "the most popular philosophical movement of post-war Japan".[1] Already in the second half of the 1960s, orthodox Marxist-Leninism began to wane due to the growing influence of a new left-wing Marxism which gave serious consideration to the theory of alienation. In this respect, a contribution to the recovery of the early Marx's more humanistic theory of alienation came from Umemoto Katsumi (1912–1974) and the Shirotsuka Noboru (1927–), disciples of Watsuji Tetsurō and Kaneko Takezō respectively. Their originality

---

1) See above pg. 207.

can be seen in their intention to critically overcome the conservative traits of each of their teachers' social ethics by advocating a humanistic Marxism.

But from the mid-seventies onward, even this humanistic Marxism, no longer captivated the young people of affluent Japan. Rather, it can be said that Japanese Marxists, whether of the old left wing or the new left wing, lost their originality and pursued the path of dogmatism. Nevertheless, there was one philosopher, namely Hiromatsu Wataru (1933–1994), who renewed Marxist philosophy in Japan by constructing an original system of thinking. Although his starting point was the Marxism of the new left wing, he was very dissatisfied with Marx's interpretation which attaches great importance to the theory of alienation. Hiromatsu attempted rather to renew the Marxist critique of reification. In emphasizing the task of overcoming the Cartesian dualistic world view, he attempted to renew the philosophical heritage of Marxism by opposing it to the various tendencies of the twentieth century. Hiromatsu's numerous publications were written with a skillful use of highly speculative terms in a manner reminiscent of Heidegger. His life work, *Being and Meaning* (Iwanami Shoten, 1982) which was intended to be three volumes, was unfortunately left unfinished due to his death from illness. From among all of his other writings, *The Intersubjective Structure of the World* (Keisō Shobō, 1972) is the most condensed present-ation of his ideas.

If one were to characterize the core of Hiromatsu's philosophy in a nutshell, one could say that on a fundamental level he criticized modern world views, whether idealistic or materialistic, which were caught in the dualistic grid of subject and object. Hiromatsu rejected the Leninist-type of materialistic theory which sees in the object the mere product of reflection of matter. Instead, he developed a new theory which recognizes the object as the intersubjectively constituted world of relations. In the background of this kind of thinking one can detect the strong influence of constitutionalism derived from phenomenology and neo-

Kantianism, as well as relationalistic epistemology of E. Cassirer. Up to the very end, however, Hiromatsu did attempt to place his intellectual effort in the center of the Marxist tradition in that he considered the world of relations not as an a priori trans-historical world, but as an a posteriori socio-historical world which stands in constant need of reform or even revolution. In any case, due to the enduring power of his speculation, his astoundingly wide knowledge and tenacity, he has been evaluated as a first-rate thinker, even by many intellectuals who did not share his new leftist ideology. Undoubtedly, he has therefore a place among the small number of original systematic thinkers in postwar Japan.

Other Philosophers at Tokyo University

2. As a professor at the Komaba campus of Tokyo University, Hiromatsu exercised much influence. Now let us touch upon other philosophers at this university.

Iwasaki Takeo (1913–1976), who for a long time headed the Japan Philosophical association, developed a unique system in which he combined Kantian philosophy with Anglo-American pragmaticism. Ikegami Kenzo's disciple Yamamoto Makoto (1924–) and Iwasaki's disciple Watanabe Jirō (1931–) produced noteworthy work on Leibniz and Heidegger respectively. Still, it can be said that apart from Hiromatsu, the philosophers associated with Tokyo University who provided most stimulation for young philosophers in this thirty-year period were Ōmori Shōzō (1921–) and Kuroda Wataru (1928–1989). These two men, who began by studying Anglo-American philosophy, each developed their own original theories.

Ōmori who taught in the department of philosophy of science at Komaba, claimed to have overcome the modern dualism of spirit and matter through the use of a radical phenomenalism and solipsistic behaviorism, which he called "expressive monism". According to him, the truth of the real world should not be thought of as something beyond the network which comes into being as the core of our form of life. Thus the designation of the object as something which stands separate from the knowing subject is nothing other than an evil born of modern philosophy. Ōmori used a kind of Socratic questioning in which he challenged many natural scientists as well as his young students. He used both epistemological investigations, which combined a visualism, à la Berkeley, and a pragmatic theory of truth, as well as keen and clear explanations, which skillfully employed examples taken from the natural sciences. His major work is called *A New Theory of a New Way of Seeing* (Tokyo Univ. Press, 1982), and more recently he has been interested in the problem of time on which he also published a stimulating book.

Kuroda, who taught at the Hongo campus of Tokyo University, attempted to overcome empirical epistemology by describing and convincingly elucidating the grasp of the world based upon active speech acts of the human subject. According to Kuroda, because the epistemology of Ōmori lacks an examination of the dimension of the so-called active speech acts of the epistemological subject, which are not reducible to perception, it ends in a very one-sided logical development in much the same manner as the empiricism of Berkeley, Hume and Mach. Kuroda responded to this by developing a theory of active knowledge by combining Husserl's theory of intentionality with the later Wittgenstein's theory of language games. In addition to this and against the tendency of British ordinary language analysis, he proposed an argument for conceiving "act and norm" from a viewpoint which understands the relationship between causality and intentionality in a complementary rather than antagonistic fashion. But before this proposal could be concretely developed, Kuroda passed away. *Experience and Language* (Tokyo Univ. Press, 1976) and *Knowledge and Action* (Tokyo Univ. Press, 1982) could be considered his representative work.

Advances in Research in Ancient Greek and Medieval Philosophy

3. In the last thirty years scholarly standards in Japan for the study of ancient Greek and medieval philosophy have improved greatly. Let us examine some of the philosophers and achievements that bear special mention from this area.

As one can read in the seventh chapter of this book, Ide Takashi, and Tanaka Michitarō led Japanese research in ancient Greek philosophy, but their disciples did not adopt their teachers' political views – in Ide's case Marxism and in Tanaka's case conservatism. Rather they vied with each other in independent speculation, which was based upon sound interpretation of the original texts. Among the many disciples of Ide, the most interesting and stimulating scholar, who also had a great impact on younger scholars, may well be Inoue Tadashi (1926–). By arguing with his Tokyo University colleagues, Ōmori, Kuroda, Hiromatsu et al, and critically using the techniques of analytic philosophy, Inoue developed the task of recovering Aristotle's philosophy as a philosophy of Grounds which vivifies the individual. According to Inoue, ancient Greek philosophy from its beginning up till Aristotle, gave birth to a philosophy of Grounds which vivified creatures, including humans, as irreplaceable individuals. This kind of Aristotelian research by Inoue, which can be called existential, was the theme of such published works as *The Challenge from Grounds* (Tokyo Univ. Press, 1974), *The Language of Moira* (Tokyo Univ. Press, 1988) and *Parmenides* (Seidosha, 1995). In the same way, Katō Shinro (1926–), who was a student of Ide and then a long-time professor at Tokyo Metropolitan University, has published outstanding research especially in the area of the early dialogues of Plato, and had considerable influence on younger scholars in this field through his rather exacting method of study. In addition, Iwata Yasuo (1932–), who taught at Tōhoku University, deserves mention for his retrieval of the study of Nichomachian Ethics. He is also engaged in the current issues of ethical thought.

Another side of this area of research is found in Fujisawa
Norio (1925–) who taught at Kyōto University. He was the most
outstanding student of Tanaka and worked as the head of the
Philosophical Association of Japan. Fujisawa saw the actual
significance of thinking in Plato rather than in Aristotle. He
thought, namely, that salvation for the modern age, which is
controlled by fragmentary knowledge, did not lie in an Aristotelian
dualistic knowledge of theory and praxis, but in a universalist
philosophy of the kind Plato pursued, which tries to harmonize the
human way of life with the recognition of the world and nature.
Since the publication of his more specialized research, *Idea and
World* (Iwanami Shoten, 1980), Fujisawa, while reevaluating
Plato's view of nature along the lines of Heisenberg and
Whitehead, continues to explain the actual significance of
metaphysical Platonic philosophy as literally meta-natural science
in a way which is not vulnerable to the anti-metaphysical views of
Heidegger and Derrida. We should also mention the name of
Matsunaga Yūji (1929–), who graduated from Kyōto University,
taught at Kyūshū University and made remarkable studies about
Socrates and Plato.

Also, medieval philosophical research, freed from the
negative image of simply being a "Catholic" philosophy has
developed significantly in this time period. Among the achievements which deserve attention are those of Yamade Akira (1925–)
who taught at Kyōto University and Inagaki Ryōsuke (1928–)
who taught at Kyūshū University.

Yamada was stimulated by Heidegger's existentialism, and
produced outstanding work focussed on Augustine's "historicity
of life" and Aquinas' "comprehension of existence". He also did
comparative work on Augustine and Shinran, and on Aquinas
and Dōgen. *Fundamental Problems of Augustine* (Sōbun Press,
1977) and *Research into "Esse" of Thomas Aquinas* (Sōbun Press,
1986) can be considered representative works. As a contrast,
Inagaki, who was influenced by the above-mentioned Kuroda,
produced exceptionally enlightened writings on St. Thomas. He

developed speculation to seek a way to grasp human experience with the comprehensiveness of St. Thomas, which has been lost since Occam's nominalism. Although he is known also internationally, his Japanese works include *The Philosophy of Habitus* (Sōbun Press, 1981) and *Abstraction and Intuition* (Sōbun Press, 1990).

In addition, the Institute of Medieval Thought of Sophia University has contributed greatly to making medieval philosophy more widely available as a common resource for scholars in Japan. A gifted German Jesuit, Fr. Klaus Riesenhuber (1938–), took over the leadership of the Institute in the 1970s and since then it has been producing various noteworthy publications. First among these is a series called *The Collection of Medieval Texts* (Heibon Press) which now includes 20 volumes. This series, in which the canon of medieval thought, beginning with the second century Church Fathers and stretching across 1500 years of history, is being systematically translated, has no parallel in the world and has won praise from Japanese scholars. In addition to Riesenhuber, there are other Jesuit philosophers who are active at Sophia University, including Kadowaki Kakichi (1926–) who pursues the comparison of Zen practice and Christian mysticism; Yanase Mutsuo (1922–) who attempts to introduce the heritage of medieval philosophy into physics; and Kitahara Takashi (Western name: Jean Frisch 1926–) who has studied the problem of human evolution by doing research into primates. In this connection, we can mention the new trend to study the Greek Church Fathers, such as Gregory of Nyssa. This school of young scholars periodically publishes collections of papers about the oriental philosophico-theological tradition called "Eikon".

Development of Comparative Philosophy

4. We also need to discuss the field of comparative philosophy and comparative thought which has produced sound results in these 30 years. The pioneer in this field is Nakamura Hajime, who

after retiring from Tokyo University, wanted to spread the knowledge of Eastern thought and founded an institute as one means of education (Tōhō Gakuen), and continues up till today as its director. Still, there is another person of distinction who has not yet been mentioned in this book. The one who most excelled as present-day Japan emerged into this field was Izutsu Toshihiko (1914–1993) who produced many internationally known works.

After graduating from Keiō University, Izutsu began as a scholar of Islamic thought and mystical philosophy. After teaching at his alma mater for a short while, he was then professor from 1969 to 1975 at McGill University in Canada and then from 1975 to 1979 at the Iran Royal Academy of Philosophy. From the time of his return to Japan up until his death, he published major works in Japanese. His publications in English on Islam include *Ethico-Religious Concepts in the Qu'ran* (McGill University Press, 1966), *God and Man in the Koran: Semantics of the Korantic Weltanschauung* (New York, Arno Press, 1980), *The Concept of Belief in Islamic Theology* (also Arno Press, 1980). In Italian he has published *Unicità del l'esistenza e creazione perpetua nella mistica islamica* (Genova, Marietti, 1991). Also his work on Zen translated as *La filosofia del Buddhismo Zen* (Roma, Ubaldini Editore, 1984) has been published in Italy.

Izutsu's aim was to raise the universality of mystical thought to the level of logos through the comparative study of Islam and Eastern thought, especially Taoism and Zen Buddhism which was influenced by Taoism. In his great work, which was published in 1983, *Consciousness and Substance – Searching for the Spiritual East* (Iwanami Shoten) he was seeking a point which would comprehend the "substance" of things, not only on the "surface level of consciousness," which appears in the mere indicative function of language, but comprehends the "Being" of absolute nothingness as such on the level of "deep consciousness". Thus, the strength of his speculative research is not only in Islamic and Eastern thought, but also in his unerring grasp of the tradition of

European thought and so one can say that he is truly an international scholar of the first rank.

Still another person involved in comparative study on the international level is the former professor of aesthetics at Tokyo University, Imamichi Tomonobu (1922–). He advocates an "Eco-ethics" which is the synthesis of thought on nature and ethics and so he has organized an annual international conference and research circle of colleagues. Then there are Tamaki Koshirō (1917–) and Saegusa Mitsuyoshi (1923–) who have produced substantial study in the area of Buddhist and Western thought.

From the standpoint of comparative thought, a thinker who has come to hold much interest in the last twenty years in Japan is C. Jung. According to Yuasa Yasuo (1925–), who taught at Tsukuba University, it is precisely the depth psychology of Jung which has found universality in the area of the human unconscious, because it can overcome modern Western rationalism with its tendency to mind-body dualism. It is just this depth psychology which can open up a horizon for real dialogue with the tradition of Eastern thought which holds the oneness of mind and body. On the basis of this view Yuasa has published a large number of comparative writings and among these his theory of body which has been translated into English with the title: *The Body: Toward an Eastern-Mind-Body Theory*, (SUNY, 1987). While speaking of Jung, we must also mention the first internationally recognized Jungian psychologist, Kawai Hayao (1928–), who taught in the psychology department at Kyōto University. He has published very interesting research on the myths of Japan.

Other Post-60's Developments

5.   Existentialism as well as the Marxism, which was so popular in post-war Japan, waned in the 60s. After this the philosophical thought of continental Europe, i.e. phenomenology, hermeneutics, structuralism etc. became the fashion especially among the

younger philosophers. These trends were spread through the enlightened writings of Kida Gen (1928–) of Chuō University, Nitta Yoshihiro (1929–) of Toyō University and Tajima Sadao (1925–) of Tokyo Metropolitan University. Let us look here though at the more original works which these trends produced.

The head of the *Société Franco-Japonaise de Philosophie*, Nakamura Yūjiro (1925–) became very well known through his many essays and writings, which are published in a plain style, as well as his many talks. His scholarship was wide-ranging and included such areas as anthropology, semiotics and drama. In this way he aimed at developing a philosophy which emphasized the *sensus communis* instead of philosophy which enshrines rationality as its core. In his view this *sensus communis*, more than anything else, has the capacity to make us aware in a synthetic manner of the commonalities of our five senses. Although this capacity was given serious consideration by Aristotle, Vico and others, it does not appear very often in the history of philosophy. Today, when the view of humans which centers on their rationality has become deadlocked, this concept of *sensus communis* needs to be rehabilitated. With this intention in mind Nakamura has published various essays related to drama, written to spotlight the genesis of *sensus communis* in the body. As we touched upon earlier in connection with the work of Yuasa, the "body" has become a prevalent theme among recent philosophers in Japan. The first work, which should be mentioned regarding this theme, is *The Body as Spirit* (Keisō Shobō, 1974) by Hiroshi Ichikawa (1931–), a colleague of Nakamura's at Meiji University. Ichikawa develops in this work a logic for grasping the reality of human spirit in the various facets of embodiment, opposing both recent idealism and materialism.

Together with "embodiment", "semiotics" also became a dominant topic. Sakabe Megumi (1936–), a former professor at Tokyo University, is conversant in modern French structuralism, deconstructionalism, hermeneutics, as well as orthodox Western philosophy. Besides this he has attempted to develop a hermeneutical philosophy which uses "Yamato" words, or classical Japanese as much as possible. According to Sakabe, a philosophy which is rooted in the everyday language of the Japanese will not develop by using Chinese loan-words, which are in fact the kind of words used to translate most philosophical ideas. A philosophy expressed in ordinary Japanese will only be possible through an original hermeneutical understanding of classical Japanese language. Based on this view, he uses a reinterpretation of classical Japanese which is rich in implications of "mask" (kamen), "touching" (furerukoto), "behavior" (furumai), and "discourse" (katari). It is an attempt both to spotlight the deep experiences of the Japanese, as well as to illuminate the hidden features of Western thought. One may regard these works by Sakabe as attempts to continue the earlier aesthetic hermeneutics of Kuki Shuzō, about whom he also published a monograph.

Nakamura and Sakabe value highly the achievements of scholars and scientists working outside the framework of academic philosophy. These include the work of Kimura Bin (1931–), a psychologist, who taught at the medical school of Kyōto University. Kimura emphasizes two things in his many interviews with clinical patients. First, that schizophrenia is not a disease to be judged in the name of science, and second that there are themes that emerge from these interviews which ought to be pursued as philosophical problems, including the precarious situation of the individual self. He develops original statements introducing such viewpoints as Binswanger's "historicity of the present", Minkowski's "temporality", Nishida's "pure experience" and "place" and Watsuji's "relatedness". Humans are not simply abstract rational subjects, they are temporal existential beings who exist within themselves and heterogeneous others, as well as being subjects who form themselves in history through time. Because of such convictions, Kimura criticizes a psychology which rejects philosophy and he argues for the necessity of a new discipline which would be a psychology of comparative culture.

Other scholars who have produced works of note include

Maruyama Keizaburō (1933–1993), a linguistic philosopher who reinterprets F. Saussure, the father of structural linguistics, in an opposite direction from the standard interpretation. He argues that Saussure is a critic of scientistic linguistics and a defender of depth psychology. He tried to develop the cultural semiotics received from Saussure; Nakata Mitsuo (1939–), who as a Japanese expert on Bergson, first got *doctorat d'État* in France and is now at Tsukuba University has been wrestling with the problem of philosophy of comparative culture; Sawada Nobushige (1916–), who taught for a long time at Keiō University and was president of the Philosophical Association of Japan, began with analytical philosophy, then turned to thought on the environment and life sciences. He has been one of the central figures in the area of philosophy of science.

Kyōto School Trends

6. Let us try to give a short summary of the trends of the philosophers associated with the Kyōto School, which has been discussed in quite a few pages of this book.

Nishitani Keiji (1900–1990), who was mentioned in the first section of chapter 7, continued right up until his death to think deeply about the significance of religion in overcoming the nihilism of the scientific technological age. His book *What is Religion?*, first published in 1961 and then translated into both English and German, received worldwide attention. Also in Japan his complete works, comprising 26 volumes, will be published by Sobun Press. Also mentioned in that same section was Yamauchi Tokuryū (1890–1982) who published in 1974 a remarkable work called *Logos and Lemma* (Iwanami Shoten), demonstrating that he was still capable of rigorous speculative thought. According to Yamauchi, if the form of traditional Western thought since the ancient Greeks can be expressed as "logos", the form of traditional Eastern thought can be expressed with the word "Lemma". In Lemma there is both the root of tetralemma which stems from

India's Mahayana Buddhism as well as dilemma, which stems from Taoist thought of China. In the case of the former the logic of the "great denial", in which both affirmation and denial are denied, becomes the axis, which then leads to a logic of "affirmation", "denial" and "great affirmation", and lastly attains "absolute nothingness", "origin" and "emptiness". In essence Yamauchi, who was critical of the intuitivistic tendencies of Nishida Kitaro and Suzuki Daitsuke, attempted to clarify his original logic of Eastern thought in this manner.

We cannot fail to mention the name of Hisamatsu Shinichi (1889–1990) among the post-war philosophical Buddhists of Kyōto. Hisamatsu developed his own philosophy called "The Philosophy of Awakening". He opened a Zen center in 1944 and in 1958 he made an international appeal for what he called FAS. F stood for 'formless self', A for 'all mankind' and S for superhistorical history. Especially in the latter half of the 60s he determined the standpoint of the center as a postmodern standpoint in the sense of overcoming modernity and he regarded himself as a postmodernist, albeit in a quite different fashion from those in Europe since the 1970s. In addition to him, Takeuchi Yoshinori, (1913–) who is also a representative philosophical Buddhist of Kyōto University, has published a work translated into English as *The Heart of Buddhism* (NY: Crossroads, 1991), which features a foreword by Hans Kúng.

Since the 1970s the metaphysics of Kyōto University has been carried out by Tsujimura Kōichi (1922–) and Ueda Shizuteru (1926–). Tsujimura concentrates on the thought of the later Heidegger and attempts to combine this with traditional Buddhist teaching. Ueda is attempting to compare and synthesize the German mystical tradition of Eckhart and others with Buddhism and Nishida's philosophy. As for the present successors of these two, Ōhashi Ryōsuke (1944–) is an energetic scholar who has completed the German *Habilitation*. Besides using his outstanding German to organize many international conferences both at home and abroad, he has edited an anthology of writings from the philosophers of the Kyōto School entitled *Die Philosophie der Kyōto Schule*, (Alber, 1988). Although this kind of philosophical trend represents one line; there is also an active research group at Kyōto University with Takeichi Akihiro (1933–) and Arifuku Kōgaku (1939–) as its center, which concerns itself with the elements of contemporary practical philosophy. They have invited leading contemporary German philosophers and held various international colloquia.

Also Shimomura Toratarō (1902–1995) who was the last to be mentioned in the main text of this book, was a very important philosopher related to Kyōto University but active in the Tokyo region and has been active in many areas. Shimomura started in mathematical philosophy and research into Leibniz, but after the war he turned to research in the area of the history of the human spirit, culture and art. Since 1962 he has written many works which deserve attention, including *St. Francis of Assisi* (Nansō Press, 1965), *Thoughts on the Mona Lisa* (Iwanami Shoten, 1974), *The Renaissance View of Man* (Iwanami Shoten, 1975) and *The World of Burkhardt* (Iwanami Shoten, 1983). Among his students, Nagai Hiroshi (1921–), who taught at Tsukuba University, has added to this production with such *tours de force* as *The Philosophical Basis of Life-theory* (Iwanami Shoten, 1974) and *The Metaphysics of Humans and the World* (Sōbun Press, 1985).

New Directions at the Kyōto School

7. Having dealt above with the philosophical tendencies of the successors to the orthodox Kyōto School, it must also be noted that other, different tendencies also centered in Kyōto have gained influence in the past thirty years. This tendency, which could be called the new Kyōto school for short, is characterized by the fact that it deals with Japanese culture from an original viewpoint. Its proponents include Ueyama Shunpei (1921–) and Umehara Takeshi (1925–), as well as Imanishi Kinji (1902–1992).

Ueyama's starting point was his research into American pragmatism, but then he turned to historical research on the Japanese nation. He emphasizes the proper way of grasping the "depth culture" which strongly determines the mentality of contemporary Japanese, and the necessity of retracing Japanese history all the way back to the Jōmon culture and the formation of the Ritsuryō legal codex. According to him, the Japanese imperial system, which was constructed around the year 700 A.D. within the context of developing the Ritsuryō legal codex, has a long tradition as a Shintō priesthood which administers the peaceful order and which differs completely from the autocratic monarchy of China. As a consequence, the imperial system since the Meiji era deviated from the main tradition, while the present-day system, in which the emperor is conceived of as a symbol of the nation, has taken over the true tradition of Japan. This kind of understanding may be regarded as a renewal of the consideration of a cultural imperial system which was previously attempted by Watsuji and others.

Umehara, who is a friend of Ueyama, received attention in 1967 when he published *Thoughts on Hell – A Genealogy of Japanese Mentality* (Chuō Kōron Press). In this work, which was recently translated into French, Umehara not only sought the core of the history of the Japanese Mind in Buddhism rather than in Shintoism, or in Confucianism, but he also classified the various Buddhist sects in the following manner: esoteric and the Nichiren sect as the thought of life, Yuishiki and Zen as thought of the heart, and Tendai Buddhism and Jōdoshū as the thought of hell. But since the 1970s he has, on the one hand, published research on Shōtoku Taishi and Kakinomoto Hitomaro, and on the other hand, he has criticized the view of a mature modern Europe as typified by Bacon and Descartes (Fundamental Thoughts on the Control of Nature, A Mechanical Natural View); in addition, he has been developing his thought which would confront this view with the traditional Japanese view of nature and culture. The thought of Umehara can sound somewhat ethnocentric but in the last half of the 80s he was active as the head of the International Research Center for Japanese Studies established in Kyōto.

One of the main persons who represents the new Kyōto School is the biologist Imanishi Kinji, who recently passed away. Originally a researcher into the mayfly, he moved progressively from research on horses to research on monkeys, eventually establishing his own concept of nature. According to Imanishi, any way of seeing which grasps society as essentially a human phenomenon, is nothing but a prejudice of Christianity. Society has to be grasped as a phenomenon which is seen not only in other animals besides human beings but also in all living things. Thus, even Darwin's idea of natural selection as the main cause of biological evolution is mistaken, because evolution includes the possibility of different species of living beings "living together" or "peacefully coexisting". Imanishi's concept is a holistic naturalism which describes specia (society of species) above living organisms, and even describes a horospecia (society of all living things) above the specia. He emphasizes that only by means of this naturalism can modern civilization break out of the deadlock in which specialists have trapped it.

On the basis of Imanishi's influence, Umesao Tadao (1921–) and others formed an ecological group which could be called the Imanishi school – so-called because they have developed a theory of comparative civilization which differs from the modern European enlightenment. At present, however, opposition to Imanishi's thinking on nature has emerged. Orthodox natural scientists criticize Imanishi's theory as unscientific and sociologists call his theory conservative. In spite of this, his idea of "habit segregation (sumiwake)" might have international appeal for the present world in which conflicts between races in various areas of the world often erupt.

Trends in Social Thought

8. Lastly, I would like, very briefly, to touch upon the trends in social thought during the past 30 years. We have already referred to the waning of Marxism, but a modernism which differed from Marxism also receded markedly in the latter half of the 1970s. Maruyama Masao (1914–1996), who taught in the law faculty at Tokyo University, exercised a major influence on the modernist movement in postwar Japan in the area of political philosophy. The diverse study which he published up to the 60s relating to Japanese political thought was translated into English and so he enjoyed an international reputation. But his criticism of Japanese culture from the standpoint of modern enlightenment seems to have gradually lost influence and instead, a more positive evaluation of Japanese culture like the above mentioned Ueyama and Umehara became influential. In addition, the writings of the cultural anthropologist Nakane Chie (1926–) who seeks the uniqueness of Japanese society in the "vertical human relationships" and the psychologist Doi Takeo (1920–) who seeks it in the mentality he calls "Amae" (fusional dependent emotion), have become steady sellers. Their books have been translated into English and attracted readers in many foreign countries: C. Nakane, *Japanese Society* (Penguin Books, 1973); T. Doi, *The Anatomy of Dependence*, (N.Y. Harper Row, 1984.)

In any event, the theme of combining the economic formation of Japan with its culture and thought became a hot issue and aroused a lot of interest. At the present time, on the one hand, there is a defense of Japanese society understood in the manner of Watsuji's ethics, and, on the other, a specific criticism of Japanese society from the modernistic viewpoint like Maruyama's thought. And these seem to cancel each other out. But both a nationalistic defense and a eurocentric critique of Japanese society are rather one-sided and misleading, since this theme needs a kind of dialectical thinking which takes the complementarity of the particularity of culture and the universality of ethics or religions into consideration. It is not an exaggeration to say that it is the most important and urgent task for the philosophers of Japan, as they face the 21st century, to contribute to international society by dealing with this difficult theme in a serious manner.

SUB-INDEX

To Appendix 1

INDEX